MAN
THE RELUCTANT BROTHER

MAN
THE RELUCTANT
BROTHER

MATTHEW IES SPETTER

THE FIELDSTON PRESS
New York
1967

Dedicated to all those men and women—my parents included—who pitted their lives and loyalty to human decency against the overpowering odds and ferocity of fascist oppression.

The courage of their resistance to tyranny and infamy will penetrate the darkness of these decades with an everlasting shaft of light and hope....

TABLE OF CONTENTS

FOREWORD

This book has not been written to formulate a system of philosophy. It is, on the contrary, the result of reflections and experience. My concern is with men and women in their down-to-earth daily struggle and I have consciously avoided endless footnotes, quotes or the jargon of academia.

Yet, how shall one properly acknowledge the influence of all those who have nurtured one's feeling and thinking?

What I have read, studied and encountered has by now blended into attitudes and thoughts the origin of which I can no longer trace. I claim no originality other than the uniqueness of experience and inner probing which have been both the burden and the basis of my quest.

My debt is great to many men and women in many disciplines of learning and, above all, to those who have helped me keep intact a capacity for the love of life.

To all of them, teachers, authors, companions, I acknowledge my indebtedness. And last, but not least, to my wife and my children.

M.I.S.

MAN
THE RELUCTANT BROTHER

CHAPTER 1

CREDO

I need truth because I was an eye-witness to the premeditated murder of children.

The killers were men of a nation much akin to my own. The children were ours.

I need truth because my generation allowed the ultimately impermissible and because such killing continues. Men everywhere, while protesting their abhorrence, are still willing to permit the impermissible, still willing to kill as "a necessary evil", still willing to appease their conscience with justifications which fasten the tyranny of evil upon their souls. The Germans called it "the final solution", a concept no one has as yet renounced. In fact all means are still accepted as permissible.

I need truth and therefore, behind the veil of language and the logic of argument of this book stands my personal urgency.

If no one is willing to renounce the murder of children how will we then be answerable for anything?

I need truth because our sons are bluntly prepared for death and we, the adult generation, wring our hands and let it happen. As if mesmerized, we trample on.

[1

The murder I witnessed was of the children of Europe in World War II. But many more murders have since been added. The killing was against children from France and Holland and Norway and Poland and Russia. They were of all religious backgrounds, though the children of defenseless minorities were the prime targets. Their very defenselessness fanned the ferocity of the killers. Some children were suffocated by gas; some children were buried alive; some children were torn to pieces by fragmentation or fire bombs; some children were given neither food nor water . . . I have seen this and I have heard the children's cries.

Some children were killed together with their parents; some children were snatched from their beds and hurled into the flames.

Our children.

All children were taken to be killed: lame children and blind children, children in hospitals and children in the street coming from school, children in light summer clothes, children who had gone for a swim. Yes, even children were taken who wept because they were afraid.

In the days of my years children were killed in broad daylight under the eyes of the entire world. All the children on whom the executioners could put their hands.

I have seen this and speak of it, not with sentimentality but with outrage and I will not permit it to be blocked from your heart.

The brutalization I witnessed is not limited to any one nation, it pervades the air we breath. Timidity has allowed the crooked marriage of rationalization and power. And now all means are justified. For at the end of brutalization is the willingness to consider murder as reasonable. The blasting of a Sunday school in Alabama is but another aspect of this malady.

Detachment from life was once the hallmark of knights eager to die for abstractions. Today, meek self-destructiveness is acceptable. Collective death wishes are skillfully manipulated so as to make destruction of life seem to be a reasonable proposition. There was certainly nothing irrational about the organization or administration of German extermination camps. The butchers could wallow in their warped aggression and the victims passively perished, inwardly defeated by the betrayal of the entire world.

❖   ❖   ❖   ❖

I was raised to believe in a militant democracy. Social progress and the inner betterment of human beings seemed unquestionably intertwined. Sacrifices which this idealism sometimes required appeared to me the price for a self-evident commitment.

Also, I was born in the land of Erasmus and Spinoza. I played boys' games under the statues honoring their memory and I grew up in the libraries and schools they also had used. A broad Humanism was handed on to me in which personal ambition was not seen as separate from the common good.

As a very young man I read Jefferson, Paine and Thoreau and it was instilled in me that man's inner attitudes can be developed in such a way that he can choose his own values and attitudes whatever the world may demand of him.

As a student, the literature to which I was exposed was steeped in the newer psychiatric insights, offering hope that if the subconscious could be unearthed and explained, man's self-destructiveness and hostility could be altered for his own good and the good of his environment.

Yet later, when the showdown occurred and the children were taken to be killed, I found that neither social idealism nor psychological awareness would guarantee a man's behavior. Many who never shared in the refinements of culture and intellectual clarification turned out to be those whose fundamental values could not be destroyed. When the confrontation came and when everything depended upon whether one could count on a man's honor, a man's word, a man's trustworthiness, the presence of social idealism or its absence and the presence of refined culture or its absence, turned out to be in no way decisive. What mattered was whether or not simple decencies were part of the unconscious reservoir of a person. Whether he saw himself as an end and therefore could never see another as merely a means.

In the years of the rule of the executioners few men turned out to be good men. Precious few were willing to risk position, prestige or economic means to underwrite their faith in a fundamental humaneness.

I have developed an increasing conviction that a primary need of our time is to experience the trauma of what Alberto Moravia called "the suffering from not being a man." Anyone who remains ignorant of such suffering escapes from the moral revolt necessary to change our lives. We need to rediscover what it is to be a man if the killing of children is to stop. By restoring the proof and pride of existing as a man, we can defy death and halt the mutilation of one's person.

By regaining the sense that we are concretely needed to fulfill something in the world, we swing the ultimate sanction from death and murder to life and compassion.

If our lives are to be rescued from the numbness of indifference and the adjustment to "fate", we must restore the conviction that we can rely upon ourselves and that the redemption of our existence is a tangible human task.

This quest is my greatest preoccupation.

When the Russian armies were approaching the camp in which I was held as a political prisoner in 1945, the executioners dragged their prey from Auschwitz to Buchenwald.

After more than ten days in subzero weather, packed in open coal tenders, seventy-five to eighty percent of the human cargo froze to death. My closest friend, a physician, and I had kept a child alive by warming it with our bodies. We had neither food nor drink to offer but we still had our fading life impulses to shelter this child.

I think that because of this my hope has not died. Of course the doubts, the regrets, the anxieties weigh heavily. More light around us is extinguished every day.

And yet, there remains the potential not to give up living and to devote oneself to life by overcoming the fraudulent and cynical. There is before us the choice, as always, to be loyal to what is human. Behind the mask of mutilation still remains the capacity to promote love.

Ancient philosophers could speculate as to whether Man existed outside of History. Today it is quite obvious that the individual is never beyond the reach of state philosophies which mold the social as well as the private environment.

Much of this molding is done by insidious brainwashing, by the faked messianism of politics which prevents men from sensing themselves as ends in themselves. The American spokesmen in Vietnam reported enemy deaths as "verified by body count." Most of us are no longer conscious of the random spiritual terrorism which keeping score entails. Dehumanization does not make a dramatic entrance, it seeps into the consciousness of man.

And yet, I am convinced that the ideologists can be stopped. Many millions, suffocated in the gas chambers, could have lived out their lives far from the ferocities of those engaged upon "historical" missions if the seepage of dehumanization had been exposed earlier and if resistance against it had been taught just as avidly as nationalism.

When will the immense suffering be enough to make us revolt?

As a Humanist I maintain that freedom is neither confirmed nor betrayed by outer circumstances. But obviously the citizen of the twentieth century is constantly forced to put his life on the line for some form of involuntary salvation. The freedom to which one is loyal because one is loyal to oneself is suspect. Millions upon millions are cheated out of their self-loyalty by promises of protective authority. Every corner of the globe is hurtled along the path of "the tyranny of progress", as Albert Salomon called it. As a consequence, the organization of society for supposedly humane purposes ends but too easily in military or totalitarian systems governed by small elite groups fascinated by the exercise of power.

No citizen in our epoch can escape the need therefore to come to terms with the realities of power and it is an open question whether reason has any influence at all upon power. So much capacity for happiness and for roots has already been swallowed by power run amok, by political control and hidden despotism. I raise the question of power because we cannot discuss our time without speaking of it bluntly or without confronting the fact that the intricacies of power weaken man's private judgment about killing.

And if that issue is not dealt with—if we refuse to come to terms with Camus' question how killing can be permitted when suicide is rejected—then we can only expect a future in which Hitler's resolve that we "must regain our good conscience about cruelty," will yet win out. For power in our time has come to look like the eternal, that which is not questioned, the permanent. And the human individual thereby increasingly appears to himself as the incidental, the "casualty." Stripped of all rationalizations neither philosophy and religion, nor psychiatry and science have removed us one inch from the possibility of universal disaster. We are as yet clinging to a world in which all we care for is threatened to its very core; we are suspended, while men of great power convince the "small fry" of history, that their private sufferings are pedestrian against the canvass of "historical necessity . . ." Power is confused with what is right and so our world ascribes an absolute value to it.

This is particularly true of the highly organized nations which in order to hold on to power must continually increase their means for destruction and manipulation. By necessity therefore all great powers are in deadly danger of seduction by militarism and statism. It is a virus of centralized authority which feeds upon the lowered resistance of mankind weakened by fatigue and fatalism.

I have only one theme: it is to expose the mutilation of the human person. I have only one cause: to arouse my generation against those paralyzing trends which make pawns out of people, and so to help rescue the human heart in which I believe. For we can be certain that the more rational the organization of power becomes, the more easily the individual will be demoted. Among the few authors conscious of this issue is Arthur Koestler whose prisoner in *Darkness At Noon* is finally brainwashed to believe that not only must he die for the system, but that his death is his final contribution to the triumph of the proletariat. Not even death shall have a personal meaning! His life, his hopes, his very identity as a person are of significance only when his dehumanization is completed, when he has become a non-being, a means to an end and nothing else.

Yet, religious and political utopianisms are never satisfied with the imperfect efforts of human beings to attain honesty and decency. They portray Man down the ages in the light of having failed to live up to what he was supposed to be. This is the supreme rationalization of mental enslavement and I assure you that I am not describing mere corruption nor a metaphysics of evil.

What is formulated here is an attempt to help in the rebuilding of purpose, to help keep alive the civilized aims that lie beyond indecision and doubt. Not the desolate talk that after this or that armed conflict things will be better. They never are until something is transformed at the heart of man's impulse for innocence. What is ultimately challenged today is not just reason versus power, but the entire proposition as to whether the institutions we have built can provide a margin of sanity, happiness and the kind of self-improvement which establishes the solidarity of our common humanity. The romantic claims of states nauseate me by their duplicity.

Neither do I know where the theologians and political determinists get their great self-assurance, for I have found that most of that which passes for fate, for the supposedly inevitable and irrevocable, is in fact rationalization. Certainly nothing in the human experience justifies the immense madness of perpetual mobilization and wars. It does not justify beliefs becoming fanaticisms, nor idealisms which turn into idolatry.

I can think of the future only in terms of recuperation, in terms of a hope for the healing encounter of each with each, the meeting of eyes, the silence of knowing, the caress that overcomes mutilation. For all negation ends in oppression and terror. Therefore, I have chosen to insist that one cannot tire, or simply claim "the courage of despair." We must live all of our epoch and use our initial impulse of defiance to create tangible means for decency, for some kind of world order, for responsibilities which, as we struggle for them, will enlighten us as to what is required of us.

It is true that one could have hoped for gentler times and it would have been a relief after World War II had we been granted a breathing spell. But this has not been so and the kind of deceit that hurried one generation twice into world slaughter has forced a few of us, at least, to turn away from the prostitution of ideas and the slick pretensions of adjustment.

Who among us can use such words as "the dignity of man" or "humanity" or "honor" without an acute knowledge of how easily such concepts can cover the sins of silent collaboration with ultimate evil or active participation in the wholesale destruction of children? We are confronted by dangers so tremendous in scope that all nationalistic prattle and pious declarations of "enlightened self-interest" stand utterly discredited. Such raw truths as will not let one sleep confront us and they must be engaged. Ignoring them would mean to prolong and probably repeat all that which led to the smothered gasps of gas-chamber victims or to the horrendous brutality of tanks crushing bodies.

THE CURSE OF EUPHORIA

The essays contained in these pages are not a testimony of easy faith or optimism. I see reasons for hope but not for optimism. There have been enough lies in our generation and enough has been destroyed. . . . The immense bloodshed of this era, whether in Hiroshima, Warsaw, Coventry or Auschwitz should compel us to be truthful.

Above all, ideological delusions or theological obfuscation stand unmasked. Their hold over mankind has collapsed and we know that only obstinate human efforts will preserve tenderness in this world. Man's safety no longer lies in the State, nor with any kind of imperial majesty. It is found in the deliberate ceaseless work of men and women who, recognizing that the failings of their elites are paid for with streams of blood, will no longer entrust their lives to such abstractions. It is obvious too that lukewarm niceties concerning human nature will not "do" either. For there is a need to speak frankly of Man and his stumbling adventure in time. Man is a solitary climber and prevails amidst great agony. By his deeds he argues his contention with the universe.

Perhaps the crucial testimony of our days was that of Adolph Eichmann as he stood before his judges in Jerusalem. Neither life nor truth had meaning for him, not because he was an evil man but because he was a man who could dutifully adjust to any authority that afforded him escape from private consciousness.

Eichmann testified that he had felt upset by a particular mass-grave in Poland: "I could see the blood spout out of the earth, it was like a fountain of blood." His discomfort was caused not by a concern for those men, women, and children, but rather by an absence of esthetics in that situation. The essence of what really happened did not disturb him. There are millions of individuals throughout the world who would assume the responsibility of executioners, who see reality only in terms of who has power over whom and are not kept awake by the problems of what to live by, what code to accept for right or wrong. We may not feign ignorance of that enormous truth.

My hope for mankind rests with those other millions in whom the sense of sacredness amidst all our incompleteness has not died. Those who in their individual lives lessen suffering. Those capable of finding still the rare islands of joy, which are their mainstay. For it is those souls who by sticking to their own desire for decency, have gained the courage to pass through what often appeared impassable and to discover meaning to their own lives because of a quiet solidarity. Their day-to-day attempts to build and rebuild lives, whatever humiliation may come their way, are proof that commitment of the heart has meaning and that human values are superior to those of the jungle. The American civil rights worker is an example, for by persistent conscience evoking resistance, he finds a means to be psychologically stronger than his oppressor. Because of that fidelity, the moment will come when the club, the tear gas and the prisons will lose their power and revolutionary change will be set into motion. It is in such effort that we find justification to see our struggles for what they are and to go on. Thus a choice is expressed, a commitment to personal strength rather than to organized power. I base my convictions upon a defiance of meaninglessness, for it has become clear that those who simply adjust to the deceit of absolute power and those who declare themselves "tired idealists" are equally responsible for the misery of our time.

I am impatient with those who because of disappointment are willing to give up the struggle for justice and the glimpses of happiness our lives sometimes yield. The self-contempt of today's literature indoctrinates us with the melancholy of disillusioned despair. Such despair maintains that since no total meaning can be discerned, private suffering is of little consequence. That very denial becomes, in its turn, the rationale for all sorts of mutilation and spiritual oppression.

I find this saturation with despair in many areas of our daily lives and particularly in the easy assumption that governments are morally sanctioned when preparing for the mass destruction of life. The hoarse ideologists of collectivism and militarism express that same desperate intoxication when they hurl their threats into the hearts of millions of innocents who, bit by bit, become numbed by the enormity of the death which is forecast. How much suffering will be enough? How many times must those who love life and justice be taught the lesson that destruction can be made into a tenet of faith?

I have witnessed the consequences of this intoxication as I scratched my nails into prison walls and retched with all of my broken body after torture. I have seen it through the web of barbed wire never to be erased from one's memory when thousands upon thousands were driven naked into the crematoria. Is it not time to speak truth to each other? Shall we not at last cry out that the deceptions and abstractions finally force the innocents to be infected by the executioners? Do we want to live in a world contaminated by total contagion of killing and death? I deny the necrophilics the right to foist their warped universe upon the apathy of the many. Therefore the struggle for the dignity of this generation is justified if despite our fears we have protested and defied in such ways as will indict those who would commit aggression against life, and if we have not adapted ourselves to their warped universe. What we should have learned then is that any realization of consciousness, any grain of happiness, can persist only if grounded in a passionate hunger for justice which can lift human beings out of the muteness of a neutral universe. Otherwise we may die, for all practical purposes, as some do who, as the chameleon, change color with any given circumstance and to whom no compromise will be too great. In the same vein, the soul of others is destroyed because they become confused amidst the complex features of reality. Their exhaustion is the prelude to their submission.

I heard a radio interview with the wife of one of the Navy pilots engaged in bombing North Vietnam. While her husband was raining napalm bombs on some Vietcong targets, she and her children, she said, prayed each night for his safe return. And, she cautioned him in each of her letters, not to expose himself to unnecessary dangers. To this good woman her husband could only be seen as the father-provider, in the military service of his country. Yet, he could not be "careful" even if he wanted to and to those below, he was as an anonymous punishing god. She could not see it that way. The absurdity was not in the woman's lack of comprehension nor in her fervent desire that her husband take no risks, it was rather in the deceit, in the camouflage of realities, which hides the truth that one cannot be a part-time killer without being tainted even when the state has sanctioned such killing. Whoever gave governments the right to rule on life and death?

I think of both this man and woman with compassion, for as individuals they certainly did not create the perplexing circumstances in which they found themselves. Yet the question must be asked also what we still feel about the villagers below, for that is the crux of the problem of our time.

Who then will raise a voice loudly enough to state the case of The People vs. Death? Who will use the knowledge amassed in the last twenty-five years about the millions upon millions of children, women, and men torn asunder by war, deported in cattle wagons, or killed outright? When will a voice loud enough become audible? The voice of those who have found that for which it is worth living and who will shout down the clamor of those who want so eagerly to instruct us as to those things worth dying for.

What follows here is written then not out of despair, but out of a belief that neither life nor human labor is without purpose. To lament the incredible darkness of this world is less important than justifying life by sheltering each other from cynical nihilism and deception. This generation, perhaps not in America as decisively as elsewhere, has paid a fantastic price in blood and destruction. It must be this generation that now establishes the irreplaceable value of life and calls a halt to the high priests of injustice. My hope is that Man has not kept himself from seeking happiness and that basically we enjoy living.

Our deepest need is not for more explanation, more things to have and to use. We know that we can be efficient, we know that we can organize numbers, build bridges, find cures, split atoms. It is not organization we lack, nor the impulse to do research and to discover every aspect of nature. What we lack is a passionate respect for the persisting concern which each generation is summoned to realize in its acts of decency and loyalty to its fellowmen. I do not mean the acceptance of moral rules only nor yet merely compassion with each other's lot. Rather the fact that in our acts of a responsive nature we partake of life not just with a will to live, but with an obedience to what we are in the totality of existence. It is a partaking that liberates us from isolation, it is a freedom to do, to perform deeds according to our choices and commitments and to be more than free. That is: to be *with* the entirety which speaks through us, our uniqueness and partnership in one. All of life is sanctified, is holy, because from the moment our parents conceived us, we entered into a bond. In our emergence we entered into a chain of being elected, privileged and known for all that which in the here and now we can bring to expression by our deeds. Our deepest need is to rediscover that sense of being known in a context of real obligations. For from the freedom which results from these obligations, evolves the hard core knowledge of our dignity and that of others.

When we give in to the utilitarian obsession with what is expedient and efficient, we always end up concluding deals by which our sanctity is bartered away. The result is confusion about our value and loss of the certainty that through us speaks an answerability which, from time to time, makes it possible to transcend our immediate needs and to complete what we are here for. A better life can unfold for us at every turn if we do not forget these roots, this origin of tangible nobility. This is the foundation of life which must be rebuilt in our generation and it can be attained by participation, whatever our doubts, whatever our disappointments and hurt. Not faith, but Man is our ultimate concern.

It took Christianity many turbulent ages to overcome its pagan Messianism. And the pagan is not dead. We need not wait for more centuries of darkest trauma before creating the fiber of new social foundations fit for conscious and concerned living.

Man is a reluctant brother, yet again and again his reluctance is overcome by daring acts of humanity.

Man is a reluctant brother, but he is a sharing creature. His generous impulses, his desire for participation are the foundation of his continuity. Those fragile moments of awareness and release from despair are measures of both his greatness and his limitations. Whatever the despair, I believe we can discover the inner milieu, the environment that can translate the passion for life into passionate living.

Isaiah wrote: "A Man shall be as a hiding place from the wind." I believe that he can. I believe—not without frequent doubt—that we can be shelter to others, and that by our daily works we can relieve the immense pressures that threaten life itself. It is this knowledge of a transformative possibility that saves me from my blackest thoughts and the fear of being overcome by the miasma of callousness that permeates our era.

FROM SELF-DESTRUCTION TO CO-HUMANIZATION

Pericles said that the main effort of Greek civilization had been exerted in "banning melancholy." In doing so, the Athenians, thus he told us, had been "lovers of beauty without having lost the taste for simplicity."

One could probably say the same about the efforts of any culture. Human beings are not reactive robots performing in prescribed fashion whenever an outside stimulus reaches them. Our reactions are also determined by what happens within us and in this is our independence.

American culture in its own fashion also works at banishing melancholy and loneliness. It too aims at finding a balance between the anxieties that beset its citizens and ways of resolving those anxieties. Yet the form which this endeavor has taken has made it desperately necessary to find reassurance that each person matters.

We do indeed function together in a social order of incredible opportunity when compared with almost any other civilization, but in that order each individual learns early that he must swim or sink. For many the promise of cooperative effort ends at adolescence. Thus, while on the one hand individuals become more able to rely on themselves, that same sense creates deep feelings of separateness. To be free often means to be freed *from* restrictive socio-economic regulations, but it does not necessarily mean to be free *for* any particular purpose. Inner satisfactions, contemplative strength appear to be pale when contrasted with what one can acquire. Inner convictions seem less important than the capacity "to play ball" and the hunger for ideas in our young is replaced by the advice to "keep things under control." Thus happiness far too frequently is defined in hollow terms, "fun" is confused with joy and interest with excitement.

Of course this applies to all industrialized nations. "Lovers of beauty" have become a distinct minority. Even our women are tempted more and more to fit competitively in the strait-jacket of a masculinized ideal in which vigor, energy and economic productivity are the main virtues. Much of our marital breakdown is due to a lack of clarity with regard to what it means to be a man and what it means to be a woman.

I say this not because I despair for American culture but because of my growing conviction that we are short-selling ourselves. Our culture, as all others, has factors which promote growth and others which stand in the way of growth. Most of the time these operate simultaneously.

The persistence of human dignity depends on whether we can still teach our children that character and values are not the products of society, but of the cultivation of inner resources and convictions. The seedbed for social health depends on private preparation. What we attempt to satisfy by our productivity and vigor does not of necessity lead to a good life nor a good community. Educational systems which raise the young primarily for ways to fit more lucratively into the existing order of things, miss the point that human growth does not always result in success or happiness, but at least as often in an encounter with pain and loss. Yet, without that realization there is personal and social stagnation. Any kind of progress occurs in spite of setbacks or traumatic realities and this is the only pathway to private courage and to an inner core of person strong enough to deal with all of life.

Contradictions and conflicts of values cannot be sidestepped. In their very dynamics lie the possibility for the survival and the strengthening of that freedom without which personal dignity is but an abstraction.

In this period of growing awareness of value paradoxes, modern Humanism may be slowly maturing in the American environment. While many remain resigned to the irrelevance of traditional religious institutions and partake of them merely in a symbolic way, others have recognized a powerful yearning for some unifying direction. To them it has become obvious that to be doers cannot be enough. I see a growing quest for things more timeless and engaging than status.

We need today therefore the reconstruction of inner-directed ideals to go hand-in-hand with our tradition of social optimism. Such an attitude of life need not be a dumb denial of the possibility of the tragic. While human circumstances have a great number of factors which cannot be changed, there is, nevertheless, a wide range with which we can interfere and thus learn that man and the institutions he has constructed are plastic and reversible.

We need to understand that nature is that which is happening, that which is in flux. Our nature often has to be enriched and we need to recognize that there is an evolutionary order of becoming. Not everything in us can be equally respected nor are all people equal in their development. I will ascribe worth to every man in all circumstances, but respect depends upon his state of human development. I am afraid that he who can honor all equally at all times can also equally negate all at any time.

This concerns our ethics. We know very well that we do not always try to bring out "the good" in others. It is more complex.

In our contacts with some we bring out the worst, know it, and somehow fatefully repeat our behavior. It is important to recognize compulsions which we all too easily parade as our "unchangeable" selves. There is the story of the man who came to see his senator. As soon as he entered the chambers, he burst out, "Senator, I think you are a thief, a robber and a scoundrel!" To which the representative of the people drily remarked: "Well, that is all right, my friend, as long as you don't impeach my honor!" Obviously "honor" is a variable!

A true test for a mature civilization is its approach to deviant social behavior. I do not plead for such deviation, but simply ask that we reserve judgment until the interrelated aspects of personality and circumstances are understood. A good example is our attitude towards those who, usually for desperate reasons, turn towards drug addiction. Our society insists that the addict be prevented from getting the drugs he craves. Upon moral grounds we find it unnatural for a man to use narcotics even though most of us have some kind of addiction to aspirin, barbiturates, tranquilizers, alcohol, tobacco, or what-have-you.

It is known that the average drug addict behaves fairly well and can continue to function in society when he can obtain the drugs. It is only when society prevents him from having legally what he craves that his anxiety grows and delinquency begins. Drug addicts are sick people; they have to be helped and they have to be cured. To insist that they are corrupt and asocial is an example of the moralistic compulsions of our society. It is as ineffective as telling an alcoholic to stop drinking. That which causes the deviation is the issue, that which warped the fulfillment of existence is the human concern and to enter into a sustaining attitude towards that single human being is the essential task. Moralistic, judgmental rejection is the exact opposite of healing aid.

Let us be careful lest our moralisms become socialized

cruelty, for that is where immorality arises. The concept of responsibility is derived from two words: response and ability, being able to respond. But what if that ability is impaired? Conscience is not a vague notion. Reasonable expectations and knowledge of what is valuable can help develop conscience with a concern in depth. Not some foggy interest in people, not sham moralism, but a crucial involvement which can reestablish the ability to respond. This is pertinent to an understanding of the deviant person.

We can probably maintain that no act in itself is ever justified but must always be measured by its consequences. This means the assertion of reciprocity between individuals. A concept of this kind which a hundred years ago passed for just a pious wish, is now proven in the clinical tests of psychotherapy. Psychiatrists and psychologists have learned that without reciprocity there is sickness, self-destruction and sometimes death. Child psychologists have concluded that children deprived of tenderness in earliest infancy, have a tendency to become mentally underdeveloped and that some of them will actually become permanently retarded. In some hospitals today, a head nurse will write the letters "TLC" on the chart, to remind other nurses that the patient must be given "Tender, Loving Care." A moral postulate is thus proven scientifically. The strength of human uniqueness is universally applicable and gains its value from experience.

This raises the question of whether humanistic concerns can create a counterbalance to the estrangement of mass living. They can, but only by recognizing that which in the day-to-day experience sustains the ability to respond. It is the consciousness that we are claimed by life and are directed and linked to each other. Each of us can distill out of his own experience the impulse of being with life rather than against it. And the faith evoked by engaging life and which is justified by it, cannot be willfully engineered. Nor need such faith thwart our reason, for rationality depends upon letting life address us as we function with others. Quest is at the heart of such faith, not exalted revelation.

It is when faith is set apart from daily experience and turmoil that the irrationalities of collectivism attain their chance. Society should have no other purpose than protecting the individual's capacity to seek a disclosure of what his own life responsibilities are. Thus man can overcome emptiness and discover his nearness to others.

The modern state has difficulty tolerating the genuinely committed man who draws upon his own resources concerning right and wrong, and who would put the probing of his own mind above the mythology of "chosen" leadership. This applies particularly to political leaders who, at mysterious "summits" determine the fate of two billion or more human creatures; the mythical fathers who can pat childrens' soft hair and growl threats of destruction at the same time. There is a need to denounce the voices of schizoid salvation.

The committed man cannot submit his life to the orgies of power because he wants to reserve for himself judgment and decision. He will be inclined to build in his children resistance against pressure and complacent respectability. He wants to escape being fingerprinted, being made an object for propaganda rather than shared responsibility. The committed person does not want to escape the contradictions of values. He knows that more is at stake in man than to be a digit in a computerized universe. Therefore, in a great number of instances, he must bear witness to the fact that he will not compromise with the menace of the collectivities—be they political, military or credal. He knows that dogmas do not create faith. It is time to promote such rebellion. The concern for human dignity in this second half of the twentieth century cannot be based upon elegant literature, but must confront the fact that there is so little regret, so little humility before the unspeakable number of innocent dead. What, in the name of all that is sane, can anyone still hope to redeem by war and killing?

I remember as a boy on a hiking trip, coming upon the first World War battlefields of Verdun. A guide told us that every inch of that soil, miles and miles around, was mixed with fragments of human bodies. We were shown a museum in which only scraps of fallen soldiers had been gathered and kept in tiny, crypt-like containers covering wall after wall, from floor to ceiling.

As I emerged from that place of horror, I was physically sick and a panic took hold of me in trying to put distance between myself and that calamity. Collectivization of conscience can only be overcome by proclaiming that unless we protect the innocent and stop the self-mutilation, we will end up in a world riddled by schizoid distortions. A world of death. What we need most is a practical affirmation that each soul transcends mere utilitarian evaluation, that worth dwells in each as an unconditional given.

Personal engagement in the process of securing economic justice, racial equality, the never-ending struggle for peace are the most certain ways to halt the deflation of human worth, the cluttering of our lives by trivia. One cannot construct a humanist faith artificially. The prerequisite is to be steeped in the longing for salvaging one's soul alive and not to be swept up in the abstractions of the collective ego or ideological brainwashing. We can escape looking upon ourselves as merely socioeconomic "units" by the realization that we owe our gathered resources, mental as well as material, to an enduring orientation away from the hustlings of the mediocre. The problem is that while our entire culture is steeped in the mythology of individualism, most men are denied the socio-economic and political means to achieve co-humanization. The more one becomes a bread-earning, child-rearing, family provider, the less the individual finds opportunity—if he wants to survive—to express the private values he may hold. Thus from the very start we go through a socialization process in which such values as honesty, personal opinions, or religious individuation are apt to run into violent conflict with what the culture expects. There is no doubt that this is one of the causes of the epidemic proportions of mental illness in this nation. It is most unreasonable to let patterns of outdated competitiveness determine how we shall live with each other. Reconstruction of human beings in society will have to be based upon our need for each other and upon the education of the young with the idea that each person is needed in a co-supportive venture. Institutionalized frustration leads *ipso facto* to institutionalized irrationality and from there to the many variations on the theme of self-destruction. The maturity of any given society can be tested to the degree to which the web of human relationships creates greater inner freedom, greater ability to love. The more institutionalized frustration and suspicion, the less the capacity to resist collectivism and ultimate centralization of authority and enslavement. Totalitarian personalities are not born, they are society produced. Men who have lost the capacity to stand up against adjustment to all those things to which no one should adjust have sold their person for a bowl of social approval and in surrendering have lost their reasons for being.

INTUITION AND DESTINY

According to Deuteronomy, in the Old Testament, when a man had killed a fellow human being he had to be held "accountable" as though he had mutilated the image of God.

We are "accountable," I think, not just for the immediate consequences of our acts but beyond that for a significance and mutuality.

When that deeper reason for being human is denied, or desecrated, something of immense value is destroyed.

The more we develop scientifically and technologically, the greater the danger that such psychic depths will be denied. Our type of civilization weans us away from the experience of mutuality. Yet, maturing human beings are increasingly in need of those participational processes which, though speaking to us in a subtle voice, help us maintain balance and sanity. We are "accountable" to ourselves. The admirable within us as well as the unlovable is accounted for and not only "sick" people suffer from guilt and anxiety. Sickness results when the sense of being needed is perpetually frustrated by warped values. All that which hinders the fruition and encouragement of the full person, all that which is silent when one should speak truth, all that which forces a man to squander his talents or his health, all that which discriminates against another, which lies or betrays, all such attitudes are based upon choices which make a man despicable to himself. For by so doing he also ruins what he is accountable for beyond his own immediate desires. Such affront against one's inner nature makes it ever more difficult to use one's pains and conflicts for the development of sounder norms.

We can define human beings linguistically and empirically, but there is no definition for the depths of their participatory possibilities. Yet, the unconscious is not some remote or chaotic realm. It is the repository to which are gathered our acts of decency and good relationship; it is an "account" upon which our potentialities can draw as our love again and again presses to be stirred. We are human because that reciprocal actualization is at stake in us as a life-giving possibility. And the first step towards awareness of such processes is to reject the notion that these reaches are somehow mysterious. Why not put trust in those resources? Why with all the conscious striving over all the centuries has so little changed in the world? The answer is obviously that despite our high degree of civilization most of what we know about human beings is still the incidental not

the motivational. So many, for example, have been disappointed
in liberal causes. People who seem to be nobly motivated venture forth but things turn out badly. One sees the same power
drives, the needs for status, the eternal eruptions of jealousy because many "angry" men and women seem frequently drawn
to good causes. Desire for changes of social structure will not
change the unconscious drives. In this unconscious, in its
images, fantasies and impulses, we have a huge amount of
dynamic strength that remains barely explored. We reject most
of what we know about the intuitive life and yet our awareness
of "soul" is the residue of centuries of experiences too important
to be denied.

We are faced with scientific, socio-economic and credal developments that have molded the outer world and paid scant
attention to man's inner realizations. Therefore, the study of
philosophy, sociology, religion, frequently remains abstract and
does not offer a way of life, nor does it add to our perserverance
and understanding. This is true also of abstract art, where free
form becomes meaningless in the light of personal experience.
We may have knowledge, but rarely wisdom. We may have
a great accumulation of facts, but rarely faith. In much of our
thinking we are tied to word-signals, not content. The more
complex our use of language, the more we are in danger of
moving away from essential cognition. Appearances may often
be highly intellectual yet their effects may be irrational. As a
matter of fact, where once "the word" set us free, as Jung*
pointed out, now the word is used to deceive us—from weight-
reducing ads to political mythology. The corruption of meaning
on all levels has made us suspicious. Because of advertising
techniques, we are actually word-*resistant*, distrusting most
men and their utterances. This is the failing of so much of
modern literature, which contains voluminous descriptions of

*Carl G. Jung, *The Undiscovered Self* (Many of the psychological insights ex-
pounded here are contained in the writings of Jung, Huxley, Jones and Stärcke.)

what happened *to* people but not what happened *within* them. One finds in one novel after the other accurate reporting of the most intimate happenings while the functional whole of the individual remains unexplored.

I do not know how many of us dare still trust our intuitions, how many of us are still capable of escaping the image we have created of ourselves as fictional personalities. That which is decent and humane and reasonable has never yet succeeded in the world, neither in families and marriages, nor in the international community except at those rare moments where the deeper insights of the inner life were at work. One person, one person who has wisdom, who knows what aches in people, who knows how to build courage and sacrifice without becoming a caricature, one such person can save a family.

There are incredible threats in our time, the disasterous possibilities for destruction cannot be stopped by an appeal to a political rationale. We would like so much to think of ourselves as motivated by a well-ordered ego, but we are not. We must learn to rely upon the fundamental two-fold reality of the intuitive as well as the analytical and this can lead to ways of life not determined by collective standards.

To illustrate more precisely what I mean by taking cognizance of our inner life, I would like to share a personal experience, dealing with the recognition of what Boris Pasternak called our being "guests in this world." He meant to say that we have no claim to anything here, that we are here by chance, and so while we may enjoy our stay, we finally must leave. An enjoyment of life is a state of being that can be recalled—it is a part of you—and it is a source of strength as well as solace. Joy is not measured in minutes or hours; it is something that suddenly envelopes us, perhaps in the midst of an otherwise trivial moment. It can fill us with an immeasurable happiness and, as with all happiness, it has within it a touch of the bittersweet.

One summer night in Massachusetts I walked along a beach

and it was absolutely quiet. The air was motionless and since it had been a hot day, millions of little cell structures were lighting the waves, each carried to an unknown destiny. While first seeing only its beauty, I later became aware of my part in this eternal returning for I perceived in it a dimension beyond the visual.

Somehow we need to be the integrators of natural experiences which underlie the recuperative power. As my life has unfolded I have come to trust deeply in that reality of endurance and recuperation. I have found it amidst the extraordinary pressures of the concentration camps. Those human beings who stay whole even when sick and starved and tortured, and who therefore can continue to give themselves to others, are individuals in whom the recuperative power is stronger than the horror which tries to crush them. The life of a man who builds such wholeness is not without conflict and setback. No, such life is full of struggle towards an integration within pain and conflict which cannot be resolved. If we can learn to draw upon those forgotten layers we can learn to claim for ourselves the greatest of all human acquirements: the strength to choose for ourselves, to be our own man.

ALBERT CAMUS: PASSIONATE HUMANIST

Koheleth, the Preacher of the Old Testament, has, perhaps as no one else, spelled out how much our life is in need of overcoming a sense of anguish and futility. Many hundreds of years later, the seventeenth century English poet, John Donne, reflecting upon the rapid changes of the turbulent times in which he lived, commented that he was dealing with the "frailty and decay of this whole world."

Anguish is certainly not known to everyone, however, and "not knowing" remains the refuge of many. What are the ways in which we accommodate ourselves to everyday realities? And, what is the emotional cost?

The problem of individual suffering overcome only in very private ways preoccupied the French author, Albert Camus, more than anything else. In his book, *The Rebel,* Camus asks for the definition of a conscious man and concludes that he must be an individual who can say both "no" and "yes." For both responses occur once the human being begins to think for himself. The moment a man finds he has a voice, even though he uses it only to say "no," he begins to evaluate particular things in his particular way. Despair may make us revolt, but unless we engage ourselves for—or against—something, our rebellion is of little consequence. We cannot deal with ourselves and our life decisions in generalities. The price we pay is too specific. Once our conscience is awakened we confront reality. We may not like that reality but it moves us to action—and whatever direction we take will express our own sense of meaning and thereby unite us with other men.

Camus' belief that there is a possibility for man to become "more" than himself, is also stressed in his book, *The Stranger.* Here he deals with a person who, almost without emotion, buries his mother in the morning, has intercourse with a girl he hardly knows that same afternoon and spends the evening in a theatre. Afterwards, bewildered by his own feelings, he kills an Arab somewhere on a beach in Algiers. When the judge asks him why he has murdered, his meek reply is, "It was the sun; it was the heat and the brilliant light." His act of killing was pure chance—like a series of incidents leading up to a phenomenon of nature. There was the bright sunshine which dazed him—and then "it just happened . . ." He did not decide anything, he made no choices. Camus asks as it were: how many decisions determining our fate are on the same level? How conscious are we, how much resistance do we have against supposedly irreversible factors?

During the trial, the prosecutor calls the man an animal without a soul. His lawyer describes him as a lifeless object. Other lawyers rush over to congratulate their colleague after he rests his defense. One has the temerity to ask the accused: "That was a fine talk, wasn't it?" But the killer confesses that he is bored by the entire circus; he has detached himself to avoid any confrontation with reality.

Who are the defendants of our world, where are their attorneys? Are we interested in the methodical decisions which anonymous tacticians have arrogated to themselves?

Or are we also detached, disengaged? At the trial everyone goes about his business "as usual." The lawyer has done a day's work at Court. He lost his case, but he made a good speech. The prosecutor has scored his points and the condemned man does not care. It is not even certain that he perceives what is happening! This, Camus states, is the human condition.

We are talked about and processed to perform in a gigantic drama, yet we are hardly aware and on the contrary, are caught up in our own abstractions.

Our generation, condemned by depressions, collectivisms and war, is granted at best the privilege of being the object of some fine speeches. Camus raises his voice against this silent rhythm of submission. He calls for commitment to those things worth living for. Man must acquire a voice again and affirm the power of conscience. When he refers to the need to rebel, Camus does not mean "to the barricades," but a transformation of Self. Man is not an interesting object for rationalization and manipulation, he is a self-transcendent agent.

Albert Camus, who won the Nobel Prize in 1957, was killed in 1960 in an automobile accident. A blown-out tire confirmed Camus' concept of the "absurdity" of death. He had grasped the anguish of our times, the loss of faith, and he sought to transcend the lure of nihilism. Out of the depth of his anguish, he forged a faith for, as he said in Stockholm, accepting the Nobel Prize: "This generation has had to reestablish, both within and without itself, a little of what constitutes the dignity of life and death."

We need not explore the evil in other men, it can be abundantly experienced in ourself. Our problem is how to shelter the world from that which imprisons us, how to struggle with the sources of disconnectedness.

On receiving the Nobel Prize, he added that what he had been looking for in life was the "fundamental man." Fundamental man who can be hurt easily and destroyed, who can be selfish and unjust but who at the same time knows the craving for peace, the hunger for justice, the eternal hope of overcoming despair. There is beauty of life within its frustration. As he put it in one of his novels, "In the midst of winter, I finally learned that there was in me an invincible summer."

Camus was born in a small farming town in eastern Algeria in November, 1913. His childhood was one of exceeding poverty. He described it by saying that he had been born "half-way between misery and the sun."

It was only after the defeat of France in 1940 that Camus, who joined the Resistance Movement immediately, was heard from by most. In his essays entitled *The Myth of Sisyphus*, he argued that however hopeless the never-ending tasks of life, it is by the quality with which we engage ourselves and do what is our duty, that we determine our dignity. The issue is not that we suffer and die, but what we do with these few poor years.

Camus was a man who, when he enjoyed life, did so behind a veil of intense melancholy. Determinant in his intellectual life, no doubt, during the war and in the early post-war period was his contact with the existentialist philosopher, Jean Paul Sartre. The first impulse of the existentialist movement was a rather desperate one. The whole world had fallen into dust, the comrades with whom one had fought against fascism had been executed or had died in concentration camps. The world looked empty. War collaborators and profiteers had survived and were fat, while decent men, and the children of an entire generation had perished. It seemed as if the rats had taken over all of humanity and this became the theme for Camus' *The Plague*. The desolate sentiments which engulfed the intellectuals had no appeal to him; to Camus the concept of a meaningless world was unacceptable!

Here it was that Sartre and Camus parted company: Sartre in the direction of a deterministic Marxism, Camus in the direction of a militant humanism. Yet, many of those who have read his works see in Camus' writings a testament of despair and find it difficult to discern his credo as an affirmation of life. Camus knew that affirmations, to make sense, have to be gained in a struggle with fate and he was courageous enough to confront again and again the realistic physical and emotional disasters in store for our generation. He warned against the ease with which we commit spiritual suicide.

When Camus died, the *New York Times* wrote of him: "There can be no surprise that our era has responded to Camus' message. The terrible slaughter of two World Wars, the unprecedented menace of the hydrogen bomb—these are part of the modern setting which made Camus' austere philosophy comprehensible and assured his memory such immortality as mere men can give."

Yet, he had summed up this "austere" creed with great force at the end of his novel *The Plague*. After the terrible epidemic siege, after the rats have taken over the city, after thousands and thousands of dead have been buried, at last the quarantine is lifted, and the little town rejoices. The physician who remained at his post reminds himself that the ancients were right. Man will always begin again. What helps the human being is his power of innocence, his capacity for dealing with pain. Still the doctor knows that the human community will always be threatened by some plague. During the periods between the outbreak of epidemics the dark days of terror are forgotten but the bacillus of the plague does not die. It is dormant, but ready to be awakened at moments of lack of commitment. Camus castigated the plague of violence in the hatred, the racism, which can descend upon any community. His message is that men do not have to be saints in order to be healers. If they are conscious of their mutuality, they can intercept the disease. Here is no naive philosophy, for Camus had seen too much to put man on a pedestal. At the same time, he insisted upon our ability to overcome and bring together what life scatters. That healing capacity is as real as our frailty.

In a short essay on his return to the town of his youth in Algiers, he made this autobiographical statement:

> "Few epochs require as much as ours that one should be equal to the best as to the worst . . . to shirk nothing and to keep faithfully a double memory. . . . A memory of the best and of the worst . . ."

There is tremendous strength in the decision "to shirk nothing," to reject nothing of life and in the courage to accept the fact that mutuality includes pain. We can lessen the anxiety about those things we cannot change by dealing with the specifics of each other's reality, without camouflage and by pitting our faith against the torment of living. Camus' most scathing criticism is reserved for those who do not care enough to take the risks of mutuality.

In one of his most penetrating books, *The Fall*, the author takes us into the life of a man who once was a judge in France, but who now has settled in Amsterdam, Holland. His is a strange sort of career, guiding other Frenchmen around in the city. He is a transient who usually lives in a bar, and that is where he tells his story. His philosophy of life is one of un-relieved pessimism, for if the history of modern man has to be written he says it would suffice to write a single sentence which would read, "Man (he) fornicated and he read the newspapers."

The moment of confrontation for this man occurred one night in November, when walking home, he saw a young woman

standing near the bridge over a river. He could make out the
back of her neck, "damp between her hair and coat collar." As
he continued some fifty yards, he heard a sound breaking the
silence—the sound of a body striking the water and then . . . :

> "I stopped short but without turning around. Almost at once
> I heard a cry, repeated several times which was going down-
> stream, then it ceased. I was still listening as I stood motion-
> less. Then slowly under the rain, I went away. I informed no
> one."

Camus, no doubt was describing not only a particular man
but Europe and the world, waiting for the dull sound of bodies
falling and finding that it is "too late," that it is "too far";
turning around, doing nothing, unrelated. Camus rebels. He
rebels against the fact that people may perform little acts of
friendliness for one another, opening a door, giving alms to a
beggar, helping a blind person; but then, when the crucial
decisions are to be made, they disqualify themselves. We have
no time. We must make money and read the papers; we must
visit and talk and make sure that we are noticed.

Man's unbelievable indifference to the values which hold his
own life and that of his communities together, almost obsesses
Camus as it may have obsessed all prophetic voices in history.
In this context, we must note his profound preoccupation with
the scientific exactitude with which Hitler killed, deported or
assassinated his victims. Camus' generation will never stop
being haunted by this, asking: "Who were these methodical
killers? What terrible weakness in Western culture made them
possible?" What is of passionate importance is not the prosecution of war criminals but why they lived as they did, why
civilization was impotent in preventing their crimes, and what
conditioned the victims for their almost suicidal passivity.

Camus tells of a German lieutenant who politely—as a
gentleman, as an officer, asked an old woman in a Dutch vil-

lage to please choose which one of her sons she wanted to have shot as a hostage! There is here a shattering total tragedy involving the woman, the officer and the men to be shot. "You choose that one? Or that one? Or no, this one?" As if executions were a matter of choice.

In the same vein, in the book, *The Fall*, the chief character discusses the fact that many people proclaim that they love life and respect the lives of others, and yet, he asks, "Maybe we don't love life enough? Have you noticed that death alone awakens our feelings? How we love the friends who have just left us?"

THE ANGUISHED HEART

Camus was not a cynic; he insisted upon the basic innocence of man, and he mercilessly exposed the self-assurance with which so many willingly participate in injustice and self-love which always comes before love.

Clamence, the lawyer is really a monstrous man who negates others in order to constantly test his own superiority. The way to do this, he has discovered, is to make others feel guilty. When he can manage to convince his listener that all men are equally guilty, then his own ambitions are no longer so evil! He confesses "covered with ashes, . . . I stand before all humanity recapitulating my own disgrace without losing sight of the effect I am producing."

Clamence is the typical false prophet of ideology and through him Camus attacks the Christian idea of universal guilt, which to him is a form of mental slavery.

Beyond the passionate attacks upon hypocrisy, Camus wants an explanation of why so many desire totalitarian systems. Throughout his work runs a belief that men are not naturally wicked but that the responsibility for the crimes of mass movements (whether Nazism or Bolshevism) rests with those philosophies which suppress the individual's capacity for moral growth and therefore see no issue in sacrificing lives for their holy grails. Camus is deeply concerned with the rationalizations and justifications for killing in the twentieth century. He is critical of intellectuals who are willing to support revolutionary movements, willing to accept violence and cruelty in the name of ideological abstractions.

Camus is not politically partisan. He searches for the human "why," for the revolt of our time must have meaning in the lives of common persons rather than demand their sacrifice. What counts are not the lofty ideological battles but the protest against the suffering of all men, women and children who write human history with their own blood. Real rebellion must be protest against injustice, for the ordinary person is not interested in transforming the world; he wants to get rid of the cruelty which crushes him and his family.

One cannot consider the thoughts of Camus without discovering a core of life, a sense of liberation beyond comfort in illusions of either a political or a theological nature. Life must be justified by life itself; it has to be made worthwhile because of ourselves. It is in this context that a total moral philosophy of life emerges, a sense of relatedness which makes for sanity, a way of facing the reality too of our own death.

Camus chose not to be overcome by the drainage of life for his credo was: "Human beings must love together, or die together; there is no other way."

Our greatest tragedy consists of suffocating each other's essence and keeping one another from using the potential for fulfillment. We need a rediscovery of all that which we can admire in the human effort.

In 1948, in one of his most creative post-war years, Camus was invited by the Dominican Fathers of Latour Maubourg to speak of his life philosophy. After reminding the good friars that "the world needs real dialogue" and that he, a non-

Christian, would not try to say anything that might be agreeable to all and therefore be worthless, he excoriated the Pope for not speaking out more courageously against Nazi persecution during the war. If the Dominicans wanted to continue regarding themselves as Christians, he argued, they should know that to him, Camus, ". . . a Spanish bishop who blesses political executions, ceases to be . . . a Christian or even a man, (but) he is a dog, just like the one who orders that execution without doing the dirty work himself."

Greatly preoccupied at that time with the death of millions of Jewish children, he cried out: "Perhaps we can not prevent this world from being a world in which children are tortured. But if we cannot get rid of evil, at least we can take care not to add to it."*

As a passionate Humanist, in rebellion against a world in which life is held too cheaply he was particularly aware of what he called "failure by default." The failure to achieve what is decent because at the decisive moment, we cannot get ourselves to do what is right.

In the story, *The Two Sides of the Medal,* an old lady is suddenly gripped by her fear of death. She is alone while her family decides to visit the theatre. A young relative she had hoped would stay with her, particularly hurts her by also leaving. Thus she remains with her solitary tears at the crucial moment of her death. Elsewhere, a person dies in his hotel room, miserable and alone, while someone next door is fully aware that something terrible is happening, but finds himself absent-mindedly studying the label on his shaving cream.

Man's greatest detractor, Camus suggests, is indifference to life, the casual approach to the fate of others. Cheap pity can easily turn to contempt and hostility but in true involvement there is *compassion* rather than pity. Compassion which says,

*This quote and others in the posthumously published collection: *Resistance, Rebellion and Death*—Frank J. O'Brien, Knopf, New York

"I know what you suffer, because I know such suffering myself. The pain in you is a pain I know myself. Therefore, give me your hand."

We are not powerless to change our lives provided we will engage ourselves without superficial dramatization. We live a brief life; there are a great many things we cannot do anything about and it is therefore a primary responsibility to do nothing that may increase the misery of another person. Camus' concern is not "soft," it is not a lamentation and there is nothing metaphysical about his passage: "We love or we die together."

There is no literary anesthesia here. His was, above all, a voice seeking pathways to personal truth.

We are confronted then with two major concerns of the twentieth century: *In the first place,* our knowledge of the self-destructive nature of hostility and our seeming incapacity to deal with it in our families, and in the world. *Secondly,* our human dislocation in an age of "efficiency" in which man becomes but an extension of a never-resting productive order. How will we survive as human beings in a technological civilization?

We must reject equally the illusion that "all will be well" in the end and the fatalism of: "there is nothing we can do." Cynicism and distrust are linked closely with hatred and fury.

In his remarkable essay entitled *Letters to a German Friend,* Camus comes to grips with what the inner "enemy" is. These so-called "letters" were written in one of the underground publications of the French Resistance movement. It meant risking one's life to write these illegal pamphlets and the Nazi Gestapo was constantly on the lookout for their author. Camus' act was one of an extraordinary affirmation of his credo. What could be more difficult than to write a letter to a "German friend" when one knew that the Germans were trying to capture and execute the author? Yet he wrote as he did, not just to expose Nazism but because he did not want the French, engaged in the Resistance, to lose their own sense of human solidarity. Hate, after all, injures the soul of the hater and makes him unfit for the enormous task of human reconstruction.

I was part of the underground movement at that time and remember that there was much discussion about these "letters." Many thought that Camus had been wrong, that one should preach unwavering hostility of the oppressor and not try to maintain a line of communication. Some went so far as to cancel their trust in him. Yet Camus wrote: "I should like to be able to love my country and still love justice." In this is the essence of his greatness as a Humanist.

For the humanist idea of love is to accept the fact that all life is marred by imperfection and that nevertheless, we must be loyal and struggle with our differences, and injuries while keeping a thirst for decency alive. If we do not do this, we will "fail by default," fail because of a lack of mutuality.

"Rebellion" as Camus uses it then does not mean denial but rather the affirmation of reasons for living. Rebellion and revolt mean conscience; just as freedom means duty and life must be experienced as purpose from day to day, from issue to issue. To live life this way is to live with dignity. Therefore the price for living in depth is to revolt against fatalism and that within us which is suicidal.

In a final thrust at his German correspondent Camus gave the reason why his resistance must continue. He cried out, ". . . you have never known what to select (to live for) but you have always known what to destroy . . . still we will have faith in another force. . ."

Humanism has been described as a "generous guidance" for life. Generous in that it invites Man to meet his own strength. Such generous guidance was the essence of the spirit of Camus. He wrote: "What is Man? Man is that force which ultimately cancels all tyrants and all Gods. He is the force of evidence."

Everywhere in the world, there are men and women who

embody that human evidence by acts of human affirmation.
They keep alive the honor of mankind by their belief that life
must be respected, that there are things worth living and dying
for. Their solidarity is the repository of hope throughout the
ages.

EICHMANN: DEATH AND THE BUREAUCRAT

". . . and still we will have faith in another force . . ." was
the challenge of Camus to his German opponent as we saw in
the previous section. The nobility of this defiance of the forces
of death and destruction was born out of rebellion against the
encroachment of cynicism and scientific barbarism.

No chronicle of this epoch would be complete therefore
without considering the phenomenon of the modern mass killer
disguised as a bureaucrat. Adolph Eichmann, the dispassionate
killer of millions, provides us with the perfect example.

His trial in Jerusalem raised once more the anxious question
whether the lesson of Nazism had taught anything to this generation. Prof. Hannah Arendt, in her book, *Eichmann in Jeru-*
salem, spoke of the "banality of evil", for mass destruction of
human life—an ultimate evil—has become an everyday consideration of political and military leaders as well as of scientists. War has been one of the persistent characteristics of the
human species and with luck one can hope for peaceful interludes of possibly twenty to twenty-five years. Yet, even these
interludes are now full of the rumors of violence and the preparation for the next slaughter.

In World War II victory could well have gone to Nazism for
the survival margin of the free nations was at times precari-
ously small. No one can predict with certainty that next time
some other warrior nation may not in fact succeed in enslaving
the rest of the world.

If we continue as we have, if we continue to speak about
"human nature" when we mean murder, if we continue to feed

the urge for calamity, if we persist in the habitual patterns, then the archaic wish for a "final" cataclysmic disaster may well become irresistible. It is for this reason that Adolph Eichmann and what he stood for needs to be understood. His incredible career was possible only because there were not enough persons in any of the countries in which he operated who were free enough of the delusions which made mass destruction of men, women and children an acceptable proposition.

Eichmann became a reality when in 1941, the eighth year of Hitler's Thousand Year Reich, Professor Joachim Mrugowsky, an honorary colonel of the SS, initiated the "Institute for Virus Research" in Germany. This was a pseudonym for a slaughterhouse the equal of which cannot be found in human history. The opening of the Institute was, in fact, the beginning of medical experimentation upon human beings in Nazi Germany. All those who participated were professors of medicine at German universities. Among them was the President of the German Red Cross, Professor Karl Gebhardt, Chief Surgeon of the world-famous faculty of orthopedic surgery in Berlin. Thousands of scholars were engaged in this program which implanted cancer cells in wombs, gangrene in the legs and ovaries of girls and infectious cultures in the reproductive organs of male prisoners. The bacteriological and pharmaceutical phase was handled by the Behring Werke, by Bayer and the I.G. Farben Industry. The laboratories were spotlessly clean; the records, especially those of the world-renowned Robert Koch Institute, were carefully kept and in perfect order when they fell into Allied hands. Eichmann was not among the participants and most of the "Herren" Professors would have considered him a lout. The first entry in the professorial diary reads simply: "Since animal experiments cannot provide us with adequate evaluation, experiments must now be conducted upon human beings."

And it was in the tenth year of Hitler's Thousand Year Reich that I saw the SS physician of Auschwitz walk into the camp on Sunday afternoons, together with his lovely, nine-year old son. With a meticulously gloved hand, while pleasantly conversing with the child, he pointed to the men, women and children to be used for the next experiment or suffocation by poison gas.

Many of the victims were simply infected and then given no treatment at all in order to learn the human tolerance to pain and fever. All of them died in frightful agony. In charge of the experiments were, among others, Prof. Siegfried Handloeser, Chief of the German Institute for Medical Science and Research, an outstanding institution of learning, and Prof. Sigmund Rascher who worked in Munich with the German Space Research Instituute, officially called the Air Force Ground Level Testing Institute for Altitude Research.* This too was a faked identity for a charnel house.**

Victims were literally exploded by air pressure, or boiled by heat equivalent to that found when friction occurs at 70,000 feet. The professors took copious notes. Male prisoners were frozen until the heart almost stopped, at which moment women prisoners were brought to them and forced to engage in copulation to measure the recuperative power of the heart. After the act, both were executed. The professors took notes. . . . Himmler came, almost a thousand miles from Berlin, with a large retinue, especially to witness this experiment. It was very popular. Hundreds of the highest medical and military authorities in Germany were present and they had a marvelous time in Auschwitz where at one time a group of Polish women were forced to participate in a "beauty contest" in bathing suits, next to the gas chambers awaiting them. Himmler sent Prof. Rascher a telegram of congratulations, wishing him continued success with the experiments, closing with, "And remember me warmly

*The Theory and Practice of Hell, Eugene Kogon
**Nuremberg, Cooper

to your dear wife. Heil Hitler." Eichmann wasn't there. But it is against this background that we must think about the Eichmann trial in 1961. These are terrible things to describe. But they happened in our generation and in a country much akin to ours. Eichmann was unimportant, he was not a devil, there was nothing mysterious about his motives. We are dealing here not with metaphysics but with a social, political and economic system, consciously chosen by a large majority of the German people with the support of intellectuals, most of the clergy, the journalists, painters, actors, businessmen and trade union bosses. We are dealing with a way of life. Eichmann was possible because of that system, not the system because of Eichmann. That system, its philosophy and most of its leaders are alive today.

In America, a film on the Nuremberg trials was a Broadway success and every bookstore was gorged with precise descriptions of Nazi atrocities. What is the origin of this fascination with the "banality of evil"?

In the film, "Judgment at Nuremberg", a clean-cut American judge demonstrates to his German counterparts how to conduct fair trials. The German judges had had an unfortunate lapse of ethical judgment! So, the U.S.A. sends a kindly American judge to help them to distinguish better between right and wrong.

I protest, because this is a metaphysical approach to a strictly socio-political reality. German judges did what they did because they elected to and because they wanted to hold onto their position. We must not be misled; the world of ideas was not involved. This must be realized since our own attitude toward the Nazi past is also, by and large, a pragmatic one.

On the very day, for example, when the film first appeared on Broadway, the United States Secretary of Defense decorated the former Nazi general, Joseph Kammhuber, with the American Legion of Merit for reorganizing the German Air Force! A convicted war criminal, Foersch, was in command of the West German armed forces. General Hans Speidel commanded the NATO ground forces, even though he appeared on the war criminals list. NATO planning was carried out by war-criminal Adolf Heusinger and Hitler's naval admiral, Gerhard Wagner, was the NATO planner for the Northern Naval Sector, with Herman Goering's aide, General Ernst Kusserow at the head of the Air Defense Staff of NATO for Central Europe! Similarly the Russians used General von Paulus and many prominent Nazi scientists.

It is important to view Eichmann against the background of these postwar attitudes for how will we fit the enormous atrocities revealed at his trial into present world realities? Who is guilty and by what standards?

There are deep grooves in the psychology of Man. The open wounds created by the disastrous events of World War II have left many numbed and unwilling to consider the realities from which they grew. Maybe certain horrors cannot be absorbed. Maybe it takes a number of generations before they can really seep down into the consciousness of individuals.

But we cannot consider the Eichmann case without the context of the sociopolitical issues that his trial raised. Professor Hans Zeisel in the *Saturday Review* made the point that Eichmann's crimes were too remote from ordinary human experience to make them recognizable and that therefore the trial put the world's conscience to sleep. Instead of preoccupying himself with Eichmann, Zeisel wrote that he would like to talk about the Czechs who, in 1938, handed over to the Nazis 300 leading social-democrats who were foes of Hitler; and the seven Archbishops of Austria who, in 1938, from every pulpit in that country called upon all faithful Christians to welcome Hitler and to support him at the time of the "Anschluss"; and the Swiss administrators of the International Red Cross who did nothing to interfere with the extermination of civilians in the occupied countries; and the Englishman who, when told that Eichmann was willing to swaps one million prisoners for 10,000 trucks, is reported to have commented, "A million? What on earth are you thinking of? What should we do with a million Jews?"

He also wanted to talk about the American Consuls who withheld visas from persecuted people saying that they might be dangerous German spies even if they were very old women or very young children; or the men in the State Department who, after the war, sent an official interpretation of the Displaced Person's Act to all our Consulates overseas saying that a special privilege status must be granted to applicants of "Germanic origin", adding that such applicants must be, "Characteristically Germanic as defined by ancestors and with such common attributes of the Germanic group as social and political associations and name."

Who is guilty? Hitler's rise to power was not an "accident" and the crimes of his regime were not accidental phenomena. It was not only the circumstances of Germany in defeat that made his policies possible. It was the careful participation of all layers of society which fastened the yoke of Nazism around Germany's neck.

In 1937 a German writer, Wolfgang Bruegge wrote a lyrical statement about Hitler's voice, entitled, "When I Hear That Voice".* He said, "During all these years I've always had the same experience when I heard that voice. It wanted me to be better, to show me the way, to make me a German. It broke through the innermost doors. It dissolved with its fervency all my doubts and it suppressed in me the faint-hearted dog and awakened in me the hero." Bruegge was not an unlettered man. He had a great following in Germany, and he agreed with Hitler's denial of a common basis for mankind. He and millions of other Germans believed that "Thou shalt love thy neighbor as thyself", had to be changed to "Kill him who is not like yourself."

*Prosecutor's Statement—Gideon Hausner, Eichmann Trial Jerusalem Record

In retrospect it is hard to imagine the climate of Nazi Germany. However, it may be important to remember that there were exhibitions all over Germany to justify killing those of "inferior" race. Everywhere there were special museums, research institutes, university lectures, handbooks, political science courses, and mass meetings making one point: "To kill is to be manly." Germany proposed a League of Nations to kill minority groups. At the same time it was greedily reaching for the property of its victims nor was it difficult to find men and women in all occupied countries itching to step into an Aryanised business or to kill a professional in order to take his job.

When the guns of Nazi Germany were silenced, when the submarines were sunk, we thought that German militarism was defeated. But racism is still alive today even while the scapegoat has been killed!

There are a few more observations to be made about the culture which created Eichmann.

Here are two examples concerning the phenomenon of war crimes and the people who carried them out.

The first example occurred in 1946 at the International Tribunal where war criminals were judged at Nuremberg, Germany. One of the officers of the SS, the "elite" group, a man with a medical degree from the University of Heidelberg, had been called upon to testify in his own behalf. When the judge questioned him about his war crimes (he was one of those impregnating uterine cancer in captive women) he gave intelligent answers which showed his erudition. Later, when he was cross-examined on some of the atrocities in which he had been involved, he offered a discourse on Nazi psychology as though he were speaking to a scientific gathering. It was a precise analysis of SS mentality fit to be heard by any class in political science. Only slowly did it dawn upon those listening that this man was in no way trying to excuse his own criminal behavior. Quite to the contrary, he still felt obliged to instruct the world as to the correctness of "the final solution".* When pressed and asked if he felt no remorse for his homicidal activities, he answered with a sharp "Nein!" The newspapers triumphantly played up this response to show that he was an insane killer. And of course everyone remarked about his arrogance. Yet, this was no case of schizophrenia but a case of political decision.

What passed for arrogance and a lack of repentance was, in fact, the expression of this man's conviction. He did not want the norms of Judeo-Christian conscience. Beneath the "Prussian arrogance" was a very conscientious, totally amoral man of the "new order". He did not seek the preservation of life as would other physicians, he had chosen to be a killer instead. This was his conscious decision and therefore, indeed, he felt no remorse. He was a "new" man with a good conscience.

The Allied judges, and newspapermen who took him to task merely offered him the great satisfaction of once more demonstrating the superiority of his convictions and choices.

The second example is one of a very repentant extermination camp commander. As this man talked before the court, he struck everyone as a sick murderer. This was gratefully received by the world press as an example of Nazi rule by madmen. But here again the facts indicated that this man was far from insane. He actually considered himself an idealist. He had a harmonious marriage and loved his children whose photographs he carried in his wallet. He provided his wife with a good life insurance policy and had hidden away large amounts of stolen funds in Argentina to insure his children's education. He was, in fact, a normally motivated family man to whom the atrocities in which he had been involved were an annoying detail to be absolved by prompt and abject confession of guilt.

Hitler was popular and held sway over the German people

*The "final solution" was the Nazi euphemism for mass suffocations by poison gas. It was also called "special treatment" in government documents.

because he could express without restraint whatever hostile wishes lived within the grocers and whitecollar workers who became camp commanders and torturers. Hitler played successfully and consciously upon one single element in Western civilization: the fact that man's savage past is just beneath the surface and can be called upon if the proper mixture of delusion, identification with power and cruelty is fed to him.

THE RITUAL OF DESTRUCTION

A very large majority of the Germans loved Hitler and could be cruel at his demand not because they were evil, but because Hitler assured them that if they were cruel, they would not be cowards, but men, part of a virile community holding the power of life and death. In order to understand the phenomenon of Eichmann, we must think of him neither as an arrogant Prussian nor as an insane killer. He was neither. He was a frustrated bureaucrat and as much as he liked to walk in his protective corsetted uniform, he also feared the authority of the dictatorship. He could be cruel without remorse to please authority and placate its wrath. This is why he could be utterly obedient and this is why an Eichmann could rise again. Neither power-mad nor crazy, Eichmann was a common man capable of murder when given the opportunity.

In Jerusalem there is a cave which is called "The Chamber of Destruction". Alfred Kazin reporting on a visit to that cave in the April 27, 1961, *Reporter Magazine*, writes that one walks into a dark, smoky room illuminated by the acrid flare of memorial candles and the young custodian seems to be almost perversely eager to show his horrors in the glass cases, religious articles smeared with blood; garments pierced with bayonets; tin cans containing hydrogen-cyanide crystals used in the gas chambers in Auschwitz. A few block away, tremendous air-conditioned vaults hold exact records of the location and time when victims met their death, and in what manner.

This seems a strange preoccupation. There is a perverse myth that it is somehow the destiny of innocents to die en masse. When we read in the Eichmann testimony that entire communities were shot in layers in mass graves, it somehow seemed that these people were destined for such a fate. For the fact is that the victims of Nazism were trapped and betrayed by the democracies as well as by the Soviet Union. Only rarely could they resist. Do victims have to apologize for having been butchered under the eyes of the rest of the world?

Just as we are not dealing with mythical factors concerning the fate of the victims, it is important to realize that there are no mysteries concerning the Third Reich. One of the worst side-effects of the trial was the revival of the theory of historical devils. If the Eichmanns were Satans personified, all of history would be an uncomplicated proposition.

Who was Eichmann? He came from a middleclass Protestant family and like Hitler he was born in Austria, not Germany. He had a thin prominent nose and schoolmates called him the "kleine Jude" (the "little Jew"). Eichmann continued to be mistaken for a Jew and he developed a neurotic interest in Jewish customs and traditions. In Vienna, he had many Jewish friends, visited Jewish homes, loved Jewish food and learned a little Yiddish and Hebrew. Think of this young man at the depth of the depression in Germany joining the Nazi party and proudly going off to do his duty: guarding prisoners at the Dachau concentration camp! It was here that his talents as "an expert in Jewish affairs" were discovered, and soon he became a prominent officer. He travelled to Palestine well before the war to negotiate ways of circumventing the British refusal to allow Hitler's victims from Germany and Austria to enter into Palestine. Neither the U.S.A. nor the United Kingdom, nor the U.S.S.R. wanted refugees. Eichmann's road towards implementing the "final solution" was facilitated by the world's indifference and this was his vocation. There is a document which shows that as late as 1941 he was desperately concentrating on a plan to ship four million people to the island of Madagascar where they would no doubt expire because there was neither water nor food for such an influx. Then, sometime in the summer of 1941, the Nazis decided upon the outright destruction of their captives in all of occupied Europe. Eichmann helped form the special killer SS commandos, about 500 to 800 men who simply moved from village to village, shooting community by community. But he complained to his superiors that this "was creating serious morale problems because the women's and children's screams disturb the SS men and are causing them inconvenience." A more efficient way had to be found. Eichmann travelled in an elegant Mercedes-Benz to the remote farming town of Auschwitz (formerly Polish Oswicziem) where he personally supervised the construction of gas chambers and ordered the Zyklon-B gas from the I.G. Farben Industry.

Eichmann lived in Hungary with his Countess-mistress while organizing the death of six hundred thousand Hungarians. Actually, when his commander, Himmler, told him to stop the gassings, Eichmann started to *smuggle* prisoners into Auschwitz. It was his vocation and neither he nor many millions of other Germans wanted the killing to stop.

Bored SS officers and SS physicians greeted victims as they arrived in Auschwitz. They always came out to see the desperate parade readied for suffocation and cremation. The chief SS physician would wave his hand, left and right, left and right, as if he were playing a game. "Left" meant gas chamber and "right" a few more weeks of atrocious suffering while working as a slave for the I.G. Farben Industry until the prisoner had lost all physical strength and was gassed anyway. Germany had become a nation of killers and wanted it so, for this is what it ultimately meant to be part of a superior race. They lived in the glow of immense cruelty. "Left, right", "links und rechts". Day after day, night after night in thousands of camps.

What had happened, why did the nation of Beethoven turn hunter of human beings? Did it exchange private madness for collective madness? The German author who wrote that whenever he heard "that voice" he felt like a hero, was as much part of the ritual of destruction as was Eichmann. Eichmann hated victims, he hated the weak, he lived by the principle Freud called "destrudo" and killed in order to sustain his ego.* In the deepest sense of the word he was in rebellion against all creation, all beauty. Because of his acts, the more dependent he became upon those he was supposed to love— Hitler and Himmler, the more he hated those who were dependent upon him, his victims. A deep sense of depression was overcome by a perpetual involvement in more and more death. However, Eichmann was not insane. Most of us would like to think that he and millions of other Germans were insane because then we, the normal ones, could feel more secure. The evidence refutes this theory. We have enough diagnostic material to conclude that the Nazis and the German nation as a whole were not psychopaths, but that they systematically chose to release their pent-up aggressions and hostility upon those in their power. The Nazis were hypnotized into becoming killers and could beat to death children and women as others would kill insects. In their trance of self-hypnosis, conscience was paralyzed.

In describing this period in his book, *That Difficult Peace*, eminent psychiatrist Dr. Joost A. M. Meerloo writes that, "The cave man had appeared once more and stood scowling outside his cave . . . Hunger, cold, his fellowman, and even his own sons are his potential enemies. Like his primitive brother, twentieth century man is engaged in total war with his environment.

*J.A.M. Meerloo, *That Difficult Peace*.

But unlike his primitive brother, he also finds that he is constantly at war with himself. What a price mankind pays for this premature sapping of his powers and for this constant burden of (guilt) and fear!"*

In Eichmann we see man totally mutilated and that is why it would be senseless to hate the individual. I felt this very strongly immediately after the war when I was in charge of the interrogation of the prisoners in the Dutch Security Section of the United States Army in Paris. I have not changed my opinion, for I agree with Supreme Court Justice Jackson who, at the beginning of the Nuremberg Trials said: "The record on which we judge these defendants today is a record on which history will judge us tomorrow." Somehow we have to escape the circle of the vendetta, the pattern of mutilation of the human soul.

If we believe that man must not be mutilated then we must also believe that all life is sacred; that to kill is a blasphemy against ourselves. If human life is really inviolable, then we cannot say "some" human lives are inviolable or are inviolable "most of the time". The real issue is the casual mutilation of human dignity every day, everywhere. It is tragically true that those who are right do not usually survive to tell their story. Still the triumph over Nazism past or present can only be won when, though an Eichmann can kill millions, the victors will refuse to kill even *one* Eichmann.

The Nuremberg Trials made sense because their purpose was to create some kind of international law concerning the plight of people in occupied countries. More important, the Nuremberg trials and the trial in Jerusalem established the principle that there are crimes against the community which will not be tolerated. This was not a question of a crime against particular victims but of crimes, against humanity. I was amazed to find a considerable amount of anti-victim psychology in the

*Joost A. M. Meerloo, M.D., *op. cit.*

U.S. Army in the postwar era. Emaciated leaders of the resistance movements liberated from concentration camps were unceremoniously shipped, over their protests, to Displaced Persons Camps by the military government. At the same time Nazi officials were put in charge of occupied cities and counties. Social-Democrats, who had taken over the printing presses at the time of liberation, were forced to hand them back to Nazi owners who came scuttling out of hiding.

No, very few are those who sympathize with victims! To be a starved, sick, emotionally broken DP was a curse in Europe after the war. To be a well-fed, well-dressed former Nazi was often an asset. Who can tolerate the claims for justice by the victims? Many are those who sympathize secretly with the executioners. Many frustrated men, deep within, shout "let him have it!" This is as true of actual assassination as it is of character assassination.

In the post-war situation too much was whitewashed to make most average Germans lose much sleep over Auschwitz. The Nuremberg Trials are still commonly referred to as the "Victor Trials" and the German public is ill-informed about the social nature of Nazism.

And so, twenty years later Eichmann sat, pale, in his glass cage. The judges told him to rise. He pleaded that he had been an honorable man who rejoined his family after the war, risking capture. He had been faithful to his military oath and this showed that he was a man of virtue. Eichmann believed he was right and that the judges were decadent democrats who were talking about morality when he had to obey orders. The problem is not limited to Eichmann.

The underlying threat to our civilization is that knowledge can exist divorced from moral implications, that skill can exist without moral principles. An example of this was the case of Dr. Mengele, the chief physician at Auschwitz, and an important SS officer, who always took all modern medical precautions when a pregnant woman was herded into the camp. He would use all the aseptic principles during delivery and then a half-hour afterwards, would send mother and infant to the crematorium. Mengele today is openly practicing medicine in South America!

Was Eichmann so different from men we know? The slick writers who create the programs that sow seeds of violence and mental distortion in our young? The businessman who will show his competitor no mercy because "business is business?" The professional man who, in the deadly competition of the academic world, destroys the reputation of a fellow teacher in some university department? All of us who live without implicit principles, without an understanding of moral obligation, become subject to life with built-in cruelty. These examples, of course, cannot be compared to what Eichmann did. But we can stop the subconscious longing for war and catastrophe.

The danger is within and for this reason I considered the Anne Frank play a blasphemy, and was revolted by the long newspaper accounts of the hushed, tearful audiences in Germany. What sham sentimentality and what a painless way to forget the gas chambers! The need to deny reality always leads to death. A part of Eichmann's success was due to the fact that millions of people had given up the will to live and, subconsciously, felt that nothing could be done, that nothing could be changed.

We must fight the nihilism that produces Eichmanns. One is alive and of influence only if there is a vigorous resistance against the negation of oneself. There can be no compromise with brutality or viciousness. The Eichmanns cannot be wished away. We can neutralize them, however, if we learn how not to mutilate each other; how to leave intact the grace of courage and the outrage against injustices.

We have an energy which we are not trained to use. It is the energy of moral defiance with which to counteract crippling anxiety and disintegration. Whatever the precariousness of life in this era our children reach confidently for our hand and for a world in which the infernal atrocities of war are overcome. Their lips were created to laugh and to kiss and not to be muted by the ashes of our emotional bankruptcy.

CHAPTER 2

THE MARGIN OF SURVIVAL

Never in history have men and women been assaulted by tidings of calamity as we are in this generation. No newscast of radio or television, no newspaper in our living rooms spares us for one minute the intricacies of threats and violence. Although we have luxuries of which our parents never dreamt, homes and cars and medical care and vacations, we are stalked even in our sleep by the intrusions of impending catastrophe.

How much endurance does the human brain have? How large is our margin of survival? If there is no safety anywhere on this globe even for those entirely innocent of drives for power and conquest, how then can we safeguard the emotional and intellectual refuges upon which sanity depends?

For some, the universality of evil is resolved by utopianism, for others, by the abundantly available means of escapism and yet all of us know that there is no security.

We find a vacation spot, away from the cities, and jet war planes scream overhead. We go to a concert and the moments of depth and transformation are ruptured by the wail of police sirens.

And yet, when death is close most of us would want to continue living, for the dream of life is still the most alluring of dreams. We know that the values of the timeless are our only hope. While life is rounded by tears and exhaustion, most of us, in the recesses of our consciousness, know that the exploitation of trivialities is our detractor and that only a renewal by communion with ourselves can reestablish our hold on existence.

True, our expectations are betrayed again and again. Our exposed flanks are quickly discovered by others and battered and quite frequently pierced. Sooner or later every human being is reduced to the animal level of scratching the earth for a place to lick one's wounds. And yet, in the matrix of our obligations to others is also the recuperative possibility which restores our hope and perseverance.

It is therefore not just the perpetuation of dismal threats that haunts us but rather the fear that all values, all principles by which we thought we could live, will be reduced to nothing. The security that all of us seek becomes too easily a casualty and once this permeates a culture, individual men sense a most brutal futility. Expectations crumble under such pressure and the balance between being related to and separated from others is disturbed.

While human beings can live under great stress, they cannot live with a continual sense that what they are doing is futile. When every value we enjoy is a target for destruction, those things we hold dear make us feel ashamed because private joys are tested against a background of too precarious a reality.

What sense does education make? What sense does religion make? What sense does honesty make if at the end of all effort, the impenetrable violence leads to chaos? Man cannot live for long without a belief in Man. For when that belief has collapsed, what else shall sustain him? What meaning shall he seek in a world devoid of all he cherishes?

Science and technology seemed to offer the greatest promise in the twentieth century. But Science is gradually being discredited. Many of us are suspicious of the technicians because they have produced an unspeakable horror in the midst of promise. It is easy to add, as an apology, that Science is also on the track of a cure for cancer. But what good is the cure if refining the machinery for destroying life remains a major preoccupation? This is a fundamental question. It is not enough to say that much of religion, art and drama—the eternal vehicles for human aspiration—are dulled by irrelevance. The real question is *what* art, *what* drama, and *what* religion could there be to help heal society?

It is in this context that one must consider the ultra-right-wing groups. Their principal characteristic is that they are inclined towards a mystique about an omnipresent enemy, and about the saints who must "save" the nation. Those who live by this mystique have chosen the irrational as reaction to the eclipse of trusted values and ambitions. In a period in which the power of enlightenment is exceedingly weak, escapism into political delusion becomes a prominent feature. The disease rampant in our society is not just a most realistic threat of war but the disenchantment of many with a world too precarious to be enjoyed. To the neo-fascist, every person who does not share his anxieties is a traitor. Hitler's genius understood this mechanism and created a state-sanctioned scapegoat for the projective needs of the disillusioned masses.

We find in our midst on the one hand those who choose suspicion and, ultimately rejection of democracy; and on the other, the cynics. Their theory states that if—and when—the bombs fall, forty to sixty million Americans may disappear in mushroom clouds, but that quite a few million will stay alive for a few weeks in their fallout shelters, to reemerge into the "brave new world" of radioactive dust! This cynicism is as destructive as that of the neo-fascist fringe in this country. It is also based upon a distorted notion void of alternative thought.

Yet, such statements are deeply lodged in our civilization.

They are borne out of the apocalyptic concept that underlies much Western philosophy. At "the end" there will be an inevitable catastrophe, a disaster that cannot be prevented. Actually the last book of the New Testament, the Revelations of St. John the Divine, illustrates how this tragedy will overtake the world and by what means the final destruction will take place. There is no more hope since all men are sinners. Life is coming to an end:

> "And I saw when the Lamb opened one of the Seals and I heard as it were the noise of thunder and I saw and beheld a white horse . . . and there went out another horse that was red, and power was given to him that sat thereon; the power to take peace from the earth and that they should kill one another, and . . . I looked and beheld a pale horse and his name that sat on him was Death and Hell. And power was given unto them over the earth to kill with sword and hunger and with death . . ."

This vision of an end without a margin of survival is awesome and in mankind there lingers a primitive fear of such absolute disaster. Think of Job, of Jesus, Oedipus Rex, of Hamlet, of Faust, of Zarathustra, of "Waiting for Godot" . . .

Yet, in the Buddhist religion there is an entirely different thought with regard to Man's destiny. The major concept here is that by detaching ourselves from pain, we annul the power of suffering. Therefore the Buddhist sees man in a sheltered universe. His is a cyclical view, the opposite of the Christian apocalyptic misery.

However, whatever the metaphysical speculations, down-to-earth pain invades down-to-earth individuals. A poet has described man's anguish as something indeterminate; always present and real as the heartbeat.

Most of us want to understand our individual despair. Usually we do so by exploring our future as well as our past, and thus we are timeless within our own experience. Through thought, the impact of the immediacy of pain is removed, and we can see ourselves in a different dimension. It is this ability which gives us the capacity to turn away from death. Despair triggers the desire to find the freedom to think about ourselves in relation to other men. This sets us free to love. Love is that autonomous potential which helps overcome the self-destructive forces within. It sustains the outreach for communion. It is true that each is a unique personality, but we are not alone! We are what we are with others, and we recognize that most keenly at a moment when one we love is taken from us, when the marrow is exposed to raw pain. Even the inexpressible in our lives is expressed because of others, never in isolation.

The Indian philosopher Krishnamurti, in his *Commentaries of Living*, speaks about "attention to life without motive." He relates this example: One night, brought outdoors by the sound of a lute, he saw an unwashed little boy in dirty clothes with an aggressively sharp and complaining face. The child, oblivious to everything around him, was playing softly on a homemade flute. Krishnamurti realized that the tune was only a trivial melody from a movie, but, the music's purity was extraordinary. The child was physically present but his mind was infinitely distant from that spot. Closed within itself, "it was untouched and clear and alone beyond the measure of time or recognition." The child was attentive to life but without a specific motive. In the same vein, that which is real in our lives is never distant but continually available. It needs to be summoned for, as Krishnamurti put it: "You can't go very far if you don't begin very near." In that context it should not be overlooked that education and culture mold our vision. Consequently, we have difficulty understanding that true freedom, the freedom to love and the freedom to achieve compassion depend on inner readiness and not chance "happenings." Our environment, our circumstances change continually, but the awareness of our being needed in mutuality remains steadfast and constant.

This sense that freedom is the understanding that one is never separated is beautifully expressed in an ancient story:

A scholar found an old man digging a hole. The scholar asked the man, "At your age, do you have to do this heavy work by yourself? Don't you have sons or relatives or servants?" But the old man continued digging and answered, "No, *this* I must do myself." And the scholar then asked, "But how old are you?" "I am 70 years and 7", he answered. "And what are you planting, may I ask?" "I am planting a bread tree, the fruits of which may be ground to flour and used as food for many." And the scholar again: "But when will it bear fruit, your tree?" And he answered, "In 17 years and 7." "But you won't live that long." "No, I won't live that long, yet this tree is needed here, for when I came into this world, it was not a desolate world. I found trees and bread and I must not leave it a desolate world, but a world provided for, as my fathers planted, so must I plant."

How much more hope there is in this attitude than in the apocalyptic image which is almost diabolical in its oppressive prophecy! The common good is not an abstraction, but is meaningful and very real to each. The common good is the sum of everyone's concerns, including the little concerns of "little" people. We must not yield to those sweeping generalizations that give man a sense of impotence and fill his heart with forebodings of isolation. It is not the "little" people who interrupt the process of living and seeking decency. It is not the "little" people who plunge the world into death and darkness.

We need to overcome the idea that the pursuance of the "greater" good must be bought at the sacrifice of private joys. The one crusade in which we become engaged should be that which can be experienced firsthand. For it is in the moments of joy, though always tinged by sorrow, that one finds consolation, not in far-off promises. There are intervals of normality, even in a world in turmoil, which can give shape to hope. The sense of the precariousness of it all can heighten the desire to make those small parcels as full as possible. It is a generative resource through which one still discovers pathways and humble achievement.

Such a measure of happiness is possible even amidst the greatest of threats. Whatever the world, the doubts and anxieties, the guilt and regrets can always be balanced by a perspective of continuity. The promise of the future however is not always in activation but often in the acceptance of quietude within. Look at the broken center one can discover in Rembrandt's self-portraits. Life has been lived, suffered and enjoyed, but the tragedy has not destroyed the capacity to turn inward for stillness. These are the truths and beauties which survive. We are never separated. As Camus put it: "Let us not look for the door and the way out anywhere but in the wall against which we are living."

Therefore the very character of this era demands a passionate affirmation of the belief in man's potential. By our work we create the basis for hope so that as loving companions we learn to span the agony of generations.

CONSERVING THE CORE OF LIFE

Each in his own fashion has some inward image of what makes for "the good life". Because of that image we conserve a core that carries us through pressures and disappointments. We cannot always articulate it with scientific accuracy but we experience it as real. To engage consciously upon the conservation of this core of life means to move from mere reflex actions to creative attitudes for living.

Nothing is more difficult. The external turmoil is reflected in the inner turmoil felt by so many. We are eager to be comforted and unsure of our self-evaluation because we find little in the world that is genuine. A great many people would like to walk away from the din of complexity. But walking away does not relieve the permanent challenge of private doubts.

In a book by Malcolm Lowry, *Under the Volcano*, we learn of the most private thoughts of a British consul in Mexico, who just before his retirement, tries to evaluate his life. His memory takes him back over decades of victories and failures, negligence and concern. While looking out over his lovely garden he sums up life's obligation in this thought: Do you love this garden? Do you love the tenderness of its flowers? Do you like the birds that nest here? Do you like the smell of the earth at night? If so, see to it that you do not destroy this garden. See to it that you conserve it!

Perhaps, instead of dwelling on those forces threatening mankind we need at least as much preoccupation with those things that hold life together, and conserve it. In genuine persons strength and weakness are intermingled and this is how most of them conserve a core of life.

I remember a woman in her late fifties who was twice widowed. When her children were grown, she decided to devote her life to retarded children living in one of the worst neighborhoods of New York City. When she left her apartment in the morning—which once was full of life, laughter, and voices—it was often difficult for her to take the elevator, walk to the bus stop, and overcome a sense of hopelessness. But when she was with the children, she conserved and continued to expand the core of her life. It was a vision of life that extended her beyond the immediate and thus engendered a generosity which overcame loneliness. It was a guidance which left the roots intact; a nourishing capacity for consolation.

This core of life is often conserved despite the most incredible conditions. Jerzy Gliksman, author of the autobiography *Tell the West*, a lawyer and former councilman for the Socialist Party in Warsaw, Poland, gives an example: As a socialist in 1939, he fled the Nazi occupation of Western Poland to that

part of his country occupied by the Soviet Union Army. He soon
learned that he was suspect, despite his socialist views and, together with tens of thousands of other Poles, he was deported
to a forlorn concentration camp in Siberia. This was ironic because just before the war he had been a member of an official
Polish delegation that had visited the USSR to inspect its system of "correctional labor camps." He had even been rather
enthusiastic about the carefully selected camps he had been permitted to visit! Now he saw the truth! He met thousands of Russians who, without due process of law, or even a charge against
them, had been deported to these camps because a brother or
sister had criticized the Stalinist bureaucracy. Millions perished
at the hands of the secret police—the millions of victims to
whom Khrushchev in an exuberant moment wanted to dedicate
a monument in Moscow. How our generation likes to erect
monuments to the dead! How the executioners enjoy bemoan-
ing their victims once they are done away with!

Gliksman saw the thousands of women who were physically
destroyed by the Soviet slave labor system, and he saw the unspeakable sadness on the faces of children who were born in
those camps, and who never knew any environment other than
the dismal barracks. When the Polish government finally succeeded in freeing him, he was not broken. He joined the Polish
army to resume the fight against fascism. Of the day of his exchange he writes, "We were a throng of bewildered people.
Torn away from normal life. Many of us were ill . . . And yet, we
were happy people. We marched in silence, each occupied with
his thoughts . . . We were now approaching a new future with
anxiety—but not without hope."

Somehow love and dignity had not been abandoned because
life mattered, because a perspective had been salvaged. The
repressive terrorism of the State had not been permitted to destroy the personality of the prisoners. Even in unimaginable
hardship they had stuck to their own values. Conservation of

the core of life is always gained in exhausting labor within. It is
a labor one cannot even begin to touch unless there is a response
to life, a postulate of worth. There is considerable doubt today
that such a concept of worth is justified or even possible. We
live in the time of "the great letdown". Many want to be "sold"
on something exterior to themselves, many are profoundly dis-
couraged about their own capacity to contribute anything. This
is a truly tragic lethargy.

Neo-orthodox religion is therefore insisting again that man
and human evolution cannot be relied upon. We must return to
the safe absolutes of old, so they proclaim! Yet, "Religion",
wrote C. Wright Mills, "has become a distraction."

In the early part of the twentieth century, the gospel of social
justice was preached from every pulpit in this country. Today
religion occupies itself with the "adjusted" society in which
neither saints nor spiritual rebels have a place. And while we
are continually admonished to be "good neighbors", we are also
reminded to do this in such a way as not to upset the status quo.
The agnostic position which looks upon man as part of nature
and as having the ability to decide his own destiny, is subjected
to severe attack.

Consideration of this kind may be found in a recent book by
a German archeologist, Ivar Lissner, in which the traditional
role of men as created by God, ready and in shipshape condition, is the remarkable conclusion of an extensive study.

Dr. Lissner in *Man, God and Magic* comes to the conclusion
that the intuition and memory of man through the ages point
towards a common belief, a common form of worship of one
God and one Creation. Lissner is only one apologist of this new
orthodoxy.

While everything in the world is stirring, while in chemistry,
medicine, psychiatry, transportation and nuclear physics the
greatest revolutions of human thinking and knowledge have
taken place, traditional religion still wants to cling to the out-

worn illusion of an autocratically ruled cosmic order. Even the "God-is-Dead" theologians hang on to Christianized world concepts.

One cannot be neutral about this. The wider life perspective demands that Man be liberated to develop his mental and thereby moral capacity, so that he can grow as a vital entity. Change is not a threat to life's security. Change is the heart of all life. This was beautifully expressed by Professor Eustace Haydon of Chicago University. He wrote: "More than any other, our generation has reeled under the shock of change. Often we stand awed and bewildered because there is no map to chart our way. The old anchors drag, the warm, enfolding arms of the dear, familiar gods have become nebulous. No more can we find the easy consolations of wish-fulfillment. Yet, we can face the hard facts of living, confident that the mind of man can find a way through to justice and refuse to yield to defeat or despair. If we do so, then we may work together, even while much of our work is performed in the twilight but we may be sure of the promise of a dawn." Is this not a more helpful perspective?

There is a difference, of course, between understanding the meaning of a way of life, and the capacity to apply it to day-to-day living. The question may well be asked, "How much realistic training does anybody undertake who commits himself to such a humanist philosophy of life?" It is—alas—minimal. One cannot, however, be really involved in that which depends on ideas unless one is willing to inform oneself about its basic hypotheses. The central question is not how to *build* new institutions but how to *use* institutions in which to find answers to the question, "How do we become 'better' people?" Obviously, the improvement of living will not be due to book-learning.

Though the advance of human consciousness is continually interrupted by the brutality of life's circumstances, this need not cancel out the hope of mutuality. "Fundamental Man" is Man who knows that within him is a unique essence which nothing can destroy as long as he affirms it.

When Buddha was asked why he so frequently wore a sombre frown, he is said to have replied, "Because wherever I go, I hear cries of anguish." It is a profound fact, however, that some people never hear such cries. It is also a profound truth that some people hear these cries and do not care.

The assumption of people's need for anything like a humanist philosophy of life can be far too easy. Most of us do not like to think in terms of opposite motivation. Still, wisdom of life is discovered only when one takes opposites as well as progress into consideration. If Man can lose the infantile expectation that one tendency must prevail, if he can learn to accept the fact that very diverse motives have to be dealt with, perhaps he will become capable of distilling a reasonable perseverance.

OF MASKS AND MEN

When an American pilot who flew a U-2 plane was shot down over the USSR in 1960, it was revealed that he carried as part of his equipment, a hypodermic filled with a lethal toxin. However, government sources in Washington assured the nation that the pilot had in fact never been instructed to kill himself. As one spokesman put it: "That decision was left to his own patriotism, his own sense of duty."

If suicide was "optional" for this man, are we not confronted with the question whether the citizen must consider his own worth as subordinate to the collective value norms of the nation? Is the private fate of the citizen less important than the group's strategy? The pilot was presented with a historical choice, a decision well beyond his on-the-spot impulse. It posed an impossible dilemma. Should he destroy himself and serve the highest social good or should the welfare of his family be the higher norm?

Is putting this choice before any citizen not in fact a form of capitulation to totalitarian inroads? Maybe such inroads must be expected in an increasingly militarized civilization, but the least one must do is to face this shift in values. Human life has become cheap, it has been said a hundred times. Yet, such devaluation should not be accepted as docile doctrine. For nothing could be more disastrous than social consciousness without social emotion.

We are in danger of developing reflexes and responses that slow the imagination and relieve the moral indignation. We have made peace with violence. There is loss of the faculty to be aware of suffering as well as of beauty; the ability to share sorrows as well as hope. The militarization of cultures always leads to the return to myths, especially the myth of death and rebirth. The young heroes must die so that a new harmony can emerge. When will we rid ourselves of the appeal of sacrifice and of necrophilic romanticism?

We still idolize the hero of our emotional infancy. That is: a heroism which is based on the idea that we can transcend ourselves by throwing our lives away. Yet, all persistent inner security results from cooperation, relatedness and the sane usage of our energies for the immediacy of individual tasks. "Optional suicide" is a sick proposition. It resembles social activism by which some persons rush from cause to cause in what is actually a renunciation of responsibility. Their fire is kindled by a deep pessimism about human potential and process. In our era the magic rituals of primitive societies have been replaced by political rituals which create an opportunity for the release of collective hostility. Yet by participating in that very release the individual agrees to moral submission.

Obviously this was the function of group myths in ancient civilizations for they provided an element of social cohesion especially in times of crisis.

Today these myths are not propagated by the priesthood of

religion but are conveyed by powerful political ideologies which in fact determine the lives of hundreds of millions. All conflict is thus elevated to devastating absolutes and as a result new high priests, those of the military industrial complex, formulate what one philosopher called "a paganistic theology" by which the individual is invited to sacrifice his life. Democracy, as Prof. Talmon of Jerusalem University has suggested, can thus be transformed into "totalitarian democracy". This means that the democratic society serves no longer as a pragmatic arrangement of liberal minds, but rather as an "ideal order" directed towards an absolute truth.

The relationship of the individual to the State thus is caught up in a tyranny in which all acts, all decisions are flavored by a messianistic zeal and in which the militarized politicos confidently determine how to make history!

In a liberal democracy freedom consists of as much absence of central power as possible. But the totalitarian democracy insists that only through the collectivization of conscience and the silencing of dissent can the individual participate in the progress of freedom. This "purification" of society is bought at the price of private oblivion, and we understand now de Toqueville's sad prophecy when writing about America in the 1840's: "I have no hope at all for the future . . . this fine century is designed for anything rather than democracy."

When the mutuality of citizens is exchanged for subordination to centralized authority we see the introduction of uniformity and of a sense of social impotence which can make such actions as suicide for "the greater good" an optional proposition.

Yet, this sense of impotence is negated only by the individual's acceptance of responsibilities for his own interest in living a decent life. Sound decisions never result from collective activism whether such activism is based upon Hegel's inevitable "unfolding of the Mind" or the promise of a pure and rational order. The invasion of our private life by snooping government agents, armed with the latest electronic equipment, is but one example of how rapidly we are going in the direction of a totalitarian democracy. Governments may claim to do all they can for the people but the share carried by the people steadily decreases, by manipulation of the truth and by a constant barrage of propaganda. The need to hate and "incoherent idealism", as Schumpeter has pointed out, are always closely intertwined.

Thus great strains have been added to the life of the individual who is called upon to sacrifice himself for the future ideal order. Men and women can become abstractions even to themselves or at best "happy ants" in a productive antheap and victims of perpetual military and ideological mobilization.

Nevertheless, any life of some sanity is concerned with far more mundane goals such as personal and family happiness, constructive relationships between the generations and hope for some basic security in one's old age. The dragons of anxiety are overcome when we liberate ourselves for the social and cultural tasks, which are but rarely heroic in an historical sense, but which in the end help keep the ego intact and provide for a self-maturation allowing for hope.

This leads us to a deep concern with mental health in our culture. Preventive psychiatry or preventive family therapy are only in their beginning stages. Yet the need for such services is glaringly obvious.

A three-year study conducted by the University of Michigan concluded that one out of five Americans believes that at one time he or she was at the point of what is called "a nervous breakdown". The large majority of the thousands of people interviewed said that the principal source of their happiness or unhappiness was economic or material. Only four percent of those interviewed expressed any concern over world tensions or the possibilities of war. External life has us in its grip and our coping with this outside world creates the majority of our emotional disturbances. The basic problem is purpose.

How confining the mode of living is which makes us concentrate primarily on the "life without" was portrayed hauntingly in one of Jean Paul Sartre's plays, "No Exit". Three people, two men and a woman, find themselves in a room with locked shutters and doors. There is evidently no way out—"no exit". These three do not know that they are dead and in Hell. They continue to follow the ambitions of their lives as they have always done. Only slowly as they go through the emotions of inner conflict do they achieve a consciousness about their real situation and a recognition that "Hell is other people." One of them says that while death settles everything, life itself is merely a suspension. It has no substance. It crumbles as we go along. If we make our happiness dependent on settled social and economic circumstances, sexual gratification, even the affection of our children, or success—then life becomes suspended. For each of these fulfillments can be taken away. The only escape, the only "exit" from the entanglement of abstraction is in accepting the burden of mutual dignity. Committed life lived with the expectation of the "within" yields enough opportunity to create the worthwhile in existence.

It is important, in this context, that in the University of Michigan study, the older people interviewed turned out to be less self-doubting. Older workers were more satisfied in their jobs. They blamed themselves and the world less, often they accepted their own shortcomings, viewed their achievements with humility, and "counted their blessings". The fever to be forever doing things had turned into an ability to be themselves. Yet, old age is often seen as an unalleviated disaster in our culture and while old people may be treated kindly, essentially this is done with a patronizing attitude. We do not see age as the time when values have ripened. We usually pity the aged and do not consider anyone irreplaceable. Sigmund Freud held out little hope for our ability to identify with each other. He implied strongly that the destructive and self-aggrandizing drives of man are primary.

But the opposite view was held by Gordon Allport, the psychologist, who wrote: "Human nature seems on the whole to prefer the sight of kindness and friendliness to the sight of cruelty . . . to prefer to love and be loved rather than to hate and be hated." Yet the quality of caring seems difficult to sustain. At the root of that difficulty is a mute tendency to see one's life goals as far from concrete. In turn this leads to a self-centeredness which is responsible for our loneliness and anxieties. Self-assertion which does not result in self-acceptance and reciprocity can not diminish loneliness.

In *Man for Himself*, Erich Fromm said: "The selfish person does not love himself too much, but too little . . ." He becomes an abstraction to himself.

What is this "real self" to which Fromm refers? What is it but the ambition in a person to seek for an order, a meaning valid for living. What else is it but an aim for a transformation of life?

In the traditional religions, love is seen as striving towards a unity with God. The One, the Eternal One, is the source of all strength, power, and grace. Man's knowledge, man's concern, and his sense of responsibility are interesting efforts, but in essence they are not crucial.

Self-denial has been taught to us as of high moral value. True love is often characterized as "self-effacing". This pious deception confuses easily what a man will consider his better interest. As a result much human capacity remains untapped or is buried in guilt-produced frustration. What are most desirable as life choices get dictated by convention or power play. It is yet another way of becoming an abstraction even to oneself. Traditional religions have encouraged this tendency.

In discussing the philosophy of Emerson, Felix Adler made

some important remarks in quoting from Emerson's poem, "Pan":

> "O what are heroes, prophets,
> But pipes through which the breath of Pan doth blow
> A momentary music . . ."

But, Adler pointed out, we are not God's instruments, we are not dust in the "throbbing light of God." Man is not a mask, not a fugitive form in which the Divine seeks expression. God is not the white light into which human beings are reabsorbed when they are worn out.

No man is an instrument! No man is an abstraction! Whatever insight we give each other must instill a renewed sense of worth with which to edge forward.

The one continual task allotted to us is to establish that kind of concern, the ingredients of which are care and compassion. Continents within wait for discovery.

All living is attaining a frail balance between human "nature" and human "nurture", between the ambitions of each individual and the exigencies of the communities to which we belong. Such balance makes it possible to affirm what a Chilean poet wrote, summing up the insight he had gained in living:

> "I have loved and I have been beloved
> The sun has caressed my face.
> Life you owe me nothing.
> Life we are at peace."

THE IMPOSSIBLE ODDS

An ideal is not the same as an intellectual opinion. An ideal is an assumption about human capacity. It combines aspiration and insight. Erich Fromm wrote: "We labor for what we love and we love that for which we labor." How profoundly true this is of any significant personal or social ambition! For any worthwhile community must have as its primary preoccupation the attempt to make human souls whole, and to generate that wholeness-at-large. In making each more alive, in helping to bring out latent qualities, the members of such community will keep a sense of identity alive among themselves.

Obviously, to survive physically we must breathe, eat, and sleep. To survive psychologically we must be nourished by an expanding consciousness. That means, specifically, to cultivate our inner necessities. We *are* our brothers' keepers and the emerging ambition in the other, his strength, his consolations are crucial to our own identity.

We reach out towards the other because it is a necessity to do so. Even those who are mute or deaf try to communicate by all available means. Words are only *one* way we can speak to each other and the essence of relationship is often transmitted without words.

There is no more incisive communication than such communion as will reveal the innate substance of ourselves. Religions of old have projected this sense upon the supernatural, but modern man can bear witness to such substantiality in the secular reality. The important question therefore, is not "What do you believe?" or "How do you believe?" but rather "By what necessities do you live?" Human decision determines human fate.

Our most precious capacity therefore is the capacity to choose, and to break the shackles of crippling fear. The French author, Simone Weill, wrote: "To love our neighbor simply means being able to say to him, 'What are you going through?'"

At the outset of life is the other. None of us is a person in general; we are particular entities; each necessary in creating a diversified relatedness. What is needed then is a development by which one makes such relatedness meaningful. Sometimes that includes valuing a person more than he does himself, acting upon the inherent substance of his character even if he does not. Men thus can help each other reach a richer state of mind in which their mode of *being* will be what matters most. This is particularly relevant because whatever judgment we may have of our culture and the time in which we live, a vital personal balance is needed to maintain perspective. Beyond the diagnoses of sociology or psychology, there is a need for a cohesive, private perception of what we are about. Human stature is gained both in our social relationships and by the aspects of intuition. The problem is that we have learned to live with a vague threat of impending calamity and that this has added to the feeling that man is erasing himself from the slate of time. Self-doubt is frequently the initial response to the necessities of change.

The German poet, Goethe, wrote that the fundamental struggle in human history is between belief and lack of it. We need to ask belief in what? For self-doubt can co-exist with belief. Only when negation is elevated to a method of behavior between nations and individuals, does scepticism carry the day. The repeated evidence of the insufficiencies of society and human nature can dull us so that we feel too incomplete to harbor any expectation.

In view of the incompleteness of the inner life and the incompleteness of the world, how can we hope to achieve any persistent sense at all?

In the Hindu Bhagavad Gita we read: "some see me one with themselves, or separate. Some bow to countless Gods that are only my million faces." I mention this because it has been the tradition of religions to pray for universal unity as if this were a cognitive reality. As a result, man's classical pose is one of feeling most inadequate before such perfection. Too many of us were raised to believe that the world's incompleteness is due to human failure. How many can testify to having experienced a persistent sense of unity?

Mystics may sometimes claim that they achieve deeply unifying realizations, but this is not a common experience and in any case non-verifiable. Most of us must therefore piece life together by trial and error and with the meager insights acquired through the years. Yet, man is by nature far less impotent and far more preserving and enduring than is often assumed.

As Plato wrote in his *Colloquy on Pleasure and Wisdom*, ". . . wisdom and mind cannot exist without soul . . . soul and mind are kingly because there is in them the power of cause." If understanding is pursued by introspection, we can discover the causes of outer as well as inner circumstances. This is possible because we are soul and possessors of the power of origin. Therefore, we can know what diminishes us; what mauls and wounds us; what it is that makes us forget that we are not just fumbling inadequates. I am referring to a confidence in life in spite of the darkness of experience. We do not want merely to speculate about philosophical grounds. We want to know about direction, cause, and power for change. We want productive conduct which helps evolve social and personal transformations.

If some call this faith, I take no issue with it, for such transformation diminishes self-negation and helplessness.

The question of social incompleteness was tragically illustrated when, a few years ago, shortly after midnight, nine women were killed in a head-on collision with another vehicle. Among them, these women had thirty-eight children. On the surface this was just another accident, another example of the massacre on the highways. But at closer inspection social duress became apparent. To the obvious question "Why were these mothers on the highway in the early hours of the morning?", the answer was that they were returning from their nightshift in a cannery!

They were typical American housewives, the wives of farmers, some of them owning dozens of acres of land. Nevertheless, in order to survive economically, they had to leave their homes each night to work in a canning factory. They were cogs in the huge economic machinery before they could afford to be mothers. There were reasons, therefore, for their meeting death in this way, at that hour, at that spot; reasons other than blind fate. In this generation much of what passes for "fate" is in fact part of social duress and one result of this is complacent mediocrity.

Our epoch has been described as living with "a cult of mediocrity" based upon the fallacy that one citizen is as good as another. Yet, one surgeon is not as good as another. One plumber is not as good as another. The tendency to consider everybody "good enough" is basically an attempt to adjust civilization to its lowest denominator. What passes for equality is often a mere taking-for-granted of the mediocre. Fundamentals for a sound society can never be created in that way. Quality demands mindedness and discriminating evaluation. Much incompleteness in society is tied in with sham equality, which suspects excellence. Suspicion of intellectual ability is one of the more blatant aspects of this tendency. Is there any possibility then for aspirations and ideals to count? Do we still possess such freedom of choice?

The world in which we live promotes a diminishing of individual stature and insists upon a colorlessness which may yet jeopardize the survival of freedom. Freedom is, after all, not a political principle. It is a mechanism, a tool to be fashioned. A free culture cannot develop if the power that organizes the social setting is detrimental to the development of this vital mechanism; if there is no adherence to any moral autonomy. In our private life too, an emotion without restraint, without some standard of limitation, cannot result in a balanced life.

I do not say of course that there are sinister powers at work in our civilization, robbing the individual and making him a mediocrity. Yet, too many of us *have* been conditioned to take "no" for an answer. I find in my own work that people who seek guidance not infrequently have a frightening lack of sincerity.

They are not dishonest and yet a response to the nature of their problems is not what they are really after. Deep down, discouragement makes a reorientation of their lives *a priori* unacceptable.

We do not seem to believe in what we ask for. Still, as St. Augustine taught us, we cannot find what—at least in principle—we have not already found!

The decline of the religious life in our time and the subsequent involvement of many people in totalitarian philosophies, is the best illustration of this lack of sincerity in our questing. We may want to experiment with truths but at the same time we proclaim that we have neither the inclination nor the time to attempt greater integrity. This is the reason for the liberal malaise in America. We too often say that we want individual stature yet at the same time are profoundly troubled by a suspicion of private meaninglessness. Thus the quest for ourselves is undermined by an emotional negation of potential.

The greatest difficulty then in the quest for stature is our tendency to short-change our expectation of ourselves.

Still, without a presupposition of the capacity to grow, the quest for stature becomes sterile. The freedom of a person is not absence of oppression but the affirmation of possibilities. In order to find a way, we have to break through the immaturities of self-negation and reach for an assertion of life. This entails relationship and the discovery that we can, to a degree, further completeness in each other. That we can stand together, that we can sustain each other, and hold on to life together. Such is the happiness we attain from time to time by trusting enough.

Tolstoy told a beautiful and meaningful story, entitled "Master and Man". A rich merchant sets out with a sleigh driver to cross the snowswept steppes of Russia in order to make an important business deal. The transaction will make millions and so the merchant urges the driver on. Soon however, the master, the man and the horse get stuck in the snowdrifts. The driver

falls into a deep sleep of exhaustion and the master uses that
occasion to unhitch the horse in order to reach the next village
by himself, rationalizing that the peasant will surely die anyway. But after much struggle, and after having glimpsed the
village on the horizon, the horse throws him. In a furious snow-
storm he follows the trail only to land back at the sleigh with
the half-frozen driver. This is where the horse had gone too.
Understanding their common plight, the master takes off one of
his heavy fur coats, trying to revive the man, and breathes into
the driver's face. As the man regains consciousness, the merchant calls out, "There you see, friend, I was going to perish
alone and you would have frozen." His eyes fill with tears. Since
he knows little else to say, he just repeats the driver's name and
after a period of silence says, "Now I know about myself what
I know." When villagers find the three the next morning and dig
them out, the merchant has died from exposure while covering
his companion and the horse. Only the peasant driver survives.
He lives to see many more years and when in the end he passes
on, an old man, Tolstoy writes characteristically, "Whether he
was better or worse off where he awoke after his death, whether
he was disappointed or found there what he expected, we shall
all soon learn."

Stature is gained in the acts of living; in struggle and sacrifice
that is the bridge between our intuitive nature, and the world
in which we live. Mediocrity, self-negation, cause the inner eye
to atrophy, and eventually go blind. Man's condition is no more
precarious now than it was in other times. Our present involvement in the outer world is no more than in other ages. The
world around us has not changed even if we understand more
about it. Human life is made possible by a most delicate balance
between these two, balance attained over frequently impossible
odds. Yet it is neither the moral nor the legal sanctions which
evoke a hopeful response to life challenges. No, it is the way of
feeling towards others and the Self which make our precarious

affirmations possible. It is the synthesis of a person, the unity achieved as we make choices which nurtures the impulse to build values fit for down-to-earth living. None of this is mysterious.

A way of life is neither inborn nor predetermined. It emerges and is defined by what it does as we build relationships and perceive those with whom we live. As Emily Dickinson wrote:

> "Each life converges to some centre
> Expressed or still. . ."

It is we who create mental space for each other because of the promise of our future greatness. The moral challenge is therefore tied to an inner response. I am convinced that men express belief or non-belief not in the creeds to which they say they adhere or not, but rather by the degree to which they are willing to identify with the life purposes of others. We are at one with the universe if we respond to the call of future excellences.

CAN WE TRANSFORM OUR LIVES?

Very few of us come near fulfilling our potential. It would be hard to find a person who could truly say: "I have probed deeply enough; I have realized my capacity to love to the fullest."

It is especially hard to perceive such goals by oneself. Martin Buber responded to the frequently heard question: "What am I suppose to do with my life?" by saying: "One is to do nothing, for *one* can do nothing." However, he added to that: "But he who poses this question with the earnestness of his soul on his lips and really means 'What have *I* to do?' he is taken by the hand by comrades . . . and they (will) answer: 'You shall not withhold yourself.'"*

*Martin Buber, *I and Thou*, N.Y. 1955.

But is it true that such guidance is forthcoming when we do not withhold ourselves? Is Buber not confusing metaphysical relationship with human relationship when he maintains that there is within and around us life to be hallowed and redeemed and that in so doing we will discover our true realistic brotherhood?

Of course, mankind is still in its mental infancy as are many of us. But the reality of the world also imposes paradoxes upon us with which it is extremely hard to deal. It is far from clear how we should use our lives.

A good illustration was offered by the CBS correspondent Eric Sevareid, who, reporting from the Scotch village at Holy Loch, told about the disquiet of the villagers who have become hosts to American atomic submarines armed with Polaris missiles carrying nuclear warheads. The lake was called Holy Loch because legend has it that at one time in the Middle Ages, a ship with soil from the Holy Land sank in view of the home port. The soil, meant to be used for the building of a new cathedral, sank to the bottom. All the sailors were drowned. The perilous journey, the anxious expectations had all come to naught. The villagers at Holy Loch are starkly reminded of that sad story as they look out over their lovely stretch of water on which American submarines now float. But what choice do they have? Shall they uproot themselves and become immigrants to Canada or Australia? Shall they say farewell to their hills, their lakes, their kirks, and the ancient cemeteries where their forebears sleep? Shall they be crushed by the dangers of humanity's paradox which is intruding into their lives? The paradox that in order to be protected they must be willing to accept the ultimate risk of having Russian nuclear missiles zeroed in upon them!

The power of the paradox of protection and terror clashes with the simple logic and sanity of a peaceful way of life. To be alive is precarious on many counts. But how to deal with the threat of total obliteration is another question! What choices remain within such "radical irrationality"?

One woeful encumbrance of human society is that a great many in all walks of life, far from wanting to "hallow" the other fellow, have proudly chosen "radical irrationality" as their modus of social behavior. They like it better that way and enjoy the sense of power that goes with the blatant hostility which usually accompanies such behavior. It is a form of social terrorism that paralyzes the environment. Let us be clear about the fact that in order to elicit the best in others we must at least be able to communicate. Many possibilities for decent human relationships die in the swamplands of hostility. It is a way of dealing not with individual men or women but with "them". I refuse to excuse this kind of behavior by pointing to its psychological reasons. We are responsible for the environment we create.

Any sane family or community will try to isolate such behavior, but a glance around us shows that this is not always easily possible. Many a business, many a family is run into the ground before the source of willful irrationality is uprooted. Lincoln feared nothing as much as "a house divided".

It is an imperative task to replace irrational drift with the more hopeful, self-respecting goals of a sane community. "Hallowed" life aims for something greater and more excellent than appeasing the shifting appetites of collectivities.

We can discern what the more promising spirit is when we make social evolution a central private concern. A great deal in life may be mystery but by human effort there is much which will not remain a riddle. Many of us have looked to social ideals to discover worthwhile life alternatives. However, it is crucial that such ideas do not become manipulative. For that has been the melancholy mistake of political and religious utopianisms which sought to unite the "disjecta membra."

We find alternatives in reciprocal relationships which enable us to live more confidently. Depth and relatedness are the key elements of such life projections.

A physician makes a diagnosis not only by considering the ailment about which the patient complains, he also seeks laboratory reports about the functioning of different organs, the composition of the blood and the psychological findings. A theological approach will not do, the approach must be functional and factual. It cannot be a prophecy, it must be considered judgment. The diagnosis must be justified by this considered judgment. If it fails in this, it may be speculative and interesting but the therapy will fail and the patient may die. So also with cultures and nations. So also with philosophies and religions, especially religions. We are at the end of the age of theology.

The patient research, the work of thousands of scientists, students and seekers, have taught us that in fact—not just in flowery poetry—Man is of the same matter as anything else in the universe; that he is propelled by the same sources of energy as the stars in their galaxies. We know that Man's biological evolution, his self-creating capacity is a cosmic capacity, and we are now approaching a new phase of understanding our role in the cosmos. We have entered the phase of what Teilhard de Chardin called the "hominization" of our lives. That means that we have started—whether the theologians know it or not —upon an entirely new understanding of Man's psycho-social evolution. Evolution is becoming "hominized". Man can—if he wants to—begin to use innumerable latent possibilities. There is, therefore, ground for hope—whatever the paradoxes.

Evidently this hope does not permit us to relax in blissful expectation of good tidings to come. The ancient Hebrew teacher, Jochanan, remarked that after the destruction of the Temple in Jerusalem, only fools could still pretend to be prophets. The disasters Jochanan had seen were child's play compared with the disasters of our own time and the disasters still in store, if we fail to occupy ourselves with the hominization process of our world. But it is also true that in terms of biological evolution, Man's presence as an organized being is probably "not much higher than a postage stamp."* We need not be prophets to see that our psychosocial evolution is young. Basically our education and our economies of artificial shortages still teach us to think and feel essentially about ourselves not as psyches, but as physical entities. We are still plagued by repressive conscience, in order to be social instead of self-destructive.

Nations are still ill at ease with the inescapable idea of world sovereignty instead of national interest. Yet all this is changing.

The same teacher, Jochanan, while rejecting easy prophecy, distinguished between these four basic human categories which still make sense today:

First, said the sage, there is the person willing to study, wait, consider and learn. Second, there is the person of less sophistication who cannot grasp complex abstractions, but who has discovered at least for himself a valid way of dealing with the questions of life. Third, there is the person who cannot help but create havoc wherever he goes, to whom destruction of others or their reputations is a means to a sense of self-importance. And fourth, the person who "never knows how to ask a question" as Jochanan put it. This is the person who has "all the answers" and who considers questions others put to him as hostile intrusions. He cannot ask questions because he is governed by suspicion of the motivations of everyone else!

How clearly Jochanan points to the inner drainage which suspends direction! Life is animated only by trying to retain one's loyalty to a reciprocity of feeling, thinking and doing for others. There is no other way to find out whether what we aim for makes sense.

When we are as brothers together, we will know "how to

*James Jeans.

ask a question". Maybe the most difficult task is to learn from others. I often think of this as the main stumbling block in human relationships, for it means discovering our powers as well as our limitations. No directedness of life is possible without the often soul-shattering experience of limitation. "The human animal enjoys nothing so much as digestion, fornication and sleep," wrote one of the pessimistic German philosophers of the nineteenth century. Can this be the whole story? Everyone, whether he can ask questions or not; everyone, at some moment, feels an urgent reality about his life. Here is the psychological moment to intensively question one's motivation, the depth of consciousness. Suddenly there arises for everyone such naked questions as: "What am I doing with my life, what am I all about?"

It may come in the fullness of life, it may come when death seems close or has struck those we love. It may come in loneliness, and it may come in fellowship. It may come at the time of divorce and it may come at the time of marriage, but there are I am sure, for each human being, moments of what I call mental emergency, a moment of engagement when we simply have to fit the pieces together or all will disintegrate. It is at those moments of existential confrontation that individuals at the crossroads may discover a relatedness within themselves to a power that is latent within them, that waits to be nourished, a power of realization.

Much of human life is stranded in the arid desert of self-centeredness and alienation, because too often we think that only by using each other can we work together. A man who works in a laboratory may spend all his life trying to understand the processes by which chemicals fertilize the earth so that plant life will be possible. But a farmer may know more about raising crops because he has lived with the land; he has plowed it, sowed it, and reaped its harvest. But to both the man who worked the earth and to the man who studied it in the laboratory, there were crucial moments of urgency that made them persist in what they did. Both had a functional, not a theoretical handle to life and to substance, a relatedness that was real and not just poetic.

WE CANNOT BE NEUTRAL

In order to understand what purpose may be served, what meaning there may be to men going forth, we need in addition to trying to achieve self-realization, to evaluate the framework in which that self-realization takes place.

Modern man becomes visible and meaningful only if we allow time for growth. It is too easy to expect security without responsibility to others. But by the mere fact that we seek security for ourselves, we have already changed the status quo. If we can be honest with each other, we must say that many people are easily manipulated, hypnotized, mollified, and swindled because they really do not want to face the real problems of their lives. The same tendency exists in the delusions of the "goals" for life that we foist upon our children. We are not serious enough about reality. In part it is because it is so much easier to accept that which does not demand discipline. Thus a kind of congeniality often takes the place of comradeship; just as glancing over the headlines can pass for absorbing information. Unless we recognize that much of our lives consists of mental vegetation instead of mental existence, we will not go forward. To overcome this, we must relate life philosophy to the deepening of personalities.

Sir Herbert Read, the author of *The Forms of Things Unknown*, has stated that any sound group life, family life, community life is built upon what is required of man, not on what is provided for him.

An oriental story comes to mind. Two gardeners who loved each other dearly and worked well together for years, were suddenly separated. But one day, one of them received a letter from his friend. He ran to his employer, a prince, and asked, "Please read it to me, as a poem." The prince looked at the letter and said, "It has only one sentence: 'Dear Friend, this morning I pruned my rose bushes.'" The gardener took the letter to his room and for months he painfully tried to compose a reply. He rewrote his letter, crossed out lines, replaced others and at last, after much brow-wrinkling, he was ready. He found that his reply to his dearest friend contained these few words: "Dear friend, this morning I too pruned my rose bushes."

The abstraction of communication was overcome, the relatedness was re-established. They were gardeners, not abstractions.

Thus can we try to communicate with each other in truth. This is what I mean by "shared life". Our questions need *our* answers. Abstraction is, of necessity, estranging.

But far too often we exhaust our lives, and the urge to live; to love and to be loved then remains without connection. Man goes forth, most often blindly. So many men, even if they do not end in direct self-destructiveness go forth without ever engaging in a dialogue with themselves. Ancient man, who lived in an uncomplicated world, could question the stars and the strange and fearful gods he prayed to, sacrificed to, and ended up hoping for the best. But modern man must learn to question himself. He must make a dialogue possible or he will not be. We cannot escape the knowledge and the reality that we are part dream, part fear, part limitation but also part mental urgency. Often we are at work on all these levels at the same time. Dream and fear, understanding and the need to be understood, self-centered day-dreams and the will to share, jealousy and generosity mingle. We are never one thing alone. We cannot be "neutral". In the end, generosity must be more important to us than anxious self-centeredness, dreams more important than fear or jealousy.

No culture, no civilization can exist only on the basis of threats and terror. It is the internal conditions of people that make for effective recuperative power in the world. It is this ferment which has stimulated the great advances of humanity, the passion of creating a human core, a human meaning within an indifferent cosmos. Thus has there been light in human history; the light not just of forming but of *trans*forming; not just of action, but of *trans*action. This means that we cannot overcome despair and anxiety without first accepting their stark reality. We cannot overcome loneliness without courageously accepting the fact that there is loneliness to begin with.

Maybe our trouble is that we try to comprehend with word symbols what we may often already know intuitively. In the famous Scopes trial, when asked by Bryan whether anything could be holy to an agnostic, Clarence Darrow said, at the Rhea courthouse:

> "Yes, it is the individual mind. It is in a child's power to master the multiplication table; in that, there is more sanctity than in all your shouted amens and hosannas and holies. An idea is a greater monument than a cathedral."

If we accept this, can we not go forth and be men who deal with perpetual crisis? The main point is that we do not lose ourselves in "things". Knowing more does not always mean understanding more.

Eric Sevareid tells about a cafe in Paris where the wine cellar is a former dungeon of the Bastille—the prison that held the French poor before the Revolution and then the aristocracy awaiting the guillotine. In the darkness of that wine cellar, so the owner of the cafe told Sevareid, still live the long, lean grey rats of the pre-Revolutionary generation.

The street above the dungeon has been repaved but the old cave remains. Is it not the same as modern man's living on a very thin layer of pavement? We climb out of the dungeon, we repair the pavement, and entrust our weight to that precarious crust because we must. Some day, we hope, it will hold us and crack no more. Will we be spiritually free enough to comprehend that day?

Liberty, so like love, is still very much a luxury and yet both are necessities for survival. We must take the power away from the frantic irrationality, from the bullies and the suspicious men, who have poisoned our world long enough and have stayed in the dungeon. Who cares for progress in general and preparation for mass death in particular? Who cares for vistas of plenty when close to five million must go without work and millions of others depend on the endless production of war industries?

Love and liberty are young in our world, but they must mature quickly in the very near future.

We have new resources available and commitment to them is one way of gathering the personal strength needed for their use. Such commitment, however, is frequently sought in desperation rather than directed by clarity of insight.

The more pressing the times, the more eagerly the world seems to follow those who say that they know exactly what to do, what to believe. Anxiety creates a hunger for reassurance. Not long ago, a professor of psychiatry at a Canadian university, Dr. Karl Stern, wrote a book entitled *Pillar of Fire* which promised such reassurance. He described how he, born a Jew in Germany, had found concrete direction in Roman Catholicism. The title of the book about his conversion was taken from the Old Testament reference to the children of Israel following a "pillar of fire" when wandering in the desert towards the Promised Land.

Dr. Stern found his promised land in Catholic theology. It is a moving book. Its affirmation speaks of the way in which Dr. Stern had overcome a sense of meaninglessness, and his discovery of new hope.

An American writer, Eric Hoffer, deals with the same kind of hope in his book, *The True Believer*. The author was a longshoreman in California and before that he had been a migrant worker and a miner in Nevada. Until the age of sixteen he was half-blind, and when medicine restored his sight, he threw himself into an intensive drive for self-education. The result is an analysis of what makes certain people "true believers" whether in the kingdom of God or in some earthly utopia. He gives this warning: "If the communists win in Europe, it will not be because they know how to stir up discontent . . . but because they know how to preach hope."

Hope and reassurance are the great attributes of political and religious eschatologies. The question is: hope based on what? No doubt, the utter despair of many today makes them easy prey for their particular "pillar of fire", their flaming guidepost in the desert. No doubt, too, the extravagant faddist despair of much of modern life is out of all proportion.

There is a memorable story about Booker T. Washington, the prominent Negro leader. He arrived one evening at a railroad station and had to get to a church for a major address. Delayed by the train's late arrival, he hurried to a carriage standing near the waiting room. But he was received with an icy "I ain't drivin' no niggers". To which Dr. Washington replied, "Okay, then you sit in the back and I'll do the driving" —which the perplexed driver permitted.

Somehow the confidence of Booker T. Washington had an electric effect. He was a man who had a job to do and the "ignorant armies clashing at night" simply did not impress him. Such confidence requires both mental and physical availability. Unwillingness to be present in depth of purpose, to be available in depth is a way to disconnectedness and despair.

To communicate concern and to be available for such communication is one way to "presence" in depth. Of course, sometimes people waste our time with chatter; but the fact that they are seeking our attention is important. How many people in marriages, offices, communities may be together, but are never really in each other's presence? The unwillingness to grant another person attention is often a way of feeding their unrelatedness. There are men and women who go thus from one fictional person to the other. They are never willing to risk their presence and thus every new acquisition feeds their further loneliness and desperation. What applies to individuals applies to groups and nations too. Once we live with an unreal picture of other nations, we find it harder and harder to see their true nature. This prevents us from changing our opinions and inhibits intellectual growth. Hitler never changed his and neither will the Ku Klux Klan.

Frequently hopelessness is preconditioning for violence and uprootedness. When large groups of men and women started to copy him, Gandhi became fearful of the superficial adherence to his cause by people who joined his crusade while rejecting the families for whom they were responsible. The Indian leader wrote sternly :"Let no one call himself a follower of Gandhi, it is enough that I should be my own follower." He proposed a bill to make it criminal for anybody to call him Mahatma, which means "the great soul"; or for anybody to kiss his feet. Gandhi knew that fanaticism and uprootedness are what blur real capacity for commitment, presence and concern.

Obligation is a central factor in any commitment, for we cannot be agnostic about loving. If a friend loses a beloved one by death we visit that friend and put our arms around him. We have increased and expressed our concern very specifically. There are no two ways about it. Our acts express attitudes.

ON VISION AND DELUSION

A young woman at whose wedding I officiated a few years ago, came to see me soon afterwards. She said that she felt "used" by her husband because his intimate affections were merely a way of confirming his own masculinity, without concern for *her* sense of self. This young woman faced a most common and real problem for the partners had shared neither mutuality of purpose nor a sense of obligation. Each was primarily interested in gratifying ego-needs which were not too dissimilar from those pursued by infantile sibling rivalries.

The ancient Greeks used three different words to describe a sense of obligation: *nomos* which means custom; *thesmos* which means statute of law; and *melos* which means harmony. Today, too, when different persons think about obligation, some will see obligation as that which society and its standards expects of them; others will see it as adhering to laws and regulations imposed upon them and which they meet, as the French put it, "contre coeur". Far too few see obligation as *melos*, as a means to harmony, as the possibility of becoming attuned to that which is compelling from the inside, and thereby leads to greater freedom.

Martin Buber speaks about human existence as the life of dialogue. God speaks to man, but man is free to answer or not, he is autonomous, he is master of his own response. I can go to a concert and only see the concert hall or the audience around me or be absorbed in the performance of the individual musicians. But I can also attend that concert and by an inner readiness be capable of hearing the symphony or the concerto. I am the master of the nature of my response.

In a wider sense this means also that by my actions I can enter into a lifelong "dialogue" with others. In doing so, each individual recognizes and affirms the potential sacredness of the other and by not holding himself back—in Buber's terminology—each engages the other in mutuality. In short, the realization of obligation can be verified in the life of the individual. By the way in which we live we prove the validity of our visions and ideas. There is no absolute truth, the engagement of one life upon another life can yield only an aspect of truth.

The need to accept this "holy" uncertainty and the humility required to comprehend it, was beautifully described in George Santayana's "The Poet's Testament" when he wrote:

> "I give back to the earth what the earth gave
> All to the furrow, nothing to the grave.
> The candle's out, the spirit's vigil spent,
> Sight may not follow where the vision went . . ."

If we can assume then that vision persists how can we improve the power of "the sight"? It is a never-ending task.

The confusion about what visions to live by is well illustrated by the "Meditation Room" set aside in the General Assembly building of the United Nations. It is a very small chamber in comparison with the spacious halls reserved for the political debates, and since it is meant to be used by people of all religions, symbols have been limited to a minimum. Actually in that room there are only a beam of light, a beautifully polished tree trunk and some rather funereal dark green leaves in a vase.

Marya Mannes, in her book *More in Anger*, tellingly described her experience of entering that room: "It seemed to me, standing there, that this nothingness was so oppressive and disturbing that it became a sort of madness . . . We had found finally that only *nothing* at all could please *all* . . . The terrifying thing about this room was that it made no statement whatever." No statement at all is, of course, some statement too, as not acting is acting by default. But we cannot live with nothingness. In her harsh judgment the author expresses, nevertheless, the conviction that troublesome concepts like sacrifice and nobility are crucial—that the visionary quality of life, lived within a context of commitment, makes sense. Sometimes the very despair about our insufficiency to live up to our ideals, is the core from which we gather the strength to go on trying.

We must ask questions therefore about faith versus emptiness for what are the alternatives? There are valid hopes and
there are delusions. There is love and the delusion of love,
there is faith and there is nothingness, the negation of existence.
Our greatest tragedy is when self-doubts, nourished by angers
and frustrated wishes, drain all vision from us.

Of course, we must know what we mean by faith, and it is
not enough to fall back on the Protestant theologian Paul Till-
ich's definition that faith is "ultimate concern". It is not good
enough for a functional understanding of human relationships.
Ultimate concern for what? Eichmann had an "ultimate concern"; so do the racists in the South. Just to be committed in
general, or concerned in general, means absolutely nothing.
Why seek refuge in metaphysical vagueness when the tangi-
bility of human lives is at hand? Faith and commitment make
no sense unless their validity can be demonstrated as conse-
quential for the lives of individuals.

It is important, therefore, to make a distinction between per-
sonalized and institutional values. When values become part of
institutional goals, there is always the danger that they will be
misused. This is a crucial question for a complex culture. Take
the example of the modern painter, or the biologist, who are
involved in highly specialized work and need to preserve the
inspiration and integrity of their craftsmanship. Yet, the result
of their efforts belongs to the public even though they do not
addresss themselves to any specific audience. Nevertheless, the
arts, the sciences, are the result of ages of human discourse. It is
necessary therefore, as the nuclear physicist J. Robert Oppenheimer maintained, that more than just a handful can follow
that with which the scientist is dealing. To Oppenheimer, a
central problem of our time is the alienation between science
and the world of human dialogue by which he meant the consideration of values. He lamented the loss of continuity between
the two, and the loss of insight about priorities. He said that,

at best, science gives us "propositional truths", which may or may not be proven by empirical methods. Yet, can the poet, the philosopher, the religiously concerned person speak in terms of propositional values? Oppenheimer was concerned not that the poet speak *the* truth, but that he speak with meaning and a sense of order, for it is out of this discourse on order, that art and ethics may arise. These highest forms are assertions based on universal human experience, on dedication and commitment. Of course, Oppenheimer did not refer to ethics without mentioning his own personal agony concerning the development and use of atomic weapons. His fear was concerned with a utilitarian ethic that speaks of destruction on a theoretical level —without recognition of the human lives involved. He appealed for a reorientation beyond technical achievement and for a mental and aspirational reorientation of life.

We must re-learn that the self will not be drowned in helplessness once it reaches beyond itself. Confidence is born when we act without limiting ourselves by cynicism. A narrowed vision of ourselves offers no shelter and the meaning and connectedness Oppenheimer sought is born and grows only when we are liberated from self-aggrandizement, self-destructiveness, and self-pity. Self-preservation demands this, as we can see so easily in the suspicious person who cannot share of himself and whose strength remains undiscovered. A warped man always finds reason for more and more doubt and hatred until finally there is the complete barrenness of a loveless life. To believe in something is to locate a center of personality and the possibility for the self in interaction.

We struggle too often in darknesss when alternatives are readily at hand. True independence is born only when we realize how dependent we are: dependent on others, dependent on nature, on society.

Real tragedy is to lose the capacity to replenish the visionary "batteries" from time to time, to lose the capacity for seeing and meaning. The real tragedy is when we are unable to love enough because of pettiness, and inflated ego. This is what dehumanizes, and strips people of their capacity to endure. "The absurd man", wrote Camus, "is the man who does nothing for the eternal." He is indeed a man caught, trapped by nothingness.

According to the magnificent biography of Sigmund Freud by Ernest Jones, Freud once told one of his patients, "You asked me for courage, but I can only give you caution." He was convinced that a cure could be effected only if there had been a *voluntary* mental movement of the patient toward cure. The psychoanalyst could be an interpreter, he could enhance the sense of capacity in the person, but he could not connect the loose ends. The final act of affirmation or rejection of life is the individual's and the individual's alone. In re-reading *Life of Freud* I was struck once more by this man's monumental personal courage. He was world-famous when he discovered that he was afflicted by cancer of the jaw, but instead of using the medical contacts at his disposal, he went to a simple clinic in Vienna, telling his family that he needed only a very minor operation. The clinic was a terrible place, the surgeon a man with cavalier attitudes about his patients. Only by a miracle did Freud not bleed to death the night after the operation. But no matter how great his pain, he refused to have his mind numbed by drugs. Even towards the end of his life, he refused to take anything more potent than aspirin, and by that time the pain was so agonizing that he could barely speak or eat. Until the last, Freud had to do his work as a physician to provide for his family. He wrote:

"Seventy years have taught me to accept life with a cheerful humility . . . I detest my mechanical jaw because the struggle with the mechanism consumes so much of my precious strength. Yet, I prefer a mechanical jaw to no jaw at all, I still prefer existence to extinction. My modesty is no virtue . . . I am far more interested in this blossom of my work than in anything that may happen to me after I'm dead . . . I am not a pessimist. I permit no philosophical reflections to spoil my enjoyment of the simple things of life."

Dr. Jones remarks that Freud died "as he had lived—a realist. From our hearts we thank him for having lived, for having done, for having loved."

The monuments of mankind are not carved out of stone; the real monuments are not in the colonnades and pillars; that which endures is within the human heart. We are here because we can do our duty as the possibilities present themselves, sheltered within the greatness of a vision. We are here because we enjoy the bond of human aspiration.

There is a faith possible which serves man's deepest longing, the longing to love. But the origin of such love is in holding fast to a vision. It is a vision with all the flaws of human attempts. There *is* no perfection; no symphony is perfect; no Leonardo da Vinci painting is perfect. We need not have remorse because we cannot achieve perfection. Remorse is justified only if we have not tried, if we have wandered so deeply into the quicksands of lack of faith in anything that no connectedness capable of strengthening life is attempted. We need not be Freuds to be nurtured by ideas that will never betray us, or set us apart from the world.

There are two simple realities to be discovered: it is part of life to suffer and it is also part of life to do and to love.

CHAPTER *3*

"WHAT WILL YOU DO GOD

WHEN I DIE?"

The German socialist sociologist, Karl Mannheim, wrote in the early 'thirties that if Man loses his ideals, his "utopias", he may reach the zenith of rationality and at the same time a social situation in which he is no longer an individual but only a "thing".

The confrontation with that possibility cannot be avoided. As one who still believes in social democracy (not just economic equity, but life as more than an alienated exercise in perpetual misery) I consider collectivism our main threat whether it comes with a veneer of capitalism or any other "ism."

We live in fear of our own power because we have been fed so long the legend that discontent, the "fall from grace", is in fact the human condition. I see in human society more than a heroic attempt at sublimation or the repression of our instinctual realities. Modern life therefore does not fill me with despair, for I see in a more reasonable social order the possi-

bilities for a renewed human solidarity. The romantic notion
—from Rousseau on down—of "moral man" corrupted by "sin-
ful" society makes no sense. What is needed is to sharpen the
appetite for freedom so that our mastery over nature, production and distribution, will not foster impotence and a sterile
materialism void of ideals. We need to turn from the abstractions of sociological analysis to the tangible presence of the
fate of men and women like ourselves.

The French say wisely: "Je sens mon coeur et je connais les
hommes . . ." (Because of what I can feel, I know all other
men.) We are cognizant, we share in all feeling and also in all
lack of feeling.

A poem of the 'thirties by Vachel Lindsay, entitled "The
Leaden Eyed" therefore implored:

> "Let not young souls be smothered out before
> They do quaint deeds . . .
> Not that they starve, but starve so dreamlessly,
> Not that they sow, but that they seldom reap,
> Not that they serve, but have no gods to serve,
> Not that they die, but that they die as sheep."

This outrage with apathy made another author ask: "If we
knew that in the next twenty-four hours we would be wiped
out, how would we spend our last day?" Some of us would
commit suicide. Others would satiate themselves with life. Yet
some, he said, would simply spend their time doing things
they had always done, responding to fear with whatever tenderness they could summon. They would remain at their tasks as
doctors, engineers, nurses, parents. For them death would have
no dominion . . . Even in the face of catastrophe, sanity is salvaged by the entirely human decision to share in all one is
capable of and thereby to know all other men. Whether the
world will be ultimately "saved" is a far less interesting question than how human beings are going to redeem themselves.

"Faith in Man" as such, has therefore always seemed a superficial triviality. What faith and which man? Neither all faith,
nor all religion lead to a trusted center for life. On the contrary,
traditionally, both religion and faith have induced men to an
abdication of reason thereby evoking a profound sense of
impotence.

Neo-orthodox theologians are prattling once more about
"secularism" and "materialism" as the causes for a loss of faith.
Yet both in materialistic atheism, as propagated in the Soviet
Union and in materialistic Christianity, as emanates from the
religious centers in America, we find faith similarly manipulated for purposes of power. Blaise Pascal already reproached
theologians for "reminding men constantly of their misery and
thus tempting them with perpetual despair". Christianity's
cocktail of "glad tidings" and dismal gloom is just enough of a
palliative to prevent any unsettling desire for social and moral
renewal. It is because of this, not because of "secularism" or
scientific inquiry, that religious symbolism has lost its hold over
men and women. Not religion but national pride and the
power to destroy worlds, is what propels the millions. When
ministerial chumminess is substituted for moral indignation,
institutionalized faith becomes a hindrance to human progress.

It is customary to forget about self-interest when discussing
these phenomena. Still, faith can be a regressive force used to
serve the interests of those who maintain status by a regression
of private conscience. Professor Miller, of Harvard Divinity
School, warned young clergymen not to be deceived by the
spectacular "success" of the churches of America. In fact, he
said, the Christian message has become "feeble and unintellig-
ible". He called the modern clergyman a man who is "chopped
into small pieces" by the petty idea of parish progress.

Institutions are always in danger of disintegration when the
power of imagination is replaced by worries about techniques.
That is particularly true for religious institutions. If faith is to

play any role at all, it will have to help rehabilitate man and society. The entire debate on whether God is dead or not is therefore irrelevant. One recent German survey showed that only 5% of those Europeans who consider themselves Christians adhere to any personal God concept. Divinity, which can no more be exemplified in human experience than other-worldly mythologies, is simply not related to the time in which we live. By insisting on the myth of eternal rebirth, the heart of what disturbs this generation is denied. If "return to the Father" can be comfortingly expected, what significance do collectivist self-annihilation, loneliness and separateness have? Yet such feelings are urgent and profound in our era. It is true that it is in the character of human beings to be social animals and therefore to build the complexities of cultures. Institutionalized God-devotion was once part of this. But no more. Those very institutions meant to make life more than merely an attempt to survive, have become in many ways sources of frustration. The Judeo-Christian tradition provides no reasonable means for transcending our crises nor can it rebuild the sense of freedom necessary for the engagement of the pressures and pains of modern life.

Of course I do not denigrate the worth of the person seized by a totality of feeling and understanding, through what he considers a cognition of the supernatural. Yet, for myself as for a great many others at this time, such surrender has become a psychological and intellectual impossibility.

"Je sens mon coeur and je connais les hommes" also means that everyone of us is Man. The amorphous concept of "mankind" becomes meaningful only because I identify with specific persons. By discovering that I am a man blessed with—at least —a tentative capacity for rationality, I become fit to discover other men and find that I am therefore fit to love and share. In consequence, I can overcome from within the traumata which threaten to overwhelm me.

It is a tragic reality that the normative models of our civilization essentially doubt this evolution, or "hominization", of experience. In its place has been built obedience, submission, and repressive rather than expressive ethics. This profound doubt in human capacity, this sense that each human being has to go through a "vale of tears", this pessimism and invitation to discontinuity, is an incredible burden upon our culture and each one of us.

It may be true that in "the shadows of tomorrow" we know that "the only lasting ideas are the ideas of the shipwrecked", yet I cannot accept this as a life condition. For precarious as our hold on reality may be, even being shipwrecked means being shipwrecked together. Since in the end there is death, there is for us only a process of "homecoming", by living! Whatever the process while we proceed, whatever the barriers and the incomprehensible cruelties that we encounter—I think of my years in Auschwitz—we have a certainty of being within each other's reach and that is enough. It is illusion to think that we can dominate life, it is an illusion particular to our cultures in which the Father is the omnipotent, the Creator, the Doer of great deeds. We humans have something to give, something for which to assert ourselves, and that "something" is in each man, nowhere else. As Rilke put it:

"What will you do God, when I die?
When I, your pitcher, broken lie? . . ."

I find this question particularly meaningful with regard to the process of healing. Is it not a most difficult task to determine what actually should be healed in a relationship? What should be restored and what not? Most of us still are influenced by the proposition that the healthy person is the person who can integrate himself within his significant communities, a notion which underlies most ontological philosophies and extends to Hegel and Karl Marx. Certainly Carl Jung's psychology seeks for the same integration by placing the individual in a larger historical, or archtypical, matrix. Health and the expression of one's full personal worth are linked closely with how one sees the communities in which one functions. The emergence of a priesthood in all civilizations, endowed with a sacred, curative potential, hints of the assumption that the disorders of personal life can be reversed by entering into a community of faith. It is not without importance that in other times the psychiatrist was called an "alienator", a man outside of the communal entity. The individual today will "find" himself not through the collective structure, but by achieving individuation. When does a person feel "well"? The answer in the Middle Ages certainly differed from what we would respond today. We do not search for an eschatological community. What then happens to individuals who live in a culture such as ours in which commitment to particular values seems often impossible? Does the Freudian method help us to return to valid norms for living, does it seek for the transformation of personality which the New Testament characterizes by the concept of the "once born" and the "twice-born"? Yes, is the proposition of sublimation a modern condition for happiness and health? Is it a condition for coping with the drainage and strains of life?

I see tremendously encouraging aspects to our increased capacity to ask such questions without ancient fatalisms and determinisms bearing down upon us.

At least, in this age, the critical issues can be understood even though current events remain baffling. At least we can sift the questions of life and death without the theological overgrowth concerning good and evil. The crises can be comprehended, notwithstanding the acceleration of developments, without the degrading nonsense of collective guilt or original sin.

Obviously, "good and evil" cannot be meaningfully introduced with regard to "democracy" and "communism". The challenge is rather, whether we can learn to use constructive forces to deal with our no less authentic destructive propensities.

Tolstoy's parable was in fact more an indictment than a contemplation. Tolstoy said that the upper class is a heavy man who sits on the shoulders of another man. The man below is the working class. The poor man groans as he is crushed under the weight of the man on his shoulders. And the man above is moved to compassion and takes his clean handkerchief to wipe the perspiration from the brow of the man under him. Later he may even give him a drink of water and some bread. Yes, he will do everything in the world except the one thing he really should do which is to—*get off* the man's shoulders and get down! Subhuman complacency too easily becomes a way of life.

Such attitudes are not limited to class struggle. Witness the prevalent crushing of individuals in the family, the prevalence of tyrannical rule in uncounted marriages. Nothing is more illuminating than to go through one's family therapy records and see the eternal repetition with which men and women kill off the love between them, by using their frustrations as the stunted means with which to get at each other. Nothing is more tragic than to listen to two people and to find that there is nothing left but hostility and bitterness, nothing but alienation and self-assertion bought at the price of self-destructiveness. So between fathers and sons, the sons struggling with the father's personality distortions and then turning around and acting exactly in the same fashion in relationships with their own sons. The same may pertain to mothers and daughters; to brothers and sisters whose never-resolved rivalries are repeated in their marriages. The world is full of such agonies and perhaps here is the heart of much of the unresolved hostility in our civilization.

WEEDING OUT THE MORAL VERBIAGE

So much of what passes for private psychoneurotic patterns, is in fact the resonance of social neuroses; disturbances of relationship. In a report of a special committee of the American Psychiatric Association about the relationships of psychiatry to industry, conclusions show how much we are dealing with social, not characterological patterns:

> "Since the emotional environment of an organization is largely determined at the top, the psychiatrist needs the acceptance, sympathy, cooperation and understanding of the top management . . . The psychiatrist has a real need for developing excellent social relations with the executives . . . "*

No wonder then that the labor movement has instinctively stayed away from psychiatric influence in labor-management problems! Yet, there is no doubt that the present economic order is the origin of a great many personality disorders. If the psychiatrist did not identify with "the top" he might be of tremendous help. But, as in the case of "adjusted" religion, most psychiatrists, by their very way of life, have little in common with lower class patients. Nor are they inclined to suggest revisions in the socio-economic order. Thus stagnation and illness rather than change and health are built into the very seats from which renewal is supposed to come. The means by which one is a "success" in our society (money, prestige, power) are frequently the cause of a deeper failure and the acceptance of drift so far as values are concerned.

Psychosomatic illnesses are therefore very often cultural phenomena, triggered by suffering because of that which is sub-human in society. The techniques of publicity, advertising and market psychology play a particular role here and one such technique is especially doubtful. If one scans the average woman's magazine (and they sell by the tens of millions) one

*J. B. Furst, M.D. *The Neurotic*, N.Y. 1954

finds *ad nauseum* the suggestion that the primary role of a woman is that of being sexually attractive; of being attuned towards sexual gratification.

Ninety percent of the advertisements point out how to achieve greater seductiveness. By emphasizing the need for eternal youth and seductive attributes, the greater inherent value of the woman as companion in the precarious struggle for life is negated. The weight of a woman's potential is shifted towards what, above all, she is not: a perpetual "sexpot". While every man and every woman know this, the mass suggestion nevertheless seeps in and gradually one starts evaluating oneself by inane standards. This, too, is a way of cheerful deception, for who wants to be desired for the shape of one's bosom? Accidental facts of appearance and the dread of aging often combine to lead a person to a loss of self-esteem.

This brings to mind a woman who was widowed in her early thirties. When all that family life meant, the care of the children, the husband, the home, fell away—when the friends of the past, married couples, shied away from visiting a lone woman, she developed an acute sense of anxiety and unworthiness. Her loneliness and ostracization by married couples—a deadly problem for anybody who is widowed—gave her the feeling that she was being punished for the death of her husband. In her mind, the idea grew that perhaps there were reasons for her being blamed for his death. This frightful burden threw her into the arms of a young man, about ten years her junior, who soon tired of her when her passions became hysterical. In the crudest possible way he cut her off, yet that very degradation strengthened her need to be "wanted" as a woman. The cheaper she made herself, the shallower her relationships and the more certain the rejection in the end. When the conflicts became too immense, she attempted suicide in such a fashion as to mutilate her face, thus creating a grim confirmation that she was indeed ugly, guilty and "paying" for it.

Her acute grief, her doubts concerning her femininity, her social isolation and her fundamentally infantile dependence upon her husband's, her father's or any significant male's approval had produced a distorted self-image, full of the deepest confusion and despair. How much hopelessness is triggered by societal suggestions; how many men and women blame themselves for ills which are—at least in part—cultural. There is a need to oppose this downgrading of human beings. Men and women can grow, so that they can learn to say "no" to accepted norms which are essentially destructive. For we are beset—all of us— with inner inclinations which drive us towards hopelessness unless we acquire a counterbalance.

I refer back to the earlier statement that our tradition has posed a polarity of the concepts of good and evil of being either inside or outside the Garden of Eden. If things were only that simple! One cannot be a humane person without counteracting the tendencies by which life feeds upon life. One cannot be seriously concerned about values without the knowledge that one is also part of all injustice.

While social amelioration is most necessary, the real need is for a new hierarchy of choice within. There is no humanism therefore without a probing of the nature of reality. Certainly, bio-chemistry is probing the nature of reality; certainly nuclear physicists are similarly engaged as are those seriously involved in the frontiers of psychiatry.

But men and women without such specialized knowledge also need to probe the nature of reality in making sense out of their lives. A humanist position wants to enrich the intellectual and emotional insight by which one can confirm present possibilities and maintain a measure of hope. No theology, no institutional activity can do this. The work, the acumen necessary, is part perception, part reasonableness, part readiness to probe the ambiguities within ourselves.

Man is more than a definition, more than an analysis! Facts

are crucial, but life emerges from the tension between facts and values, alternatives and choices.

It is not too difficult to maintain that one's primary concern is Man, but it is not enough. For there are the opportunities of life expansion but also of attrition. That is no less a human concern. An earnest life-attempt is not about gayhearted saints shouting "hallelujah" because they have found the "true" way! It is about a mental confrontation which includes pain.

During a visit to Hyde Park I heard Mrs. Eleanor Roosevelt mention a haunting example concerning "accepted" destructiveness in the human community. She spoke of the many adolescents who were relegated to overcrowded cells in the houses of detention of New York City. These are frequently young men and women in their 'teens, packed like animals in airless, dark cells, frequently together with the worst deviates of society and waiting for months before their cases come up for trial. This wastage of life is, in fact, based upon another anti-human tendency in society: the idea of retaliation. Frequently society seems almost to be in a conspiracy to deny change and growth their chance.

Behind the verbiage of "moral" language stand the ambivalences of our social character. There is no greater joy than to have found, from time to time, that one is achieving a transformation of person: to get beyond anger, to overcome the rankling of a desire for revenge; to become able to awaken new strata of relationship and to act differently. Such capacity is the heart of private sanity. It is counteracting the devastation of continual self-doubt based upon polarized oversimplifications of "right" and "wrong". Ethics is a method of dealing with the issues at hand, not by proxy but by the discovery of an immediacy within. In the torment of making choices involving others we can discover that each life is significant.

Such progressive humanism is neither weak nor pious. It will not become regressive because it is forever questing at the frontiers of knowledge and feeling and doing. It matters very little what we say we believe as long as we know what we are doing. Longfellow said:

> "So nature deals with us, and takes away
> Our playthings one by one, and by the hand
> Leads us to rest so gently, that we do
> Scarce knowing if we wish to go or stay
> Being too full of sleep to understand
> How far the unknown transcends what we know."

The dark uncertainties of life need not frighten us because sometimes as we tackle them, they help make us human. This is the claim humanism can make for a trusted core of life. It is a claim which can be illustrated by a great many examples in human history. Some of the precedents are so well established that they are barely remembered. Take the fate of Giordano Bruno, condemned to death by the Roman Catholic Church in 1600 for having stated that "the sun is a star as all other stars, space has no limit and is filled with galaxies, all of them are worlds driven by the powers of nature." He refused to recant this statement before the Tribunal of the Inquisition which was to subject Galileo to similar pressure in 1633. When Bruno was sentenced to die, he said, "You have reasons to be more afraid of the judgment you are imposing upon me than I can ever be to hear it." Humanist faith, neither weak nor regressive, taking darkness into consideration, has not been found to be wanting.

This also applies to the life story of Sir Thomas More as por-trayed in the play "A Man for All Seasons". More lived in the sixteenth century and was first a favorite of Henry the Eighth, yet in the end he was beheaded by that paranoid tyrant because of his stubborn humanism. What motivated More's courage was not an abstraction, but the conviction that there are certain principles in society that must not be violated lest we become degraded by the sub-human. Thomas More was a scholar, a lawyer of tremendous insight. In his book *Utopia,* he railed against the tyranny of absolute monarchy and also pled for the beggers and others who for the slightest offense were hung in England. This book is actually the first social psychology of poverty and analyzes the relationship between crime and poverty.

It is significant that in the drama, Sir Thomas More's personality is most profoundly challenged by the "Average Man", a personage who appears in all scenes of the play. This "Average Man" is Sir Thomas More's servant, who talks with him about the weather and business and then sells his employer's secrets to the Cardinal's spies. When he later becomes a servant to the Cardinal, he sells *him* out in turn to Cromwell. He wants his comforts, he wants these big men to fight it out for themselves and he will make sure that he will not end up poor. His aimlessness, his lack of principle, one day gets him appointed as More's jailor. He now proudly represents "authority" which wants reformers safely behind bars. And finally he consents to be the executioner, the man who will actually swing the axe! As Thomas More ran the gamut from scholar to Chancellor to victim, so the "Average Man" had run his cycle from servant, to jailor, to executioner.

No, I have no illusion that a humanist commitment is easily lived. Yet, we cannot say: "I will keep the best in myself for that day when I can be beautiful and good." The work is now and we should not confuse *desiderata* with motivation. There is a frightful discrepancy between prayerfully expressed ideals and what people actually do in their day-to-day living. There is enough of this discrepancy to throw up one's hands and cancel one's membership in the human race. . . .

However there is one restraining factor: man's moral growth is part of an evolutionary process. This process depends upon learning painfully how not to repeat suffering. "Human beings cannot build cathedrals every day," Malraux wrote. Man is the

interrogator of the unknown and if he is a rebellious interrogator, his life needs no embellishment. We can teach ourselves that the real secret of being alive is the discovery of
resourcefulness and resistance. One does not purposely make
such discoveries. As Karl Jaspers put it, we can discover
"tragedy which shows man as he is, transformed at the edge of
doom." The sense of helplessness can be overcome by individuals interrogating eternity. Blissful expectations of salvation
can be replaced by a revitalization of the mind, which is dependent neither on the gods nor on metaphysics, but rather on
effort, ambition and a psychology for living.

The messianistic hopes for harmony are doomed to failure.
Their expectations were based upon supposedly competing
forces outside of human nature. It is magnificent when the
shifting harmonies of individuals merge into a symphonic work
but even if they do not, we can still engage upon a life in which
expectations outrun the pains of disconnectedness.

One can live by the diversified vibrations of many hearts
which have in them all variety of intelligence, skill and motivation. We need not be angels to try. Understanding this variety
of the human canvass is to respect the contribution everyone
can make. It is discovering a fidelity to life because of the power
which brings more and more of our resources into play. Thus
obligations may become elements of a hopefulness of living
which can lead to concrete actions; tangible idealism instead
of prayerful aspiration. It is not enough to thirst for humaneness
in the world. There must be a rediscovery of the trusted centers
of life, a clarity of private horizon. The cry for humanity is
never so meaningless as when that cry comes from people unwilling to discipline themselves or to accept the sacrifices necessary to make choices.

A different internal climate, a different internal milieu is
possible for as the Buddhist maxim reads: "a river does not
become less a river because it flows into the sea." Human en-

deavor is no less privately significant because in the end it
merges with a more total destiny. Our lives can fall into place
if we know that we, in our time, in our turn, did our share in
being a tributary to a "mighty stream" of humane effort through
the ages. This is more than a hope, more than "a faith in Man";
it is a method, a way of life, of and by itself capable of sustaining us in moments of despair.

Of course, the counteracting forces are tremendous and they
invade our private existence at every turn. It is obvious, for
example, that our generation needs to remain deeply aware of
the shadows of obsessive hostility. Self-aggrandizement and
raw aggressiveness are taught as virtues to our youth. We are
in fact continually at war with ourselves, for every act of overt
hostility is merely an expression of great conflict within. Actually, mass participation in the ideological preparation for killing
seemingly lessens the awareness of the inner war. When brutality is sanctioned by society there is a sense of relief, for then
the personal drama needs to trouble us less.

BEYOND THE FROZEN IMAGE

The twentieth century may well be remembered as the century of incredible destruction of human life. Ushered in by
pogroms in Russia, with the slaughter in Kishinew as their gory
zenith. Followed by the terrible persecution of Armenians by
Turks, described unforgettably in Franz Werfel's *The Forty
Days of Musa Dagh*. World War I saw the killing of about
fifteen million souls by poison gas, flame thrower and such
idiocies as the battle of Verdun where along the "Voie Sacrée"
about one million French and Germans were sacrificed. Then
followed the executions of the Russian revolution and Stalin's
starvation of the "Kulaks" and the civil war in Spain eternally
symbolized by the destruction of Guernica by Hitler's Condor

airplanes. More recently, the German genocide, claimed about eleven million souls; then the use of the atomic bombs against Japan; Chiang Kai-shek and Mao's killing of Chinese; the Moslem-Hindu fratricide after the formation of India and Pakistan; Korea, Vietnam, the slaughter of three hundred thousand communist suspects in Indonesia in 1966 and so on and on.

At one time man had to be continually in a fight-reaction relationship to his environment. Today, the inner fears, the surrender to the false prophecies of nationalism turn man's aggression against himself. Brutality has become the symbol of the collectivization of conscience and it seems at times almost impossible to escape, whether in literature, science, or the arts. There is a rage close to the surface of the consciousness of our time which at any minute can be mobilized for murderous collective violence.

A Catholic humanist, Gabriel Marcel wrote, "We seem nowadays to have entered upon the very era of despair . . . (for) we see the ultimate failure of all techniques to save man himself." The paradox, Marcel points out—is that while we have by no means lost our confidence in technological progress, we have failed to devise a technique with which to deal with brutality. Hope is a commodity hard to come by. Examples of brutalization are numerous. One, particularly striking, occurred in the Fall of 1962 when a great number of Chinese families were turned back from the border of Hong Kong and returned to the Communist guards to be punished as traitors. How pitiful was the U.S. refusal to give refuge to these "Asiatics" because of the racist intent of the McCarran-Walter Immigration Act! When we acceded at last, saying that we would let in a handful of refugees, Washington carefully stipulated that we would *only* take the healthy, young, and skilled workers. The older people, the weak and sick ones, and the children were left to rot in overcrowded refugee camps! The champions of freedom tacitly accepted the barbed wire in Hong Kong as easily as the Russians did the wall in Berlin!

Another striking example of collective brutality occurred in New York City when a boxer was killed in the ring, a tragedy also seen by tens of millions of people on television. The boxer was hanging unconscious on the ropes but his opponent kept pummeling him to death. Now this man was killed under the delighted gaze of a national television audience. The crowd wants the collective catharsis of seeing one man stretched out in shock, on the canvas. Its brutal orgasm must run its full course before the crowd is ready to go home, back to the frustrations of everyday living. As Thomas Wolf said in *Of Time and the River:* "How have we breathed him, drunk him, eaten fury to the core . . . uncontrollably forever swelling in our soul . . ."

Thus life is abused and many of us are the passive abusers. And yet brutalization is not all. What people hope and slave for in life is equally well established. It is when the more hopeful strain is frustrated that distortion sets in and the growling caveman reemerges. Alas, while hate, aggression and brutality are easily communicated, ideals of decency and hope have to be struggled for. To make the pursuit of meaning fruitful, each man must balance his inner aggressions with his capacity for maturation. Without a continued effort to achieve this, concepts such as love, constructiveness and an aim for peace cannot become his. It is our unformed infantile side which aches for battle, revenge and the infliction of pain. Surrender to these forces does not really relieve the inner compulsions, the separateness. All higher teachings whether in the Hebrew-Christian culture, or in the oriental philosophies, aim at defeating the apathy and immaturity and at making men capable of accepting the freedom to be responsible for their acts.

Dr. Horace L. Friess of Columbia University, has written in

this context of the similarity of the writings of St. Paul in the New Testament and of the Buddhist Rig-Veda which sums up thousands of years of Indian human experience. Paul, in his First Letter to the Corinthians (13:13) says that until we will meet God face to face, there remains for Man these three great resources: "faith, hope and love—these three—and the greatest of these is love." Hope is not a generality. It is found only in the specifics of human commitment, and there is no commitment without love. Hope must be a vital function grown in the very human condition which could also set us to despair. To be helpful in actual life circumstances, hope has to be grown amidst the recognition of limitations and deficiencies.

In the Buddhist Rig-Veda, this topic is dealt with extensively. What are the blessings, for which Buddhists pray? They pray for children, for wealth, for health, for a long life, for release from guilt and punishment, and for care of their memory by their children and grandchildren so that they will not be neglected after death and live in hell. Do we perhaps as much entrust our lives to governments and "experts" of all kinds as Hindus do to their gods? Do we not sacrifice heavily in order to achieve what we think we want? There is no doubt an underlying continuity in the values we seek. Who could take issue with Buddha's concept of enlightenment, with his wish for the blessed state of Bodhisattva, when Man will have become truly compassionate and enlightened, capable of spreading deliverance to others, willing to undergo the endless suffering of existence, the cycles of creation and re-creation so that compassion may emerge?

"Faith, hope and love. . . ." In modern society—in addition —we also have to create the mental posture to overcome destructiveness. It is not easy, for we virtually live with a cultural suggestion of emptiness. It appears "sophisticated" somehow to have no hope at all. We are bombarded with the suggestion that man is powerless, that individuals cannot change anything, least of all themselves. We are told that civilization must be balanced on the brink of disaster, that the individual must be willing to subordinate his desire to be left alone, to live with his wife and children, to the great "historical tasks". This is hogwash. It is the hoax of all types of dead-end materialism.

A recent French motion picture entitled "Last Year at Marienbad" makes this suggestion of emptiness very strongly. I call it a "fascist" suggestion because the whole opus is aimed at undermining faith in the dignity of the individual. It deals with a group of people in one of the old nineteenth century European resort towns where in a massive Victorian hotel, swanky men and women are destined to meet. Yet, all corridors are empty, lakes in the park are frozen and what the mirrors reflect is marred by cracks in the glass. Everyone's footsteps disappear in deep carpet. Those who converge there are not people but masks; they live no real lives. They have gathered, festively, as if waiting for a party to begin, but in fact they are marionettes manipulated by the strings of Death. Death is portrayed as a man who gambles at the card tables. Death always wins. . . . The principal woman in the drama is supposedly seductive, but she too becomes a victim. She hides in a strange costume of feathers, a wispy umbrella of illusion in which she will die like a languishing swan. Even when dying she will neither cry out nor show pain. She is killed by a pistol shot, the sound of which is muffled by the feathers and she dies without a sob; her finger rests on her lips as if begging for silence. She represents muffled Humanity, bereft of all feeling.

As in so much art expression of today, this picture is anti-woman in that it denies the existence of tenderness and the capacity to bear life. It is a fascist outlook because in this imagery all validity of courage is denied. In addition, it is a propagation of sexual deviation. When men and women embrace, when they might be uplifted, it becomes clear that instead they stand at the portal of self-destruction. I pay this motion picture this much attention because it received the highest honors at numerous film festivals and was advertised as one of the "best pictures ever made". It has reached many millions of people with its desolate message.

Our world is not an empty castle in which time is frozen. Our lives are not just absurd movements towards death. The fluid impulse is not what is essential in us; we are not caught desperately; we are not doomed animals. Everything does not crack in the mirror; everything is not a mask.

If there is one thing sane people must oppose, it is this creeping, suicidal destructiveness foisted upon us under the guise of enlightenment. It cannot just be fought with words. For most of our destiny is shaped by our own acts and decisions. It is true that there is much we do not control. Many things no doubt happen *to* us; we cannot change their course. What may befall us, what may be in store for us is often a frightening thought. Nobody with real emotions can feel entirely secure in a cosmic situation so full of unknown factors. Who knows of what his days will consist, what strange happenings will not influence his life? We plan, we arrange our lives, and we try to bargain with fate, and we know not!

Who shall speak lightly of human tragedy? We do not have to read Greek classics to feel utter pity for all human trials, blindness, and lack of charity when a word or a gesture could have liberated another. We are not as unique as we think, nor as important in our own particular suffering.

Then how shall we understand the cause of that silent and compelling power that so often seems to pull people away from each other exactly at the moment when they need each other most? To be able to love even that which is problematic or unlovable in the other is nevertheless the secret of all persisting relationships. The unlovable is as real as the lovable; that which frightens us is as real as that which brings us contentment. None of it exists in isolation.

Faith, hope, and love belong together and are born in great tribulation. It is misunderstanding of this balance between the components of human character that makes hope so easily shatter. It is this misunderstanding which makes us give up when our effort is needed most to have any chance at all in this brief and often terrible existence. When the understanding of the need to balance fulfillment and disappointment is lost, when the understanding of the limitations of what we may reasonably expect is blurred, we face true despair. And yet, we are in each other's charge. Hope consists of man's capacity to go down to the abyss of pain and to return to the tasks of life. The "tasks of life", of which the first is pity for the lot of us all, compassionate pity, not sentimentality. It is recognition that even though we may not always be conscious of it, men and women weave between them in their down-to-earth little acts of life, the destiny of generations. We cradle life between us. We are never without the other.

Men and women who come together when the soul aches for a gesture that will say, "yes, I have chosen you above all others; we will struggle through pain together," express by such commitment a much wider meaning than any couple may comprehend. When we come together in this pity for our mutual vulnerability, we hold between us the curative wisdom of all generations. "Oh, world, I cannot get thee close enough. . . ." Compassion is not some shoddy sentimentality, but a recognition of limitations, "for better or for worse". We are entrusted to each other in order to engage those compelling forces which so frequently pull people apart in hostile recrimination. It is a way to discover a sense of life-intention. It is a way of regaining the power of the heart which we know so well when life smiles upon us. Yet, the impact of that "smile of life" can be discovered amidst great tension as well. The other remains the eternal challenge of our own better capacity.

These are vital layers of subsistence which must not be violated. The problems of life do not wear us out; it is the short-age of love that does. The poet Constance Carrier wrote:

". . . crippled, groping, the hand
will seek again what it knew
the hurt foot moves, like the heart
through a land it stains with red.

Heart and heel and hand
armor is not for you,
We cannot choose what we shall feel
We are vulnerable . . . or dead. . ."*

We cannot help being vulnerable—it is a condition of life to be vulnerable. Nevertheless, within our own vulnerability we may distill a sustenance, for we are happiest when we replenish the reciprocal facets of our nature. We are happiest when we share, work together, eat together (passing food around, not hoarding it). Often we are happiest when we are most vulnerable. Such is human tragedy and nobility. So also when we love, when we care enough to discover the other beyond what the other means to our particular needs. It is then that we are happiest, when we help heal, when we encourage.

Faith and hope are not luxuries. They are lifesavers, necessary ingredients of sane living. It is not essential to have more faith, but it is essential to become more conscious of the life forces, in the other and therefore in ourselves. Not more dependent, but more intensely directed toward a humanization of our existence, making our humane instincts more important than the reckless animal which also houses within.

"The moral fight", said William James, "must be a real fight, not a token gesture in which the outcome is guaranteed and neither a token gesture of defiance or resentment meant to show that any outcome is impossible." "The moral fight must be a real fight." What is meant by "moral"? Certainly not

*New York *Times*

piety. The "moral" is that for which we take responsibility. Not good intentions, not just standing up against ugliness and injustice. The moral fight, to make any sense at all, is the fight within our own psyche as we assume responsibility. To refuse to be responsible means to misuse ourselves. We cannot blame this misuse on others. No abstractions will do—there is just us and the reality of life tasks. In truth, we are more often misused by ourselves than by others. We can learn to do so less and less.

In Maxwell Anderson's play *Joan of Arc*, at the climax of her life when she stands before the court which is intent on sentencing her to death, she defends herself before these highest authorities saying, "In all the world there is for nobody any authority but his own soul."

The Inquisitor bends over, he scents the possibility of a verdict of heresy and he growls at her, "So then, Joan, you are choosing death?" And Joan of Arc answers, "And *what* if I offer my life for this choice? I know it. Every man offers his life for what he believes. Every woman offers her life for what she believes. One life is all we have and we live it as we think we should, and then it is over. But denying what you are and living without belief, that is more terrible than dying, that is more terrible even than dying young."

Living with belief "without denying what you are." That I think, is the true nature of man and in this is our hope.

A Schumann sonata suggested this poem:

RECLINING BIRD

My tender friend of folded wing,
    Who hides in furry sway
And hunched, all through the burdened day,
    Call to my heart and sing!

My friend of shrunken flight
   Behind a sheltering screen
Of life within, unseen
   As bedded for the night.

Call now my shrunken heart
   That hides in bent-down wing
And call and call and sing
   And let us both depart.

I know a hollowed wood
   Of trees in muted reach
I know a silent beach
   And of my hurt the roots . . .

Come friend of folded wing
   Who rests in bent-down heart,
We turn as we depart
   And shrink still as we sing.

Beholden to the sky
   Now breaks our sudden death,
What holds our fragile breath?
   Where do birds hide to die?

I know, the waxing spring
   Will turn to folded fall,
Light splashed against a wall,
   Yet must we sing and sing . . .

THE HEADY WINE OF HATE

My fundamental concern is with the actual ways in which individuals live together. James Baldwin addressed himself to this question in an article in the *New Yorker* magazine (11/17/62) when he spelled out the humiliation every Negro experiences each day in American culture. Expressing his dismay about the fact that "so few people are willing to shoulder the burden of their lives," Baldwin nevertheless concluded that, yet:

".. . at the bottom of my heart . . . I think that people can be
better than they are . . . One is responsible to life; it is the small
beacon in that terrifying darkness from which we come and to
which we shall return."

The damage done to Baldwin's sense of human dignity has
obviously not destroyed his own capacity to relate to others
with some kind of hope, some kind of perspective. Yet, how
many, whether Negro or "white," can claim such persistent
inner assurance? The barriers are formidable and most of us
carry battle scars.

Outstanding hindrances to strengthening that "beacon" are
disproportionate anxiety and hostility. Unless we are willing to
look at hostility realistically, moral theories are of little avail.
There is much anger and fear in us largely put there by our
churning unhappiness with ourselves and our feelings of in-
adequacy.

Why is disproportionate anxiety such a primary obstacle?
Anxiety and hostility are frequently intertwined. Persistent hostility kills the confident impulse; hatred and hostility are like
heady drinks: they deter a person from his better performance,
they discourage solidarity with his fellowman, they make him
feel alone and trigger self-destructiveness.

A dominance of hostility makes it impossible for a person to
feel what James Baldwin characterized as "one's responsibility
to life."

There is a wealth of psychological and clinical material describing hostility, and much of it emphasizes the fact that the
more hostile a person is, the greater his anxiety. It is a vicious
circle.

One of America's leading psychiatrists, Dr. Abraham Kardiner, in his study of "Plainville"* describes a community in
which hostility had become the primary emotion expressed by

*Quoted in Rollo May, *The Meaning of Anxiety*—N.Y.

the different strata of society. On further study, he discovered that this hostility, which had ripped apart the community, resulted largely from gossip. Kardiner showed that the gossip occurred in those groups who were also isolated and the more they gossiped, the more anxious they became. Despair and lack of communal goals was the result. There was no remedy, but mental decontamination. Of course, what was true in Plainville, U.S.A., is true in the world at large.

Nations isolate themselves by hostile propaganda, and then they find themselves the victims of hostile counter-propaganda—thus anxiety is increased in circular fashion.

Hostility is the easiest of emotions; it pulls people together in irrational company. Events in Little Rock, Arkansas, and later in Oxford, Mississippi, in Harlem and Watts, California, during race riots illustrate how isolation leads to anxiety and suicidal hostility.

Some people, who may be only vaguely aware of their feelings of anxiety, can be drawn into disastrous and destructive associations. To hate or despise others is often a unifying agent that thwarts personal development. In his book *The True Believer*, Eric Hoffer said:

"Hatred is the most accessible of all unifying agents. We do not look for allies when we love, but we always look for allies when we hate."

Since this is a world problem of the first order, we need not speak in abstractions. We know that some persons are compulsively hostile and cannot help themselves; they are like those suffering from obesity and who cannot stop eating since vague anxiety is continually triggered by the slightest hunger pangs. We also know that most people can be "better" than they really are. Anxiety is not the entire story. What matters rather is to find out what blocks the channels of greater self-confidence. To explore this question means that one has to adopt the attitude of a teacher starting a new semester—he must have faith that his students can be taught. He cannot *know* whether they are teachable, but he has faith in their availability. He prepares himself even though he does not know in how far each of the students is in fact available. His self-respect is involved in his trust that he will be able to reach them and no disappointment will stop him because he has a task to perform. He tries to be a guide, knowing full well that the results of his efforts are not guaranteed. To know and to understand what judgment is and how one can put it to work is a crucial task. It takes continual self-examination, and conscious appraisal of the meaning of our interpersonal relationships. We cannot oversimplify our notions of human nature. Not everyone can be reached and it makes little sense to drain one's energy and mentality trying to elicit responses in those who are not able to respond.

The heart of a humanist attitude is not sentimentality but courage to read facts and to recognize limitations; not to seek the perfect person but the person willing to engage upon the discovery of mentality; not the person in need of conformity but the person willing to do the think-work that goes with independence. It must be open to all, at all stages of their lives, and at all phases of their emotional and intellectual development. People who are mature enough to have the desire for decent relationships do not have to watch anxiously whether they themselves or others "measure up." The practice of judgment is a tough, precise discipline.

Take an example of functional ethics: it is not too hard to make friendships. However the demands of decency, foresight, carefulness, and mutual trust that friendship demands can be very difficult. A person who sacrifices himself may think he is a noble influence, but he may in fact not act wisely at all. A mother who sacrifices herself so that, at the expense of her own happiness she can promote what she thinks is best for her children, does not necessarily display sound judgment.

Humanist consciousness depends upon the response to one's own conscience. It does not offer an easy way out. To maintain that man is autonomous is a far cry from pretending that "everything goes." The principal asset to be gained is the recuperative power of character and human resourcefulness applied to whatever life turns out to be. Only when we demand much of ourselves and others do life goals become clearer.

In New York City, a state training school for youngsters is available only for children twelve years old or more, provided that they have no diabetes, are not mentally ill, are not crippled, and are not pregnant. But what is to happen to those who are? What about the abandoned children whose parents will no longer assume responsibility? By the end of 1962, there were 2,071 children classified as neglected or abandoned in New York City. Most of them had to wait in City shelters but nobody knew what they were waiting for! We may agree on social services, but do we agree on what ethical duty is towards those at the bottom of the social structure? What is the community willing to do about the causes of such misery? What is it willing to do to break the taboo on birth control instruction, especially for parents who are economically or psychologically helpless?

Humanism deals with the causes of right and wrong, and with ways of improvement. Humanism then is about the growing edge of experience. It is about the promotion of meaning and a liberation from that which diminishes a sense of selfhood. It is based on the firm conviction that there are in each person vast mental resources, vast possibilities which have not been realized.

In one of his militant discourses, Dr. Channing, founder of the Unitarian Church, remarked on the self-satisfied manner in which the Christian Church deals with poverty as a problem of charity, but refuses to go to its causes.

"The Christian would not have it otherwise. He learns too many lessons of resignation and faith and hope from the poor; he enjoys too much satisfaction in administering to their necessities; he receives too many admonitions to his pride; he is made to feel his own privileges too gratefully, to wish that poverty were no longer known on earth."*

This insight of the Unitarian reformer about how conscience can be lulled to rest, to a feeling that all is well if we just show a little kindness, did not endear him to his own parishioners. Dr. Channing, now celebrated as the prophet of Unitarianism, complained bitterly that the Unitarian Church deserted him in such vital matters as the slavery question.

Humanism is not inclined to accept the order of man and society as it is. Rather does it want to test again and again what Man and his world ought to be. At the heart of all social reform is the need for a personal passion for transformation.

Our world is tired of seeing better practices postponed. "Kingdom Come" has no true meaning in the twentieth century. What is needed is a plan for justice, for social and personal progress, not a blueprint for perfection. What is needed is a quest for new social institutions, not for ideal standards.

It is true that anxiety and hostility exist. It is also true that growth of personal strength has at least a fighting chance.

During the Cuban crisis a number of Soviet and American scientists met at Andover for a conference on communications. Shortly after President Kennedy's address announcing the U.S. blockade of Cuba, the participants at the sessions drifted into the conference room. No doubt the Russian delegates were worried whether they should stay on. Many must have thought of the possibility of being separated from their families in a nuclear conflict.

At the beginning of the session, the American chairman made a short speech. He said that everyone was probably preoccu-

*As quoted in the Unitarian-Universalist *Register*, 1963.

pied with his own thoughts now and that he would understand it if delegates wanted to terminate the congress. He asked for a show of hands of those willing to stay. At first shyly, then firmly, all hands went up.

All Americans and all Russians voted to stay and to work on the task at hand. The dynamics of their relationship were stronger than their anxiety and—from that moment on—said one of the participants later, "we were closer to each other as human beings even though our political debates and differences might have become more outspoken."*

It was a triumph for sanity, for individual identity over collectivism. There is no maturing life in isolation. We are continually in danger of taking our doubts and turning them upon ourselves instead of seeking newer ways to deal with what legitimately troubles us. No one can as yet define human nature yet we have some idea what elements are needed for human nurture, as Lawrence Frank wrote.

The cultivation of attitudes conducive to a life of some happiness and balance and of institutions to sustain such balance is definitely within our scope. But obviously not everything that passes for culture supports the cultivation of a better capacity. "Evil is not inherent in human nature . . ." wrote Ashley Montague in *The Humanization of Man*, "evil is learned. It is not human nature at fault, but human nurture."

As a species we have, in fact, not yet started to scratch the surface of our humanity nor learned to guide our lives away from the obstacles of hostility. Still, men can learn to become allies. Men can teach one another functional methods, techniques of human development.

Felix Adler compares man with a surgeon in a hospital during the time of war. He serves in his country's army but he is first of all a physician. He devotes his skill to friend and foe

*As reported in the *Saturday Review of Literature*.

alike. He will not inflict wounds but heal them; his functional reality provides the perpetual human bonds which surpass temporary enmities. His healing capacity is not overwhelmed by the poison of fanaticism or dogmatism.

Humanism would rather foster such trust in the individual. Traditional religion based itself upon the idea that there exists a permanence beyond the natural realities of being born and having to die. The philosophers have called it "totality-of-being."

But today we can learn that there is only process. A vital balance must be achieved now, while we are journeying. There is no fixed destination, only the destiny worked out together with others. We need the confidence that we can trust ourselves, and that we can learn to have the courage to be imperfect but human.

In spite of the mythology of economic success, we can enjoy life by shaping character without guilt or the frustrated expectations of flawless perfection. By being capable of forgiving as well as being forgiven, by rejecting nothing in life, a maturation occurs far different from mere "adjustment." The question is, after all, not whether we fail but whether we will try again.

SOLIDARITY AND SELF-RESPECT

Albert Einstein wrote that our short sojourn on earth needs to be directed towards the happiness of "those upon whose smile and well-being our own happiness depends." . . . In short the world is a social world and the "smiles" are not just a refuge from loneliness.

The uncharted capacities of others are not an emotional provincialism but a precious innerness. By our capacity for choice we insist upon a fundamental oneness, we are not victims but identifiable persons. The neurotic compulsions which seduce many into self-defeating loss of solidarity therefore threaten the specific cause of an improved life of individuals.

The issue is never, as someone wrote, whether the medicine tastes bitter but whether it will make us well. If we feel obligated to get well, because we recognize the need for health for ourselves and for those dependent upon us—"those on whose smile we depend"—then we will take the medicine, whatever its taste.

This is what is meant by the "courage-to-be," the courage to make reality decisions. A man who believed in democracy had to volunteer in World War II's struggle against totalitarianism even though others might try to dodge the draft. Thus also do we stand up for a person who is wronged whether we like him or not. The respect for what "ought to be" in relation to him is not merely a matter of taste.

Such self-created obligation is not related to metaphysics. It is an attitude which suggests: "Whatever I recognize as norm for myself I will respect for another, for without it I am not a free man." To recognize the worth of the other and the inviolability of his character thus becomes an inner need. In order to have self-respect, one must recognize the self-respect of others.

Quite naturally, this includes growing in one's trust of people, and developing a quality by which one will be able to entrust oneself to others. This is very different from a naive assumption that the other "means well." Obviously, when we meet someone who wants to brutalize us, it would be most unethical to close our eyes and hope for the best. If a man is not to be trusted, we had better not trust him; if he is out to hurt us, we had better make certain that he will not. Mark Twain once remarked: "If a man tells you he just can't help stealing watches, before you discuss his plight, search him!"

Trust is a quality to be gained, not bestowed, for "growing in trust" is the result of experience. We read about man's "aloneness" in the world, as a stranger in the universe or part of a "lonely crowd." The trust to which I refer will not accept this diagnosis as universally valid. For is it not true that from the moment we leave our mother's womb we are far from separate? We have a past and we have a future in concert with others, we are not alone; we are, in fact, always related. We are not, and will not be totally separated until death claims us. Therefore, to possess identity is not enough—what is needed is identification with persons significant to us and with worthwhile purposes. Biological or psychological relatedness does not tell us enough because the meaning of each life depends on the quality of the relationships built by commitment of character. We are and we are becoming at the same time; we are part and creative partner at the same time: we are unto ourselves yet have our being in others. This is where aspiration and choice join. Painful as this often is, we cannot avoid having judgment.

A most definite indication that a person is emotionally troubled is that in his relationships his destructive feelings, his suspicions, become increasingly dominant. Of course, the person so afflicted cannot always help himself. His hostile sentiments more often than not may easily become self-destructive as he convinces himself that he is deprived of emotional ties and as sorrow over "life lost" feeds his discouragement and eternal discontent.

The more mature person is capable of inter-personal relationships dominated by expectations and judgment, by the knowledge that he is doing his best. By nurturing his uniqueness as an individual he finds pathways to happiness and thus he affirms life in the process of living.

It is crucial therefore to grow in one's capacity for appreciation and gratitude. The more we can do this the more we learn how to give our trust and thereby we overcome the thoughtlessness, the cruel and the destructive in our environment. To mature as a person means to discover that most life questions are open to—at least—partial solutions and that even the unbearable can be surmounted.

In this context I think of Albert Schweitzer's philosophy as expressed in his books *Philosophy of Civilization* and *Civilization and Ethics*. In these works he developed his theory of "reverence for life" not because of naive sentimentality but because of insight and judgment.

The first book was written between 1914 and 1917 when Schweitzer and his wife were interned by the French. (Having been born in Alsace-Lorraine, they were arrested as German citizens!) I think that Schweitzer was moved by nothing as much as the notion that while he was building a hospital to save lives of "savages," Europeans of supposedly civilized nations were killing each other by the millions. The circumstances of the world are utterly unconcerned with our hopes and often smash our expectations. Yet we must choose to live and work.

Schweitzer based his universal concept of ethics upon "reverence for life", because human beings can know that they share "a fellowship of pain. All those who have known pain", he wrote, "are joined together in an effort to relieve it; and can therefore learn how to prevent pain for themselves and others. . . ." Here is a "golden rule" not consisting of "do's and don'ts" but of a faith in human capacity.

One thought stands out in Schweitzer's thinking. It is that all of life is dependent upon all other life. To him, as to Martin Buber, all real living is "encounter" and therefore the dignity of everything in creation must be respected. Each creature must be cared for and when any life is to be disturbed, it has to be done not thoughtlessly but with a sense of sadness. It has often been thought that Schweitzer was pushing this idea to somewhat ridiculous lengths. When a new wing was built to the house for the lepers in Lambarene Hospital, he did not want the wood to be treated with chemicals against termites, but insisted that such lumber be found as would resist the termites. So also did he not want cut flowers in his rooms, but only plants. The fact that the flowers had been severed from their roots took the joy of their beauty away from him. He agreed that a creature could eat another creature only if it could not survive without feeding upon that other life. But he himself had become a vegetarian. One day friends brought a young antelope to him which they had bought after its mother had been killed, and when they asked him what they should do with the young animal, he replied, "Give it unsweetened milk, air, sun, shade and love. But, by the way, what did you do to the hunter?"*

No wonder, then, that he called atomic weapons not only a sin, but "a desecration of man". Schweitzer had a deep sense of the way in which all life is intertwined. Whenever a new assistant joined the medical staff in Lambarene, he would ring a big bronze bell. And when such an assistant left, the bell was rung again. For the beginnings and endings of life have to be celebrated and life is not an accident, but sheltered within the sanctuary human beings can build. Every meeting is also a farewell, our potential greatness is in facing this without complaint.

Schweitzer is most relevant not in his theological theses but in his revitalized moral vision. He helped others follow an example and thus he handed on a spiritual power. In fact, he was a man willing to make all the sacrifices necessary for the exemplification of an ideal. Therefore, it is neither important whether one agrees with his philosophical or theological ideas, nor whether his hospital could have been run more efficiently. *He* ran it in the steaming jungle and his critics stayed home!

Out of that sense of commitment Schweitzer rejected relativism. Commitment must not be overcome by compromises between what we consider just and what we consider necessary.

*All this in Erica Anderson, *The African Years, Saturday Review* Sept. 25, 1965.

Reverence for life includes therefore a deep sense of responsibility, a faith reinforced by reason. As there is progress of knowledge and technology, so must there be progress of man's socialization-process.

Therefore, man belongs to man, is entitled to his fellowman even though circumstances may create estrangement. As we act and suffer and progress, we have a chance to prove our substance as people. Now we can leave the coldness behind, the estrangement, the thoughtlessness and express gratitude, which may lead to happiness as the product of trial and error. This is how a man can develop inner awareness and concern, and escape the curse of being only partly alive and plagued by resentment.

We do not have to consider Schweitzer to find examples showing how little that inner awareness is as yet practiced in our culture. One of the finest judges of New York's Children's Court, Justice Florence Kelly, recently revealed a medieval practice which makes it mandatory to have children charged with some infraction of the law in order to have their situation adjudicated. Without this the Court cannot take jurisdiction! Thus children neglected by their parents—something over which they had no control—have to be charged with being neglected children and stand as respondents answering that charge! From then on this will be part of their record.

In the same fashion, other children have the word "delinquent" pinned on them. It will stay with them for the rest of their lives as a black mark imposed by society.

Still, as Justice Kelly put it: "I have not seen a case, of my own knowledge, of a child alleged to be delinquent whom I didn't think in some way was a neglected child . . . I am convinced that the most creative and effective source of help for troubled and troublesome young people lies not in the Courts, not in institutions, but in the community."

"Reverence for life" is not just a lofty theory! It is the cornerstone of communal sanity. Each person called upon for help and who responds positively steps thereby into an essential relationship of "meeting". At least that is what I think Martin Buber meant when he said that before a man can ask "what is truth?" he will have to first ask "Who am I who asks this question?" And in order to know who "I" am, two types of relationship are possible for me. I can be in relationship to other human beings, people with whom I work, my husband or wife, my children, my fellow-citizen, in an "I-it" relationship. It is much the way in which I relate myself to things, to a chair, to a table, to money, to security. A manufacturer can look upon his workers as extensions of machines, a businessman, a doctor can look upon his clients as means of getting money, in which the other person has hardly a human existence; the other is to be used for one's own ends. Buber said that the impersonal kind of relationships which lead to emptiness and which in the long run make mass-murder possible, need to be replaced by an "I-Thou" relationship. Then love becomes possible because a personal "I" meets a personal "Thou" and such love can be used, in order to live in an authentic way, aware of the other as a full person, and thus we can meet ourselves. We are no longer at the mercy of our hatreds and anxieties but become capable of giving without fear and of loving not just the perfect in the other but all that which is less perfect and even that which may sometimes be pretty bad. It is because of that "I-Thou" relationship, said Buber, that men can really meet God, the God of an ideal, not the God with the long white beard to whom one sends prayers asking for deliverance, health or happiness. While the usage of the word "God" has little meaning to me, I see in both Schweitzer and Buber the evolution of a humanist idea. This idea affirms that even though we live in a universe of which we cannot know the meaning, we can at least create meaning for ourselves. We have in us the capacity for adaptive changes out of which character is built. Emerson's

"Each man is one more lump of clay to hold the world together", is still as good a guideline as any.

Also, if we can learn not to add to the misery of others, we can achieve the maturity to perceive the other lovingly. We can sustain one another and in that is a service to man at least as majestic as the ancient services to unknown Gods. We can learn from our sad experiences in life that far too often we take each other for granted—our husbands, wives, parents and children. Frequently we only appreciate them fully after they are gone. It is a special task to learn how to move from being merely related to active relationships, for no person can become human by himself.

Since there is nothing to our knowledge that justifies belief in immortality, how much more urgent the task to make these few years worthwhile for one another! We are indeed, as J. Ramsey MacDonald wrote: "Road menders and road makers, opening out ways for human feet and human aspiration. . . ."

Only by commitment do we discover the meaning of compassion and how to deal with our own suffering. For in a way each of us is responsible for how other human beings live.

Choice and aspiration, reality and ideal join when we strive for such common ground.

To quote Emerson once more: "This is our centrifugal force; we cannot be adrift because of this, and out of its sight we cannot go."

HOW SHALL WE READ HISTORY?

Human existence is drenched in a general notion of time, yet life is never lived in general. The impact of our experience is immediate and makes us an individual within a shared community of individuals. We are never "this human being" only but always conscious of being human as such. Since we perceive universal characteristics via the personal, our own expectations fit within a framework of human expectations to which each adds by the fullness of his diverse personality.

While there can be no guarantee of achievement, there is an emergent strength when fitting oneself into a context of readiness to share of oneself. Such aim helps disclose a fuller capacity in every human encounter. Vital, moral concepts for living reveal each person as a person, each life as a life in particular. There is therefore no happy, smooth, unfolding of one's life experience, nor of man's historical experience.

Only in retrospect do events seem to fall neatly into a pattern but we can never feel this way about our own life nor of the times in which we live.

Even the turbulence of the 'twenties, for example, and the catastrophic events of the depression, or World War II, already appear as so much more understandable now than the 'fifties and 'sixties.

There is almost an optical illusion at work when we consider ourselves, for past events seem to have clear outlines while the present is utterly confused. Yet Man is that being who wants to be heard whatever the unsettledness and it is especially by what happens to an individual, that he attains meaning.

As we evaluate our own experiences it appears as if we can understand where we are going. Yet, when suddenly our private expectations are interrupted by setbacks or tragedy, all signs become confused again and the quiet of what we thought to be our direction eludes us.

Take the couple who, after ten years of marriage, found it increasingly impossible to live together. There had never been much compatibility between the husband and wife. They had married . . . Well, why do people get married? She was twenty-eight and had started to think of herself as a spinster—a fact which her family did not for a minute let her forget.

The man, then in his forties, had very set ideas about women and marriage, but was strongly under the suggestion that something was physically "wrong" with him for not yet having married. Marriage was now a matter of "one woman is as good as another". Still, he courted the girl very romantically. In the first year or so of their marriage, however, he used to drive her to irrational jealousies by continually boasting of his many pre-marital "affairs".

Two children later, with an increasing economic problem facing them, there was a complete breakdown of communication between them. They spoke to each other only at the top of their voices, full of acrimony and never-ending references to past hurts. The demoralization of the particular was destroying their capacity to see the universal hopes with which they once had groped for each other.

All their guideposts had broken down; they lived in abject depression and, of course, this hurtfully influenced their children.

Their road to personal perspective had seemed so clear only a few years ago! To get married, like everyone else, to have a home, to raise a family—but it was now "all in pieces, all coherence gone". What had seemed such ordered progress of events was now a completely chaotic reality.

In the midst of all this, a doctor's report of a fatal disease in the woman. Strangely now, there was a turn in their psychology. Life once again had a pattern. Because of that catastrophic diagnosis, things fell into place again; the signs of private life could be read again; the neurotic interaction of the destructive earlier course could be intercepted. Whatever their tragedy, the ground for mutual change could be plowed again.

Marriage, with all its difficulties, weaknesses and problems of understanding, can remain nevertheless a matrix to sustain life, and the worthiness of ourself and our partner. The main condition for this possibility is the decision to address ourselves to the immediacies at hand. The solution to our doubts and tensions are found in confrontation which verifies our will to overcome the void of withdrawal.

Coherence must be discovered and rediscovered in endless struggle. In that way the hope between partners can become justified and not just remain a lofty emotion. There is no real life without the strain our hopes impose and there is no completion without pain and labor. To hope is not enough, to have faith is not enough, to love is not enough. They are all ingredients in making sense out of the disorder and suffering which life is to such a large extent. By themselves they have no staying power.

Hopes are, of course, often cruelly tested. In one of Brecht's plays, dealing with the life of Galileo, we are made starkly aware of this.

The drama focuses upon the Pope of Galileo's time, on the morning before a very important meeting when the Holy Father, attended by two monks, is being dressed for the occasion. Also in the room is the Cardinal who functions as the Church's Inquisitor, and he requests permission to bring Galileo to trial.

"No", replies the Pope, as the monks put on his first layer of holy vestments. "No, keep your hands off Galileo!"

A new garment is hung on the Holy Father and another and another. As his appearance becomes less and less that of an ordinary man and more and more that of a Pope, so also do his opinions about Galileo change.

In the end, as the monks place the holy crown upon his head, he tells the Inquisitor, "Just show him the instrument of torture," knowing full well that a mere display of the torture chamber is not what will satisfy the Inquisitor at all.

Galileo's students wait outside the torture room. They are sure that their teacher has not gone back on his theories. Watching, we feel our own emotions waver; we hope, above all, that the old scientist will not be tortured too much.

In the end, the bells of Rome ring out jubilantly for Galileo has recanted and the Inquisitor has triumphed.

The scholar's students turn sadly against him and shout at him in anger, "You have dirtied your hands and our hands." But Galileo answers, "My hands are better dirty than dead." How shall we read history? Was the Pope the coward? Was Galileo the coward? Did not the Inquisitor save Galileo's immortal soul from damnation? Even in retrospect the signs of reality are often more easily seen than understood or read.

And what of our own time? We have come to accept the fact that there are always a few million unemployed. Close to ten million people are somehow involved in what has been hygienically designated as "distressed areas" where the "culture of poverty" reigns.

Yet, when World War II broke out in 1939, one out of every six in our work force was still out of work and only after 1941, with war production in full swing, did the nightmare of unemployment end. Not many Americans like to remember that period for it is human to want to forget the ordeals of national catastrophies.

Most of us benefit today, whether we want to or not, from the prosperity which results from the perpetual mobilization in which we live.

Senators, trade union leaders and Chambers of Commerce immediately protest when the Executive wants to cut down on war production in some sector because the spectre of unemployment is a deep and terrifying emotion.

The feeling of being useless, the feeling of seeing one's children without food and clothing is more intolerable to us than reading the signs of what the perpetuation of war production really heralds.

As a result, we are in danger of becoming indifferent to the fate of others when our own fate seems to be threatened. This paralysis of conscience is precisely what all totalitarian regimes are aiming for. The signs of our epoch teach to him who can read that more and more people in Western civilization are willing to do anything to anybody, to oppress, to segregate and eventually, to murder, provided that the larger segment of the national entity feels secure about it and is given the ideological slogans with which to rationalize it.

The Spanish philosopher Ortega y Gasset often spoke not only of the "revolt of the masses" but also of the "rage of the masses". He was not so sure that humanity was not willing to endure more and worse than the horrors of World War II. Obviously, the mass culture set into motion in the 'thirties by the overwhelming totalitarian regimes still has an important traumatic influence. We have seen them use this power to make continents fall into line. To forget this misuse of social hope and political idealism would be a deadly mistake.

All that Jefferson could imagine as possible dangers of centralized power, all that de Toqueville could warn against in terms of the lack of conscience in mass civilization, was genteel in comparison with what our eyes have seen.

We must be willing to admit that the old liberal methods of social control are not enough; that the "people" can be bamboozled, misled, lied to at will and manipulated beyond measure. There is destructiveness in the human psyche which must be taken into consideration by any ethical theory worth its salt. Obviously, a more humane world cannot be externally imposed. It can only evolve from the actualization of that which frees man's potential and thereby overcomes the disintegrating ambiguities. If we really understand this, we start to grasp that coercion by force should be taboo in this world of unspeakable destructive power. The "realists" who count on a "survival-ratio" after the next world conflagration are dealing with delusions. Today's world cannot be understood by directions and controls valid for the world of yesterday. There are those who without dogma hold fast to this central credo: that the individ-

ual man has in him a natural capacity for goodness and humanity. That Man has the capacity to respond to truth and has been
endowed with a capacity for love and beauty. This is a humanist credo in all simplicity. Is it enough to live by? That is the
central issue, for our choice of values will determine whether
we will live at all.

In this context I would like to call for a humanist impatience,
for a militant, not a timid, humanism. Because we live in the
confusions of the here and now and do not have the luxury of
historical retrospect, it is often hard to see the trees for the
forest. But the trees are there. It would be more reassuring if
we could see the end of the road, or at least a glimpse of fulfillment. But no generation can and what we will have to settle
for is the hint of a pathway.

Liberals, non-conformists and radicals are in the habit of
stressing the need for change, and the more hopeful aspects of
what will be realized once such change occurs. They are therefore in greater danger than most of turning cynical when what
they believe is needed does not come about. For such individuals, humanism is a disappointment because guarantees do not
exist. For many, the strains of hope are too much; they want to
hope and then witness fulfillment. This, a desire human enough,
cannot be satisfied if we insist upon intellectual honesty and the
eventual character of that which can be achieved by the humanist impatience. It is an impatience for the actualization of
inner freedom. Everyone discovers in the long run that others
frequently do not pull their share, or that they even oppose the
good one had set out to accomplish by placing their private
pettiness above the best one could have hoped for. To know
this, with quiet determination, is to remain as a person in the
community of persons.

When we sulk and retreat from the company of others and
let them know in no uncertain terms that we have "had it",
that we are "through", we in fact consent to our depersonaliza-

tion. To engage in bitter criticism from the sidelines and ultimately in sarcasm about everything and everyone, seeing the
world in term of "Oh, everyone has his angle", is a certain way
to self-defeat. Yet, when we maintain that what we are doing,
whether our dearest hope has been outraged or not, is done
because of and stimulated by an inner necessity, the world
can never be estranged from us.

From this emerges a private perserverance, a life-attitude
which can be thought of as religious.

"Often our deeds are dreadful," wrote H.G. Wells, "because
so frequently our minds are in darkness." There is no reason to
stop at this dictum, for as we know darkness, so do we know
light and as we are creatures of error and cruelty, so also can we
be creatures of the agitated heart and humaneness.

For every Hitler there is an Eleanor Roosevelt. For every
racist there is a determined integrationist. It is not naive to
respond to the simple decencies in the world nor need we turn
our backs upon each other because so much is as yet unfulfilled.
The insight with which we recognize how much remains to be
done is a creative power: to make the unapparent apparent; to
make the crooked whole. It is a fortunate strain stronger—in
the long run—than the roadblocks.

CHAPTER 4

SILENT TERROR AND THE
FUTURE OF FREE MEN

Implicit in this nation's culture is the assumption that the liberties of the citizen are fundamentally safe. The Bill of Rights and the Constitution are considered solid cornerstones. Yet freedom is more than its legal expression. Monumental documents are crucial but the essential question for the survival of freedom is whether it is personally experienced by the citizens. When freedom ceases to be a privately-felt reality, no document and no court can safeguard it. As a genuine ideal, liberty expresses hope and ambition by which the individual can strive for growth and for happiness. All totalitarian dictatorships block the process by which men and women unfold their capacities and instead there emerges the domination of a power elite and the submission of the many.

Freedom is continually challenged in America. There is always the danger that individuals cannot experience it as an integral part of their self-fulfillment. To many, liberty is a burden rather than an opportunity and collectivist ideologies, which are fundamentally anti-individualistic and anti-life, often have a deadly attraction. National communities do not end suddenly. Yet, their essential fabric can become so weakened that, given a mixture of unresolved tensions and social problems, their essence is destroyed. When social change is not brought about by intelligence and compassion, it frequently occurs through the eruptive and violent impulses which though hidden behind a reassuring veneer, are always close to the surface. Freedom's basis is concern for human beings, and when life has lost its meaning for enough individuals, a deep-seated need to surrender freedom comes into play.

This chapter will deal with a variety of challenges to America's freedom. It will also try to hint at the promises which the concept of liberty still holds, for at the core of my reasoning is the assumption that the health of a community must, above all, become apparent in the private lives of its individuals. Can that be claimed for our culture today? There is reason to be gravely concerned. Utilitarian values now predominant in America are a poor antidote against appeals of non-reason. The concern for the whole Man as expressed in the Bill of Rights will remain alive only if continually used to enhance human dignity and love rather than to uphold outworn facets of the status quo.

Since such determination depends on whether freedom is still a personal experience and not just a political slogan, the wish to guarantee a good life for every citizen cannot be grounded only in social legislation, but needs an "externalizing" consciousness of what Man is for. When such deeper freedom is limited, a part of the personality suffers. Therefore there is no such thing as "partial" freedom.

In the very early years of the Republic, a man called Elijah Lovejoy settled in the valley of the Mississippi, where later he was hated and despised as defender of the anti-slavery movement. Elijah Lovejoy came from the pioneer reality of America and its boundless sense of freedom. But in the end, in Alton, Illinois, he was shot down by those who thought him an "apostle of the Devil." The sanctity of human worth, so obvious to him, aroused murderous passion in others. The same applies to the civil rights workers, Chaney, Goodman and Schwerner, brutally murdered in Meshoba County, Mississippi, with the open connivance of local police officers. The Bill of Rights had absolutely no meaning for these killers.

Therefore, just as the attainment of freedom is a personal experience so does its defeat affect the total stature of the person concerned. Thus, on the day of Lincoln's assassination, the Houston (Tex.) weekly *Telegraph* could write: "Not a soldier nor a woman with true heart in this Southern land but feels the thrill electric and divine at this sudden fall in his own blood of the chief of our oppressors." When we speak about Lincoln as a towering historical figure, we must not forget that just as in the case of Franklin Delano Roosevelt and John Fitzgerald Kennedy, some people jubilated when the President lay dead. Lincoln knew that freedom had to be personally felt and so— tragically—did John Brown. Yet, John Brown was executed, Lincoln, McKinley and Kennedy assassinated.

In a speech in Baltimore in 1864, Lincoln said: "Plainly the sheep and the wolf do not agree upon a definition of liberty and the same is true of human creatures." So also in our time.

The blackmarket in such words as "democracy," "liberty" or "the people" has further obscured freedom as a decisive characteristic of human fulfillment. The irrational mass movements and their profound herd-appeal have put the individual on the defensive. He is hard put to define for himself (let alone for others) what freedom means. This may be a fundamental historical issue: not to consider freedom as a political abstraction, but rather as the passionately-lived reality of human beings who must choose again and again where they will stand—with the wolves or with the sheep. When all is said and done, the struggle between Man's innocence and Man's social cowardice, is a question not merely political, but one of personal decision.

Woodrow Wilson, the Presbyterian Princeton professor turned politician, who said that the best day of his political career was when somebody somewhere in a New Jersey crowd yelled out, "Hiya Woody, howya doin' today?" was not just a naive Yankee when on Christmas, 1916, he sent Germany and England a message urging them to stop the war and conclude a "peace without victory." This was a most striking concept and understandable only within a personal comprehension of ethical principles as they apply to freedom. Of course, the German Kaiser laughed at the American "dumkopf." Neither did England's Lloyd George react seriously to what British politicians must have regarded as another impulsive American gesture, innocent of power politics. And—alas—in the Vietnam war, Wilson's revolutionary concept *has never been* considered.

Wilson was deeply disturbed when, on returning from Congress after the 1917 declaration of war against Germany, he said, "My message today was a message of death, death for our young men. How strange it seems that (the Congress) should applaud that."

I stress this point of freedom-as-personal experience because here is potentially the most creative aspect of our culture.

When Wilson went to Europe after World War I, hundreds of thousands of people surged forward to touch him and literally to kiss the ground upon which he had walked. They recognized instinctively a leader of vision although nothing human, including vanity and fear, was alien to him. People were looking to America for a liberation, for a "rebirth of freedom" for the disenfranchised, who had been told for centuries by the ruling elites (in Lincoln's words): "You toil, you earn bread and I will eat it." Freedom is difficult to define. At its center must be a concern for the whole person. Such freedom particularly is endangered in this era because in a culture of specialization, our lives are regulated by forces largely outside our influence. Industrialization has led to an impersonal money economy in which the relationships, between producer and consumer are utterly distant. We live by mortgage interest rates, and the daily fever of the stockmarket ticker tape, which is the electrocardiogram of success. We are regulated by what unions and corporations decide about prices and wages, what banks decide about mergers, what defense spending the government wants to undertake. What personal experience of freedom is left? Who has use for a person who is good and kindly, poetic and loving, or rich in inner life? The stature of what a person *is* interests us least of all, but what status he *has*, what he possesses, what influence he may have with other people from whom we may hope to get favors, that is what interests us! Who among us openly associates for long with those who did not "make it" in society, who have no bank accounts, no property, no status? We do not feel secure with such people; they frighten us. When freedom is no longer a personal experience but only a political slogan, the fabric of a free society is in danger. When competition is deified, human values and the valuation of the individual must suffer. The aged cannot provide for themselves in such a society; they must be helped to maintain their dignity. The farmers cannot survive without parity payments and soon millions of workers—both white and blue collar—thrown out of work by automation may join the "unemployables." Will anyone speak honestly about money and its relationship to freedom? Unless and until that happens, the rest will remain pious hope.

Countries like the Scandinavian nations, Holland, Switzerland, and Australia have chosen some form of social democracy for a reason. They are not wildeyed revolutionaries. They have found that freedom must be given a new content, if it is to again become meaningful in personal terms. Economics are not heavenly-ordained arrangements. It is most dangerous to assume liberty is secure because of sanctified documents.

As early as in the year 1798, the Alien and Sedition Acts, passed by Congress, gave the government the right to deport all aliens and made it necessary for any foreign-born person to have lived in America for fourteen years before he could be naturalized. The Sedition section was still worse, for it permitted the State to arrest men accused of sedition which, by and large, meant criticism of the government!

Actually, the Civil War accelerated the demise of a type of freedom that had existed in early America. Few of us are aware now that under the government of Abraham Lincoln, an estimated 38,000 men and women were arrested and brought before military tribunals charged not with crimes, but with controversial expressions of opinion in speech or writing. In 1862 so many arrests had been made that Lincoln had to grant an amnesty! Only a few months later, however, the President himself ordered a general suspension of the Writ of Habeas Corpus which made the preservation of private freedom most questionable. Even though imprisonment was usually of brief duration, this form of enforcement of power illustrates how much freedom was challenged even then. The eternal question arose whether the law operates to maintain the existing order or whether it is the dynamic instrument by which the people seek the realization of ever more meaningful liberties.

Behind the emotionally charged concept of freedom often lurks a misunderstanding of the ethical impulse necessary to have it remain meaningful. Freedom is very different from "being-let-alone-provided-we-don't-hurt-others." Instead, freedom is a matter of living as a person in the community of other persons so that each is thereby encouraged to give of his own best potential.

The most meaningful self-actualization of which each is capable is the one which furthers the first-rate affirmation of

others. The test of whether such freedom-to-affirm is worthwhile is the degree to which it evokes the courage to claim
that freedom for others. Freedom is an instrument as much as
love. The universal and the particular are always intertwined
and democracy and freedom must presuppose a commitment
of those who proclaim them.

When such moral commitment is removed, democracy dies
within individuals as well as within the nation, as we know
from the Weimar Republic in post-World War I Germany.

Laws, constitutions, declarations, are means and methods.
But the heart of a political system lives or dies in the community of its people. In fact, democracy appeals to a moral order
excluding none. In freedom, responsibility for everyone is a
crucial prerequisite. Democracy is therefore a hopeful system
although its flaws sober us repeatedly. Yet, the enemies of
democracy speak its language when trying to justify their use
of power.

The modern totalitarian regimes have created the impression
that democracy is on the way out, and that the impulse of
freedom as a way of love which adapts itself to down-to-earth
social and personal needs, is a "bourgeois" weakness. Still, much
of the tensions of our time can be deduced *linea recta* from the
American Revolution and ascribed to the tremendous attraction of democratic ideals.

COMMUNISM: THE DEAD-END OBSESSION

There is reason to believe that the problems of the world
can be tackled effectively by the pro-life forces of democracy
rather than by the anti-life forces of threat and oppression akin
to dictatorships. Democracy's main attraction is in its accom-
plishments and it is therefore unfortunate that compulsive notions about bolshevism have created so much fear in our midst
and have drained so much energy which could have been put

to better use in expanding human fulfillment. Nations gripped by fear respond to the worst in those who oppose them, as we have done too often. Democracy's strength is the activation of the desire for personal growth which thereby counteracts the lure of surrender and submissiveness. Only a nation confident of its freedom could initiate the Lend-Lease program of World War II and it is this confidence that we are doing right that must be regained. It is necessary therefore to evaluate the pressures of our time as part of a larger tableau of history, a canvas on which the American experience is another and, yes, vibrant streak of color, but not necessarily a dominant one. The universe does not revolve around us and there are no "American" solutions for all world issues. Dreams of omnipotence belong to infancy and we should have outgrown them long ago. Totalitarian governments are deterministic governments, their thinking snarled by inflexible theory (e.g. the perpetual prophecy about "the end" of capitalism even though nineteenth century capitalism no longer exists). Yet, if we believe our own propaganda our thinking may become just as stale. Even in Russia, today, voices are heard pleading for more flexible relationships between consumer and producer. Men like the economist, Liberman, would rather be in step with economic evolution than suffer history by dogmatically insisting upon Marx's production theories. Many of the situations challenging the United States were not created by communists. Communists did not drain the natural resources of South America and turn a goodly portion of the commonfolk of that continent against us. Communists did not help Hitler's Germany arise and create the power vacuum in Europe into which the Soviet army marched. Communists did not create the tensions in Indonesia, or the Congo, or Algeria, even though they tried to take advantage of upheaval. The "devil" theory of history leads nowhere. No, the fundamental challenges are those of freedom which were set into motion by the American and Industrial Revolutions. It is we Americans who have created the ambition for abundance in the world; it is we who have created the technology which has perfected mass communication; it is we who have started the development of atomic energy; it is we who have gathered immense food supplies. Rather than feel frightened and guilty, we need to involve ourselves confidently in what this nation initiated.

Without the Western push in industry and also without the Western theory of Marxism, there would be no modern Soviet society. We are the harbingers of the greatest revolution of all time: namely, the revolution of an industrialized civilization based upon technology and science. There is reason to be proud of this as the most fantastic achievement in world history, potentially the instrument which can make man human instead of a beast of burden. It is the revolution which can make humane the economic and political relationships between individuals and nations. This is where our strength and capacity reside.

Freedom has to move, to expand and therefore it creates tension. The point is not whether the communists will fail or be successful, the question is whether the democracies will be able to identify and deal with the needs of people in a changed world community. Sometimes this may mean that we will have to make decisions seemingly contrary to traditional national sentiment.

Nations, as well as individuals, will survive only if from time to time they are willing to act beyond their immediate likes or dislikes. This means that we must be willing to share the world with regimes whose ideologies go against our grain. Our preoccupation with communism is a dead-end obsession and the anxious analysis by "Kremlinologists" of every word uttered by communist spokesmen is a waste of time and intellect. This is not what the world reality requires of us.

Democratic freedom obviously cannot survive by stale ad-

herence to the status quo. It can be deadly for a democratic
community to be maneuvered, by totalitarian imperialism, into
reactive power politics in which domination and manipulation
are central factors. That is the tragedy of America's Vietnam
intervention. It is historically the wrong track. We did not enter
that conflict as imperialists, but we have been finagled into an
imperial posture by bankrupt military rulers.

Obsessive preoccupation with communism becomes all too
easily the fanatic and ideological pursuit of abstractions. Yet,
what distinguishes a powerful democracy from a powerful totalitarian state is above all the understanding of human as well
as social responsibility. When that is lost through ideological
ferocity, the aims of the democratic community are undermined
by a subversive arrogance of power. Freedom depends not on
counteracting the communists everywhere but upon building
commitments towards a cohesive caring world community.
Democracy is not a theological but a pragmatic arrangement.
It depends upon making "deals", arrangements of a practical
nature to make liberty feasible. "Deals" are not dirty, they can
be sane live-and-let-live agreements of people existing in partnerships. If there was not one communist alive in the world, we
still would have to answer the question whether we can build
a world partnership for plenty and opportunity. If we can do
that, communism is no threat to us. As Secretary Henry L.
Stimson pointed out in his book *On Active Service in War and
Peace*, there is no longer room for merely grudging or "limited"
participation in the world. Americans need to learn the tolerance to accept other social structures, other political worlds.
The time of a monolithic communism is gone.

Nor are all American military actions "clean" and all communist military actions "dirty." Many revolutionary movements
in southeast Asia or South America which we consider "communist" think of themselves as nationalist. We are not appointed
the world's pest exterminators, going after the communist "ver-

min" wherever it raises its head. What the world scene shows above all today is a rebellion against Western domination. When we say that "no human power can force us from Vietnam," we are expressing the same historical rubbish that made the ancient Greeks vulnerable and that twice defeated the German Reich. The majority of mankind is fighting to liberate itself from domination and with the exception of Portugal, all major western powers have at last understood the lesson. The French, the British, the Dutch have relinquished their colonial roles and the Japanese are through as a colonial power. To speak about "native revolutions" as some kind of communist ecumenical movement is a distortion of reality and it pushes us into the wrong corner of becoming "anti-people," against the common people, who want to be liberated from the big landowners. These nations want neither Russian nor Chinese nor American domination and we must avoid becoming the heirs of obsolete colonialism. In identifying ourselves with military dictators and blackmarketeers, we are not true to America's heritage. We must wake up to the fact that the imposition of military power is the ultimate humiliation, imposed by the West upon non-western nations for the past four or five centuries. We must stop dictating to Asians how they shall live and what kind of government they are supposed to have. They do not want salvation by American arms. They are "natives" no longer.

In addition, all wars have in fact become civil wars. While World Wars I and II were the clashes of powerful Christian nation-states, almost all conflicts since 1945 have been fratricidal. That was true in Greece, in the Middle East, in Korea, the Congo, Cyprus, China, Vietnam, Santo Domingo and Cuba. Aggressive imperialist wars, once accepted as a fact of life, are not what plagues the world now. It is the small, cruel, internal conflict. The idea, therefore, of a Holy Grail against communism finds no echo in the world, nor does the slogan "better dead than Red." The communist nations have lost their monolithic characteristics. Yugoslavia, China and the U.S.S.R. do not agree at all upon communist strategy. The communist world is polycentric now too and this opens up possibilities for political instead of military confrontations. This is the fundamental reason why General de Gaulle revised the NATO alliance in the 'sixties and what is needed is a realistic appraisal of change, instead of an angry sense of being frustrated by "ingrate" allies.

As former Ambassador to Moscow Kennan put it:

> "Our country should not be asked and should not ask of itself, to shoulder the main burden of determining the political realities of any other country . . . This is not only not our business but I do not even think that we could do it successfully."

AMERICA WITHOUT APOLOGIES

The greatest challenge to freedom is to learn to overcome the inhibitions of the past. There is much excess baggage of a tribal nature to be disposed of by all nations.

The fundamental opportunity is to build a dynamic peace in a revolutionary epoch in which the capacity for destruction has reached insane perfection. That issue is the central ethical task of all nations.

I have confidence in the American future because ours is a culture of "homo faber," man the maker, the fabricator of solutions. Also we are a generous culture with a sense of stewardship and obligation towards the world. Perhaps the Romans nourished such sentiments too at one time, but I think that our civilization is different. Most Americans feel that we are custodians of something immensely worthwhile. I see a quest for meaning underlying America's foreign relations ever since the conception of this republic. It is because of that meaning that I am so critical of the distortions of power and warn against the trap of militarism.

It took many anguished voices before the nation listened to those who said that we were upsetting nature's balance by the indiscriminate use of insecticides. But then we sat up and listened. In the same vein we should not rule out a "sitting up and listening" where international relations are concerned. In short, there is in the fabric of America's society a wish to conserve life, but it is not without its ambiguities.

For example, our adherence to the Protestant business ethic is fundamentally conservative, while the momentum it creates sets revolutionary social forces into motion. In the wake of increased productivity follows social mobility which while praised to the skies, also threatens the rootedness necessary for stable family and community life. We are part then of a culture which in many ways is divided against itself. What does this mean for the future of freedom both on a national and on an international level? We have high productivity and an incredible distribution of goods and still more than forty million of our citizens live in a "culture of poverty." We take this somehow for granted. A large majority of the workers (and that includes a great many white collar workers and people in sales organizations) have come to live with the possibility of periodically losing their economic substance. Of course, the never-ending number of strikes show that a raw class struggle still exists. There is very little consciousness that such clashes of interest are the result of faulty economic assumptions and that "layoffs" and contract fights could be prevented by adequate social planning of human as well as of economic resources.

To speak of these shadow-sides of American society almost invariably invites harsh rejection. It is not considered good manners to stress the paradoxes in our production system.

Of course, opportunities within this system still can be fantastic. The dream of "making it" keeps the "drones" forever hopeful that by moving on they will be "getting somewhere." But "where" exactly is less clear. As a matter of fact, to pose that question smacks of rhetoric since it preoccupies very few persons. Wright Mills called us a "cheerful ant-heap" which is an oversimplification but not entirely beside the point. If a man's value is, by and large, measured by his status in the market place then one would expect a culture in which ruthlessness would be publicly acclaimed. Yet even the very wealthy in America try to camouflage their acquisitiveness and hide their accumulation of wealth behind a facade of dedicating playgrounds, nursery schools and flower shows. Thus, while money and status are terribly important, they are not *all*-important. Perhaps this is responsible for an intercommunality of classes which has made the pursuit of freedom respectable in America and, for that matter, in most of the Americanized nations of western Europe. The question then remains how to reconcile the self-evident acceptability of this sense of freedom with the obvious lack of personal involvement in the political processes of liberty. Americans wholeheartedly want the mobility and opportunity of freedom, yet have to be coaxed by advertising gadgets to exercise the discipline of liberty. Hobbes' prescription was certainly more "logical." He saw the enforcement of order by a strong government as the only radical remedy against the impulses of human nature. What he proposed was a development of internalized authority by way of ultimate control. The question today still seems very much related to this problem. Freedom and inhibition are preached simultaneously. The Republican farmers who cry out against "creeping socialism" are the first to gratefully invest the government check sent to them periodically for *not* tilling the land! We are afraid of intelligent rulers and at the same time we crave leaders. We idolize personalities rather than social principles and this is what conditions our thinking.

This issue of paradox will have to be met if much of our social unrest is to be dealt with. Quite obviously this will not happen because of exhortations. Certainly, Americans do not consciously want to live with impossible contradictions. Certainly, Americans do not want to sell each other moral "bills of goods." And yet the paradox is the climate in which we present ourselves to the world and the world is upset and bewildered by it. The blessed "Great Society," this new Jerusalem, on the North American continent, very often appears to the world like a giant with a split personality, powerful beyond words and yet proclaiming its abhorrence of sound social planning. It helps us little to speak of the sanctity of the individual and the sanctity of freedom if our functional channels for achieving them remain closed for so many individuals. Each era in history has a symbol of the forces of disintegration forever present in all human organizations. In ancient Israel, it was theocracy, in ancient Greece, self-centered "hubris," pride; in ancient Rome, all that which was symbolized by bread and games. The danger symbol of our age may well be our fear of putting to work in the world the creative impulse of freedom we set into motion.

This is not intended as a morbid criticism of America. For though we are not the only hope of the earth, we can be proud that as a community we have not yet soiled ourselves with violence and killing to the same degree as have most European nations. There is a genuineness about us which may still sustain our chance to use our power and wealth for the preservation of freedom. Yet, who can know whether history is on our side, whether history is in favor of our attempts? Very few wealthy nations have made the grade in history. Our chance lies in the eradication of poverty and the accursed racisms and nationalisms once more rampant. Our chance is in breaking down the trade barriers so that we can help the world acquire the means for producing wealth, for on this spreading of wealth depends our survival. If there are chains around America that keep us down, they are not chains of steel. They are chains binding our minds.

Lincoln's greatness was his acceptance of the tragic element without seeking those uncertain supports that are beyond man's nature. His idea of a Divine Providence was that humanity has within it a power for right and justice which each generation has to rediscover for itself. It is more than significant that a secular saint like Lincoln could rise to the height that he has attained in our history. But his was the sainthood of a man and therefore tainted with the imperfections of a man. Lincoln's greatness was that it was achieved as much in the White House as outside of it and it consisted of facing up to and not evading social conflict. How easily might not Lincoln have been overwhelmed by the tragedies of his private life? Who would dare to say that this man did not know moments of utter despair? Wearied and sick, tired and often frightened, it was he who decided what his bent shoulders could carry. Lincoln was not making history, he was living out his own life without apologies.

So also that most tragic life of our generation, the life of John F. Kennedy. After his assassination, his brother told a nationwide audience that the President had never known a day without pain. Of course, his was a daring, great, personal ambition. But there was also a sense of "noblesse oblige," a commitment to bring America into closer relationship with the great revolutionary changes of our era for he knew that no nation can persist today in total sovereignty. If democracy is to make any contribution at all, it has to be in what it actualizes for the individual and his inner safety.

Lincoln was assassinated, Elijah Lovejoy was shot to death, Woodrow Wilson died of a broken heart when his dream of a League of Nations was defeated, Franklin D. Roosevelt died of the overexertion imposed upon him by his office, John F. Kennedy was assassinated. They were all very human, very imperfect. They were loved and hated passionately. But each was his own man. We need not be one of the "chosen" nations to add to the dignity of the human race. All men are answerable for their own future, all men are part of a reality that transcends what they think they built just for themselves.

A HOMEBRED FASCISM?

In times of national crisis, it always seems as if there are only two choices: surrender or war. When faced with a relentless opponent, like Soviet Russia, the temptation is especially strong to accept such oversimplification. For such attitude pinpoints the enemy and creates an excitement mixed with stomach-gripping fear. The desires and hopes of common people to make a living, raise their children, provide for their old age, suddenly appear like colorless goals. Yet, when the pursuit of private happiness is pushed aside for larger national purposes, it behooves the citizen at least to ask some questions. It is in this context that we must consider a new potent right-wing which has been clamoring for all-out war with Russia. It is a political faction that wants to divide the country by accusing the government of carrying out a gigantic conspiracy. This right-wing, once considered a lunatic fringe, is today well-financed and organized and speaks through hundreds of radio stations and millions of pamphlets. It consciously seeks the destruction of democracy. It is a group composed of respectable men as well as of political fanatics. Its outcry is for blind nationalism and for oversimplified action in international affairs. Its myth is that the American people have been betrayed by their leaders.*

*The documentation contained in this section has been obtained from a great many sources, among which are: "The Man Behind the John Birch Society," Chester Morrison, *Look* Magazine; "The Ultra-Right Wing Today—Problems in Containment," Prof. Alan F. Westin, National Community Relations Advisory Council; a speech by Rep. James Roosevelt, 12/31/61; "Operation Abolition" published by National Council of Churches; "Right Wing Retreat from Freedom," National Council of Jewish Women, Oct. '61; "Strawmen on the Right," Greenberg, in *The Reporter*, 7/6/61; "The Liberals Have Helped the Radical Right," Schechter, *New York Times*, 4/29/62; "The New Know-Nothings," Tristram Coffin, *Progressive*, 12/61; "The Rightist Crisis in Our Churches," Louis Cassels, *Look*, 4/24/62; "The Ultras," Fred J. Cook, Special Issue of *The Na-*

How far has this sector of the right already influenced public thinking? How far is a lack of daring approaches to the world situation due to a desire to appease this vocal extremist wing which wants to abandon international aid programs, liquidate the NATO alliance, and get rid of the existing political system? Anti-democratic forces in America, fed by irrationality, slander, and terror, are encouraged for the same classic reasons which made fascism possible elsewhere. Their reaction to pressure and change is one of heightened anxiety and polarization. As a result they are suspicious of progress.

What is at stake, as Erich Fromm put it, is "preserving the world, and bringing men of good will, men who love life, together to form a united front for survival"* so that this plagued globe can be pulled once more from the abyss of self-destruction. There is no doubt that the values of democracy are vital and yet lack of faith therein can destroy their viability. This has happened before, it can happen again. Faith in democratic values presupposes the recognition of a reality principle in political life rather than the fanatic flight-or-fight reactions.

A good example is the rightwing contention that psychiatry is a plot; or as one of their spokesmen said before a Congressional hearing, psychiatry is a "Jewish plot," meant to brainwash redblooded Americans. Just as the right wing believes in a conspiracy in Washington, so does it see mental health clinics as sinister institutions. The Ku Klux Klan and local anti-Semites in Montgomery, Alabama, succeeded in having public meetings of a mental health clinic stopped. They successfully peddled the story that the mental health society was out to

---

tion, 6/23/62; John F. Cronin, S.S.Dept. of Social Action, National Catholic Welfare Council; "Dan Smoot Speaks" *Look Magazine*, 4/24/62; "Who's on the Far Right?" Fletcher Knebel; "New World Drive By Nazis," Irving Spiegel, *New York Times*, 10/29/61; "Birch Brass," James Wechsler, *New York Post*, 10/5/61; "Crusader Schwartz," *Time Magazine*, 2/9/62; J. Edgar Hoover, before the Senate Internal Security Subcommittee.

*Erich Fromm, *May Man Prevail?*

lure good Southern whites to a secret clinic in Alaska where lobotomies would be performed in order to make them accept integration and communism! The radical right also charged that the Mental Health Bill for Alaska would be the beginning of what they called "Siberia, USA," the beginning of massive secret connivance by the Federal Government to railroad those opposed to communism into insane asylums!

Ludicrous as all this seems, there *is* in this country a segment of the population that believes such allegations. There are two hundred and sixteen radio stations in forty states that unceasingly peddle suspicion and fear to millions of listeners. America's reactionaries cannot be wished away. It is a movement that is not as yet united as a political party, but is extremely well-financed and can in no way be written off. The aggressiveness of the John Birch Society and its well-organized campaigns was illustrated at the time when President Eisenhower was planning to visit the Union of Soviet Socialist Republics. Birch Society members sent the President thousands of postcards reading, "Mr. President, if you go, don't come back." In the Boston area the Birch Society conducted a campaign to blackmail shopkeepers. Customers found among their groceries from shops of which the Birchers did not approve little cards which read, "Always buy your Communist products at this store." Civic intimidation of this type has been proven quite effective. In California, a law was proposed to punish members of "subversive" organizations and of course, who was to be considered subversive and who not would be left to local authorities! Yet a proposal like this easily received the 500,000 signatures necessary to put it on the ballot.* We have here the beginnings of an anti-democratic movement. What are its roots? Can a democratic order fight it successfully?

At the heart of any form of fascism we find frustration and these are times of great collective frustrations. Faith in our-

*N. Y. *Times*, October 25, 1962.

selves and in our destiny as a nation has been badly shaken. Frightened and bewildered, many contemplating the loss of control in the world seek the comfort of simple explanations. The right-wing offers such an explanation. Therefore, its voice is heard at military seminars, business conventions, and luncheon clubs via spokesmen who claim to have "an answer to Communism," by "exposing" the communists who supposedly run the Federal government.

It is impossible to understand the great variety of right wing organizations without considering their main thesis: that this nation is the victim of a vicious plot. For example, when Senator Strom Thurmond ended a speech at the "Congress of Freedom," organized by the right-wing "Soldiers of the Cross," a woman rose in the audience and shouted: "I don't know why all this time is being wasted on talk. The best way to get rid of our problems is to kill all the damn niggers!" While very few of the right-wing spokesmen would go this far in public, the bloodthirsty outcry of this woman conveyed something crucial: primitive hostility always determines the right-wing strategy.

Fascism is not just another political ideology. Fascism has no coherent theory; it is rather a state of mind, a way of feeling about the world. Fascism is the outcry of men who feel beset by problems for which they cannot find solutions and who must therefore blame their troubles upon some outside evil. The external chaos of fascism mirrors the internal chaos of most of its followers. Fascism is a way of life that denies any other. One is either in agreement with the fascist mind or one is a "traitor." Fascism denies the equal validity of all human beings and therefore automatically offers its followers the sense of being "chosen" or "superior." It is a way of life and those who accept it have chosen to hate. When one tries to argue rationally with an authoritarian personality about his pet hatreds, he will smile and when one disproves his misconceptions, he will say, "And I *still* hate the Jews, the Negroes and the Catholics." The fascist has chosen an existence of suspicion and delusions of power with which he identifies. Debate irks him as "intellectual" and therefore subversive. His psychology is based upon admiration of power and disgust for "weakness," "do-gooders," "longhairs." He wants to dominate, and strongly identifies with those who do. Ideas annoy and upset him. (In Nazi Germany, one could actually be imprisoned if the police chose to "assume" thinking contrary to official policy.) The fascist will always expect victory to be his and that it can be attained easily. When one defends oneself against his accusations, he will say that this proves that one is guilty. Fascism is a state of mind. It is a psychology in which fatalism plays an important role. In essence, the fascist personality does not resent restrictions upon his freedom but rejoices in subordinating himself. What happens in the social, economic or political reality is always seen as the result of power relationships, factors imposed from without. In consequence, the fascist personality does not feel that human effort has much influence on future developments. They are foreordained by forces beyond human control, by fate, by "Schicksal," by unavoidable centers of power. A famous song of the Nazi period was "Es kam wie es kommen muesste," "it happened as it had to happen."

Perhaps one should speak of totalitarian personalities, as Dr. Overstreet did, for as he remarks, their world is one of "anger, not of thought; anger and the need to be on top of some heap." Such a personality also resents the intrusion of reality and not only wants to disagree with an opponent but must demolish him completely. His world consists of those who command and those who take orders. All human relationships must fit in with his concept of the weak and the strong. This will color his attitudes towards the sick, the poor, the helpless, the persecuted. Their presence infuriates him and, not infrequently, this mentality carries over into his sexual attitudes. While there probably are ways of describing this kind of personality in terms of psychoanalytic insights, it is important to stress that the fascist personality feels better, happier and more fulfilled in a world structured around his emotional needs. The fluidity of a democratic society frightens him. In Nazi Germany, the S.S. built a deliberate social psychology upon these presuppositions which was of tremendous influence not only upon the common S.S. man, carefully trained how to behave in this rule-and-submit universe, but also upon his victims. In the end, those who were to be slaughtered were frequently relieved at being caught since they had come to prefer dying to living amidst never-ending demoralization and terror.

Radical reactionary movements espousing the fascist way of life can no longer be ignored in America. Their message reaches millions each week through more than 7,000 radio programs. Fascism can be foisted upon any nation which has lived for a long time under stress and fear and which hungers for a simpler, vital response to its difficulties.

There is danger when newspapers feed a sense of the impotence of the parliamentary system and when mass communication media are permeated with tales of violence. A vital effective democracy is the most decisive antitoxin against totalitarian inroads. All societal institutions need to express the affirmative ideals of a participative social process. If they do not, a sense of being overwhelmed will grip numerous individuals. It is crucial to remember that the fascist personality is not a deviate personality. Recent history should teach us that fascism and Nazism have a powerful appeal for all those who feel frustrated by the complexities of modern society, those who have lost hope, those who feel cut down by an impersonal economic structure, those angry with the world, resentful and longing to "be a man again." At the heart of fascism is self-doubt. The person who cannot trust his own motives, who lives in perpetual conflict, can easily be made to assault the motives of others. There are many who suffer from a deep doubt concerning their capacity for personal and social progress, justice, or humanity. Fascism depends upon an amoral type of social organization. It is psychologically and economically deterministic.

To understand right-wing thinking, it is important to pull together all those arguments which culminate in its central thesis of the nation victimized by a conspiracy. Whatever specific group affiliation he has, the man on the right believes that the world outside his country is the menacing breeding ground of hostile powers. He sees conspiracy therefore in very precise terms and argues that war with Russia and its allies is inevitable since good and evil cannot share one planet. We must abandon the United Nations, throw out income tax, social security and foreign aid; get rid of teachers and ministers who are concerned with social and political problems; uphold segregation, forbid fluoridation of drinking water, and "bleeding hearts" welfare policies.

The John Birch Society describes as communist and dangerous: the United States membership in the United Nations, the World Health Organization, the United Nations International Children's Emergency Fund, all foreign aid, the TVA, federal aid to housing, *and* United States government savings bonds.

THE SUCCESS OF UNREASON

Central to all this is a deep hostility towards progressive legislation. The "logic" is that both political parties—Republican and Democratic—have been captured by subversives who are creating a socialist America. This scheme, it is claimed, has been put over with the help of newsmen and intellectuals who are hoodwinking the public. Hostility to the "press" and to "commentators" in general is a consistent rightwing characteristic. Censoring of libraries and burning of books always have high priority.

One of the key men of the right is a "respectable spokesman,"

Dr. Fred Schwarz, a self-appointed Australian leader of the Christian Anti-Communism Crusade. Mr. Schwarz, who started out in this country in 1953 with ten dollars, now runs a million-dollar-a-year business of anti-communism. In Los Angeles, Schwarz' crusade scooped up more than a quarter of a million dollars in ninety days. The "take" in Philadelphia was $100,000, and in Phoenix, $40,000. Schwarz has predicted that by 1973, the United States will have been conquered by communism. He warned the people of San Francisco, he said: "that those who would not be dumped in the Bay might be put in the Nevada desert!" This nightmarish thinking of the liquidation of people is typical of paranoid projection. In one of his exhortations, Schwarz cried out: "Christians to arms! The enemy is at the gate! Lift high the blood-stained banner of the Cross and on to Victory!"

Where Schwarz arouses the masses, Robert Welch of the John Birch Society moves in to instruct the fearful what to do with their hatreds. Thus also does the "respectable right" and the radical right work hand-in-hand with the lunatic fringe of Rockwell and his vest-pocket Nazi Party which is stoking the fires from the lower depths. Thousands of young men in Chicago, in the summer of 1966, were waving swastika banners in anti-Negro demonstrations triggered by attempts at integration of housing.

The right wing believes that those leading the churches, trade unions and businesses who seek integration, lack patriotism and racial pride. "Big government" is the enemy of the betrayed "little" men. There is a need therefore for secret organizations, propaganda and calculated violence to spread terror. In addition, "good" Americans will soon find out that the civil rights movement is a "Jewish-Communist" plot to bring about "mongrelization."

The strength of these arguments can be easily understood when one reads in *The Politician*, the book by Mr. Welch of the

Birch Society: "In my opinion, the chances are very strong that
Milton Eisenhower is actually Dwight Eisenhower's superior
and boss within the Communist Party . . . There is only one
possible word to describe Eisenhower's purpose and actions.
That word is treason. My firm belief that Eisenhower is a dedicated conscious agent of the Communist conspiracy is based on
accumulation of detailed evidence." But then so were Franklin
D. Roosevelt, John Foster Dulles, General George C. Marshall
labelled as part of the great conspiracy.

Robert Welch and hundreds of thousands of Americans who
agree with him are deadly serious. They believe. And this is
why the rightist movement is gaining ground in many sections
of the country.

When violence is organized, when veiled threats put fear in
the hearts of minorities, it is time to take this movement seriously and to ask why irrationality and anti-intellectualism are
so popular.

While Schwarz only mournfully criticizes Washington, other
potent preachers of the right show no such finesse. Their success is phenomenal. One Wayne Poucher, a minister, has a daily
program called "Life Line" carried by two hundred and sixteen
radio stations in forty states. The program is sponsored by an
oil millionaire, and the heaviest concentration is in Texas where
fifty-seven stations carry the program. His word, according to
an article in Look Magazine, "is gospel to hundreds of thousands of Americans." His battle cry is that socialist planners
are waging war against the American people.

Why is there a tendency on the part of so many to be vulnerable to this kind of political neurosis? An impressive analysis
was offered by Professor Allen Westin of Columbia University.
Westin said that America's adult population can be divided into
at least three parts:

1. The sector committed to a civic-minded democracy—a
   sector of about forty-five million people.

2. A partially committed sector, of about fifteen to twenty million people.

3. An apolitical sector, of sixty to seventy million people.

The civic-minded participate regularly in elections; they join voluntary civic organizations and endorse the political system of checks and balances of free inquiry, debate and a free press. The partially committed sector joins very few organizations, is responsive to irrational appeals and panacea solutions and votes, by and large, in presidential elections only. It is a group of people which can be swung one way or the other in an election. The apolitical sector, however, rarely votes. It is the largest sector. Those within it do not join civic organizations and regard the dissent from orthodox versions of "Americanism" as disloyal.

When there is no crisis in the country, this fundamentalist group has little impact on the nation as a whole. But in times of stress and frustration, when depression or war threatens, the apolitical community is stirred and enters the political process. They will not join existing political organizations but seek out groups that respond to their fears. They distrust the cumbersome process of democratic voting and elections. Westin maintains that the right-wing is a constant realistic factor and that there is a perpetual threat that it may destroy social progress and democracy.

If democracy is to withstand the onslaught of the right-wing, the liberal, civic-minded community and the partially committed community must be able to maintain a political dialogue and work together. If they cannot, the vacuum will be filled by the anti-democratic forces which see no hope in the present political and economic system and are easily convinced that some anonymous powers are betraying the nation. This apolitical community yearns, therefore, for a pure nationalism which will "repeal" the stress and strain of the twentieth century. They blame the complexity of the world upon the evil machinations of liberals and "One World Advocates," or, as the Birch Society calls all opponents, "Com Symps" or communist sympathizers. The method is very similar to that of the bolshevist parties which used suspicions of "cosmopolitans," or, in China, of "neo-feudalist revisionists" to nourish fear and hate.

What is the future of the right-wing groups in America? It is obvious that they are on the upswing and only at the beginning of their influence. The takeover of the Republican Convention in 1964 was but a symptom of their strength. Welch of the Birch Society is aiming for many millions of members. The Birch Society raises a budget of about thirteen million dollars a year. If we compare that with the budgets of any liberal organization, we can readily see the potential. The right-wing sacrifices money with great devotion and dedication while liberals still starve their own organizations, as they have always done, remaining an impotent factor.

Neither should it be forgotten that the far right of today is better structured than that of the 'Thirties. Many very large corporations support rightist campaigns. The corporate illusion that right-wing groups can be "used" has, of course, deeper socio-economic reasons since the corporate structure is distrustful of social experimentation.

Obviously, in modern America, with the means of mass communication at our disposal, political reaction can be sold as well as razor blades. If this takes us out of the political realities and into a nightmarish world of conspiracy and secret organizations, some corporations at least consider it *good* business. The Schick Corporation is a good example of the blending of commercial purposes with propaganda.

Thus we find also a college in Arkansas which is practically sponsored by right-wing millionaires. From this place, Harding College, emerge propaganda movies such as "Communism on the Map." According to this alarmist picture, says Fred Cook, in an article in *The Nation*, "Communism today dominates the entire globe except for West Germany, Formosa, Switzerland and the United States." Even Great Britain is considered "pink" and no distinction is made between social democratic governments and communism.

The challenge to freedom from the right becomes the more threatening when we realize how many military seminars and how many private organizations have been deluged by its propaganda. It took a special directive by Secretary of State McNamara to ban military participation in right-wing seminars which had been carried on indiscriminately among reserve officers and other trainees. Rightist propaganda has created the danger of division in America by suggesting a fear-ridden approach to communism, by discrediting our own government and accusing prominent Americans of being communists, thus threatening the morale of the nation, and, a well-worn fascist technique, expounding the theory that the country is "stabbed in the back" by its own leadership.

Are we faced then with the makings of a genuine fascist wing in America? While it is wrong to underestimate this danger, it may be equally wrong to exaggerate it. On the basis, however, of a great amount of documentation, we can say that while we are certainly not yet challenged by the European type of Nazism, a neo-fascism *is* afoot. As happened in Europe, the fanatics and the lunatic fringe have the silent backing and financial support of many respectable right-wingers. Among them are some very wealthy men and a few retired military leaders. Also, the right-wing in America, as did its European predecessor, lives by garbled emotionalism and fantasies. And just as in Europe, the American right spouts a fanatic nationalism, blind to the realities of the twentieth century, which equates all liberal thought with communism, and which cries for one decisive blow to slay the evil in our midst, thus securing a total victory regardless of the cost. To this right-wing movement have come the hate-mongers, the professional anti-Catholics, anti-Semites, white supremicists, anti-income tax and anti-mental health-mongers. They have not yet focused upon a scapegoat and are still in search of a dramatic leader, but in many communities, the new right-wing is powerful. It is dedicated; it censors books; it harasses librarians, teachers and ministers; its avowed purpose is to destroy democracy.

A Catholic priest, John F. Cronin of the National Catholic Welfare Conference, pointed out the paradox: the forces of hatred seem to be most potent now that the internal threat of a Communist Party is least. Those who sow the seeds of over-simplification and the right-wing fanaticism are, according to Father Cronin: ". . . more than dishonest; they are divisive. They weaken our democracy by spreading suspicion of treason in government and by asking Americans to use communist tactics against fellow Americans. If carried far enough, these movements will paralyze American diplomacy. For whenever discussion with communist powers is considered weakness or even treason, then we are left with only two stark alternatives: surrender or war."

This frank statement has, of course, drawn the wrath of the fanatic right as have the critical and warning voices of many others who have stood up against the modern, "know-nothing" movement. The rightist columnist, Buckley, has repeatedly suggested that Pope John was "soft" on communism! Homes of critics—two Protestant ministers—have been bombed. The scars of the McCarthy period have hardly healed and we must keep in mind that it was Republicans, not liberals, who brought him down! Actually, many American liberals headed for the hills in impotent self-defense. There are reasons why the right-wing might really grow overnight. If we do not have war in the very near future, one can at least predict a continued rise in pressure from Communist China. Our position in the United Nations will become less and less dominant; the new nations will become more and more vocal and militant; there will be continual upheaval and social ferment in Africa and South America. In short, the conditions for the further growth of national frustration which feeds neo-fascism can be easily predicted. We must add to that the racial issue in our own country. In the next decade there is no doubt that the color problem is going to move North. As more Negroes achieve middle-class status, they will want to move into middle-class neighborhoods and they will increasingly become economic competitors with the white middle-class for well-paying jobs. The lip service to integration on the part of many a Northerner will be put to the acid test and this again will lead to tensions and frustrations. The theories of racial superiority and the John Birch Society's position against forced integration could well become focal points of right-wing success in our Northern states.

These are powerful emotional issues and they will swell the ranks of the right-wing groups if no counter-strength is planned now. As has been pointed out cogently by Dr. Harvey B. Schechter of the Los Angeles Anti-Defamation League, the failure of American liberals to lead an intelligent fight against all totalitarianisms has created a vacuum that is now filled by the neo-fascist right-wing.

If liberals do not educate the nation as to the history and origin of totalitarianism, they cannot be surprised that political extremism has a growing appeal. Authoritarian political power has to be answered by democratic effectiveness in politics and in the economy.

It is necessary to heed the comparison drawn by California Judge J. E. Barr of the Siskiyou County Superior Court, who likened our present situation to the atmosphere of suspicion and unreason which accompanied the decline of Greek civilization in the fourth century B.C. The Greeks, in their frenzy over subversion, banished their great General Xenophon, and the two admirals who had won victory in the Peloponesian War, Acipiades and Thycydides. Then, according to Judge Barr,

". . . the suspicion of these ancient far righters fell upon Socrates, one of the great minds of all times. His sin, in their view, was that he was a non-conformist, a questioner of facts. He was tried by a special court of five hundred and one jurors, found guilty of subverting youth and the Gods, and he was executed."

What was alarming about this persecution was that it was not perpetrated by a dictator or a foreign tyrant, but by a democracy. And another frightening facet is that the chief victims of that day were the intellectuals. As Judge Barr says,

"The right-winger, when he becomes crazed with fear, will invariably strike out at the intellectuals whom he cannot understand and whose non-conformity he must, in his terror, equate with treason."

In a time of heightened crisis, extreme vigilance is necessary if freedom is to survive. Freedom to think, to ask questions, to suggest alternatives and to liberate the nation from fear and hatred—these are goals for a liberal America. Their realization demands the commitment of persons and not of ideologies.

YOUTH AND THE SOCIAL APPETITE

The anthropologist, Margaret Mead, has repeatedly expressed the idea that the world has moved to such interdependence that we Americans must consider ourselves the guardians of all Russian children and that our own children are, in fact, the responsibility of the Russian people.

This powerful thought had been formulated some years before by the psychiatrist, Dr. Frank Freeman Smith, at a conference with Russian psychiatrists in Moscow. Dr. Smith told how impossible it had been, even between men working in the same field, to use words and ideas that did not arouse anger or suspicion. Then the idea occurred to him: "If we adults do not trust each other and can hardly speak to each other there is at least one thing we *can* do. We Americans can be the protectors of the Russian young and you Soviet adults can be the protectors of our children." This suggestion received an ovation and it triggered a new spirit at the conference.

Can we accept that "their" children are "our" children and vice versa? What do we know about each other's youth? Perhaps if we increase our understanding of our own young people, we can get closer to seeing how they and Russian youth can discover a community of life, rather than be conditioned towards fateful hostility.

But how serious is the adult generation? A recent Federal budget shows that we spend about one cent to the dollar for education. This baffling figure indicates that as a nation we care little about the nurture of our young. Of course, this does not correspond with what each parent feels about his own children, but as a culture we do not as yet value our young to the same degree that we value comfort, defense or investments. Yet many adults continually deplore the lack of concerns shared with the young, and are always willing to condemn an entire generation when some youngsters strike out against society.

Such indignation makes it possible to neglect probing the deeper causes why some young people want no part of the existing social order. Every civilization develops its own process of socialization, its own pathways by which youth can move from dependent childhood to more adult obligation. What is it in our culture that makes it so difficult for many youngsters to ease themselves confidently into the values and expectations of the existing order?

This is a question asked by worried parents and not only in the "Western" world. The British have their "teddy boys"; the Dutch have their "Provo's" (from provocateur); the Russians their "hooligans"; we have our "beatniks"; the Argentinians, a reborn Hitler-Youth Movement; the Israelis, their special juvenile delinquent camps.

And while a great many young persons do not participate in

such groups, there are a great many others who see in them a valid way of registering their complaints against the adult world. Their complaints are justified. For our society, as much as any other, wants to postpone dealing with it most troubling characteristics. When youth points out our inconsistencies, we act as if the world would crumble unless they too accept what we have come to take for granted. But young people cannot accept the adult compromises as gospel; youth cannot help realizing that the adults want to ignore those factors causing the greatest emotional strain. Yet youth, as it makes its way in the world, suffers most deeply from such psychological depletion. The tremendous discrepancy between the values preached in our civilization and those we actually live by cannot be hushed up. Youth will point to the oratorical mediocrity which oozes from the commencement rituals and which they are asked to swallow wholesale as values without which society would disintegrate. Adults often think of youth's unrestrained frankness as irresponsible. Yet, how else shall the young react? They have been raised and educated in a world radically different from that of their parents; with just their college education they have incredible opportunities and yet their social matrix offers exceedingly few opportunities for a solid value base. Everything, literally everything, is in flux and so their adulthood is postponed.

What are the processes by which we transmit values to our youth and what values do they actually receive? What do we really know about the inner life of young people and sometimes even of our own children?

This brings to mind the story of the Reverend Kumalo in the book, *Cry the Beloved Country* by Alan Paton. The Reverend Kumalo is a minister in a small African village, and he is a charitable and gentle man. Yet his son has deserted a pregnant mistress and his sister in Johannesburg has become an alcoholic and prostitute. The Reverend Kumalo travels to the big city, hoping that he can at least bring his sister back to the village. Arriving in Johannesburg, he hears that a white city engineer, a fighter for Negroes, has been shot. When the police round up the suspects, it turns out that Reverend Kumalo's son is the killer. In his misery, the pastor speaks these moving words: "To think," he says, "that my wife and I lived out our lives in innocence in our village, not knowing that this thing was coming step by step . . . Now we can see, but we could not see then."

Even the most loving and concerned parents frequently have to make this tragic confession. It is not that they do not want to know what occurs within their children but rather that the initiation of the young into society is more often than not accidental. How does one convey the values one lives by to one's sons and daughters when the pressures and strains of society intrude continuously upon the intimacy of relationship? It is clear that a society, a culture, will only persist if its members choose aims assuring survival. Whether or not we do this in our culture is open to question. The increase in suicide, alcoholism, drug addiction and crime are classical symptoms of societal decay. Yet, there is also the Peace Corps, the struggle for human rights, the sweep of technological progress. But do our young people feel part of those more hopeful aspects of society? Many are the complaints concerning loneliness, social vacuum, insecurity and the incapacity of the older generations to make the newer feel that they are trusted and counted upon.

If we want to avoid the drift of the young towards submission to hostile leadership and cynicism, the purposes of society have to become far more explicit in terms of personal experience, personal opportunity.

The goals and means of a free society must fit in with the hopes and aspirations of private individuals; the communication of social ideals must come about by the involvement of all generations in attainable purposes. One of the problems of our particular culture is therefore that there are sub-strata of society which do not, in fact, participate in social intercourse. These persons—and this is especially true of unemployed youth—do not feel part of society. It is but one step from social insecurity to a psychology tainted by self-doubt, self-negation and finally, self-destructiveness. The riots in many larger cities, with the poor making other poverty-stricken persons their primary target, is a most dramatic example of this self-defeating rage.

Let us consider closely the disenfranchised youth in our culture. President Kennedy wrote, shortly before his death, "I am particularly disturbed over the serious plight of the nearly one million out-of-school and out-of-work youth." Former Harvard President Dr. James Conant spoke about this same group of young people as "social dynamite" and the then Secretary of Labor, Arthur Goldberg, called it the "most dangerous social condition in America." Yet, if this is the diagnosis, what is the therapy and can it be provided by our present order of society? We have recklessly created a new sub-culture of millions who will never participate in the economic or democratic processes. They are isolated. They never "get along"; they never belong within a framework of expectation and, as outsiders, they can become easy victims of irrational and hostile mass appeal.

It should be obvious that the question of gainful and meaningful employment is of crucial significance. Basic changes have occurred in the total economic structure in the last fifty years and nowhere have these changes been as decisive as in the sector of unskilled young workers. If we agree upon the value of meaningful labor as conducive to a sense of social identity and self-respect, the absence of labor opportunities should concern us greatly.

Where once liberals actively opposed exploitation of the young, child-labor, the deepest worry today is youth-unemployment. In that evolution lies the complex nature of the ethical issues involved. Obviously, the economic forces operating haphazardly through "bust and boom" have not been able to fur-

nish society with the stabilizing factors which at one extreme
will not exploit the young and at the other will not doom them
to mass unemployment. Yet this is what seems increasingly
ahead for the many millions of youngsters who will not have
the basic training and skills to fit within a computerized corporate economy.

Can we agree that the provision of labor is as much a social
responsibility as the protection from exploitation? Or will cries
of "creeping socialism" frustrate every attempt to plan sanely
for the younger generation? Fifty years ago, child labor in this
country was widespread. In 1910 one out of every seven children aged 10-15 worked, usually 10 to 12 hours a day, at starvation wages in the most unhygienic and degrading circumstances. Many thousands of children, six or seven years old,
worked under intolerable conditions; children were crippled for
life daily in the ruthless economic upsurge and because of the
insatiable appetite for unskilled labor.

The dangers today are not for children between six and fifteen but perpetual unemployment of youth sixteen to twenty-
one years of age.

During this decade, the 'sixties, about twenty-six million new
young workers will enter the labor force; 40 percent more than
in the 'fifties. By the late 'sixties this will mean about three millions new young workers each year as compared to two million
ten years before. If one adds to that figure the 65 percent of the
youngsters now living on farms who will move to cities looking
for work, one becomes aware of a mass problem for which a
decent society must provide solutions.

In addition, the number of youths not finishing high school is
increasing. The estimate is that in the 'sixties about eight million will not finish high school. A large number of these young
people will never be employed and will instead join the steadily
growing army of unemployables which now totals four or five
million people. Unemployment is one thing, but to be tagged

as "surplus labor" at the onset of life is deeply damaging to anyone's self-respect. It will color a young man's entire life, his relationships toward his family and community, and his attitude towards marriage.

In his excellent study, *The Other America*, Michael Harrington wrote: "The millions who are poor in the United States tend to become increasingly invisible. Here is a great mass of people . . . somewhere between forty and fifty million . . . They were poor. They still are . . ."

Nothing could be less productive than to approach these issues with the clichés of nineteenth century "laissez-faire— laissez-aller" economics. These theories have simply lost all validity and they probably never applied to America in the first place. Lenin's penetrating analysis of capitalism in *Imperialism, the Highest State of Capitalism*, may have applied to Europe in its most imperialist phase, but it has no reality base in the United States economy. The "surplus capital" which he said would never be used by the capitalists for raising the living standard of the "masses," has, in America, been plowed back into precisely those industries which made possible a spectacular improvement in the living conditions of the workers. American capitalism was never imperialistic as was the British or Japanese and therefore the perspectives of increased prosperity must not be hampered by an outmoded fear of socio-economic planning. The economic order is not ordained from on high and its transformations are well within the reach of human intelligence.

The social inadequacies which have created the under-employment of youth will respond to pragmatic innovation and need not be delayed by the evasion of facts. We have not so hampered foreign aid and we must not do so concerning employment opportunity.

Today's youth lives in a new world already more interdependent than any previous generation's. Our young people must be trained so that they can play a venturesome role in that interdependence. Massive programs like the Peace Corps are the answer, for such involvement guarantees participation in the democratic process. To give our young the immense opportunities of a world at peace demands more than the angry polemics of ideology with their Soviet counterparts. Socio-economic questions are personal questions. The opportunities we seek for our own children must be made available to all. This cannot be done without recognition of the need for the transformation of some crucial aspects of today's society. The question is whether such transformation will come about because of social disaster or as a result of forethought.

THE CASE FOR TRUST

Each culture finds its concrete destiny through the values emerging from the lives of its members. This is so, whether or not that culture chooses these values. What individuals do, not what they profess, will determine the character and future of any society. Whether or not a philosophy of life has truth to it is decided by the way in which individuals treat each other, by the way in which they seek to practice what they profess. This is particularly relevant in the attitudes of the adults towards the younger generations. To preach desirable virtues is senseless unless such virtues become functionally visible. Therefore when individuals are isolated by an incapacity to participate in the life of a culture, something of personal value is drained from their lives and all of society is traumatized.

Those who must stand aside, without a way of communicating their frustrations, suffer. The withdrawal they may show, the suspicion they may feel towards others—is born out of the fear of being found too weak to stand up for themselves. Those who rebel against the fabric of ordered society and, who may seem threatening in their rejections—as witness the street gangs—

actually want to "belong." They are like individuals who cannot take the risks of trust. Still, without such trust, life is brutal and pitiful.

Our wretchedness is not in our condition as vulnerable creatures but in the hell we make for each other. It is obvious then that social attitudes, the community's state of mind and economic factors are intertwined. How can we promote among our young—by our example—the capacity to live in peace with others, particularly the oncoming generation of the Soviet Union and China? How can youth unlearn the memories of the adults' cruel past? How shall we teach about past injustices, blunders and inhumanities without poisoning the young? How shall they know the past in order to use it for the future?

Any person, nation or group who wishes to do so can make a long list of the injustices perpetrated against his particular group. There is plenty for everybody! Yet when resentment is handed down from father to son what will be gained?

If Margaret Mead's proposal has merit, namely that we are responsible for the future of the Russian children and the Russians are responsible for ours, we have to unlearn many evils and try to formulate a constructive way of dealing with our individual and group unhappiness.

Surely, the American civilization has enough inventiveness and vitality to create better pathways for its young than those martial perspectives necessitated by our military posture throughout the world. I do not agree that the unemployables should be fitted into some para-military service, as the government has suggested, in order to "make men" out of them. The only masculinity worth thinking of is the one which promotes personal dignity and self-realization. A society which wants to remain free needs to engage in furthering self-sufficiency. If we do not learn how to carry this out we will be deluged by a mass civilization in which all liberalism will be overpowered by irrational mass movements. There must be an end to the commercial exploitation of the teenage urge for status without social ethics. The "seduction of the innocent," the corruption of youth for gain, is a most questionable "privilege" of the free enterprise system. Freedom is a result of a societal climate. Hunger for freedom depends upon example and habit; therefore, the standards of our civilization need to be consciously raised. Youth has a right to be initiated into a world in which it wants to live, not into a world so torn by its conflicts that it becomes impossible to make valid choices. Youth needs roots in a community of concern and mental health.

We must not forget that the pressure of a culture hell-bent on success creates a deep sense of dependence in the many who cannot be successful. The more pressure and resulting dependence, the more danger that persons will be swayed to what it is suggested they should desire and thus self-reliance is destroyed.

In that context we have to learn that to make mistakes is not fatal; that to be less than perfectly adjusted does not mean that one has no worth. Hostile minds are always ready for wholesale condemnation, but the wiser person uses his sense of proportion in remedying mistakes. Youth needs to know that it too has a right to be imperfect and to make mistakes. Our young have to be given the opportunity to learn the meaning of forgiving and forgiveness without which no balanced life is possible. It is the ABC of human reality that we are fallible and often anxious and that nevertheless we have a right to come back and expect to be trusted again. A child's world is shattered not by being confronted with his or his parents' realistic failures but by the insistence that the adult world cannot be wrong. A framework for making mistakes without disastrous consequences is as important for individuals as it is for nations. Self-righteousness is the breeding ground of all intolerance.

Therefore, among the attitudes youth has to unlearn is nationalism. The time has come to teach the history of human achievement rather than of human debasement. Of course, careful study of the details of history is necessary, but much of our literature and history are still based upon Man's quasi-heroic combative characteristics. The power of the mind should be given a chance in education, over the power of muscle or the notion that a nation can only get ahead by disadvantaging another.

Why do the street gangs in New York slums call themselves the "Bishops," the "Dragons," the "Egyptian Kings," the "Royal Kings," the "Cobras," the "Sovereign Overlords"? The reason is obvious. In a world where display of power is central, in a world in which "cornering" a person or a nation, "pinning them against a wall," putting them "over a barrel," is considered manly and strong, in such a world those who feel left out need to think of themselves as Lords and Cobras. It gives status to empty lives. But the pursuit of power is a dead end street. It offers no avenues for personal growth.

If youth cannot identify with the adult culture, then adults need to remedy the dynamics of that culture. It is not a question of pampering the young but of the survival of a shared reality. If our youth cannot believe that the world handed to them is a good world, then they will reject it and themselves because they feel hopeless. This is the vicious circle of self-destructiveness. "If I can't get what I want, I will destroy what matters to you." What we see in disenchanted youth is a warning to society as a whole. The breakdown of mutuality as a value in society is the first step towards disintegration of individuals. And just as it does not make sense to generalize about persons sixty-five and over as "aged," so it is wrong to aim general criticism at youth. We desperately need a genuine reconstruction of individuals, regardless of generation and new ways of believing and acting together. "New ways" can be based upon enduring values which will strengthen the individual's capacity for a meaningful existence. Parents and educators are always in danger of seeking the acceptance of youth by tossing central values overboard. In their eagerness to respond to change they further weaken the value base of the new generation. This makes the young people still more insecure and still more confused about what matters and what does not.

Values which served to build backbone in the past need not be abandoned in order to respond to technological, scientific or philosophical change. Such values have to be reinterpreted so that they can serve to formulate new ideals, new dreams, new societal goals. Transformation cannot occur without foundation. Youth needs a trusted core in order to stretch its own imagination and commitment. The generations can attain continuity if what must be changed remains based upon what has been found to be essential in the past. This will require restraint and foresight and love. Carl Sandburg formulated the challenge most sensitively when he wrote:

> "There is only one child in the world
> and the child's name is: All Children."

Are we willing to accept that?

LOYALTY AND DISSENT

Each civilization formulates its own myths and each citizen, consciously or unconsciously, holds a view of the world in which he lives. The American proposition, from the inception of the Republic, has been that human nature is plastic and that civilization can be improved and transformed.

All through the nineteenth century the dominant thought pattern in politics, sociology and economics was nurtured by a fundamental optimism which proclaimed that, by rational agreements and checks and balances, a desirable world could be built. The pessimism of Feuerbach or Spengler found little acclaim here as William James and Dewey became the philosophers of a democratic view of human character and of the

potential for a cooperative order. In a sense even Freudian insights were bent to this optimistic framework for a better understanding of the subconscious was seen as yet another means
to improve society.

It is only now, after two shattering world wars and after the
steady growth of world-wide irrationality, that we begin to
doubt that capacity for reformation. Following the McCarthy-
ism of the 'fifties, increasing nationalism and political intolerance have seeped into the American fabric and revivalism is
only one aspect of the distrust concerning rational and scientific methodology. Yet our better hope, I am convinced, lies in
those aspects of our past which boldly proclaimed America as
a unique experiment. Popular democracy had never before been
attempted and therefore the emergence of this Republic seemed
tied in with the forward motion of history and of life lived for
greater ends than just material opportunity. And just as the
human personality must be seen as the sum of continuous
processes, so does the history of any community result from
process. The way by which a nation relates to process determines the goals for which its individuals will find it worthwhile
to live. Group existence does not emerge from an ontological
"nothing".

It is the product of human relationships, group consciousness and a community of fate. America spelled out a hitherto
unheard-of-principle: because of the process of history, future
governments would persist only with the consent of the governed. The immense appeal of that notion in the enlightenment
period must not be underestimated because the citizen had not
ruled since ancient Athens and that truly revolutionary document of our beginnings stated that: "we hold these truths to be
self-evident . . ."

This has not ceased to be revolutionary language even though
Americans as a whole have become reluctant to consider revolution as akin to their own way of life. The American experi-

ment was unique both because it voiced a faith in Man's capacity to uplift himself and because from the tenets of this experiment flowed the consequence, that the American ideal was simultaneously an ideal for all of mankind. Thomas Paine wrote proudly: "We have it in our power to begin the world over again" and this has since been affirmed countless times. In personal terms, it enabled all men to become free enough in a material and spiritual sense to remake themselves. This world aspiration was doubtless the most disturbing feature of the American revolution for all those abroad who wanted to hold on to feudal power. It has remained similarly the frustration of all reaction in American life, whether of the Know-Nothings, the American-Firsters or the John Birchers.

Loyalty to America then, as a spiritual aspiration, is not dependent upon the status quo but rather upon a revolutionary "gospel" which did not ask about race or color but only about the urge for freedom. As Thomas Wolfe wrote: "So, then, to every man his chance, to every man regardless of his birth, his shining, golden opportunity—to every man the right to live, the right to be himself, to become whatever his manhood and his vision can combine to make him—this, seeker, is the promise of America." What stirred the immigrants from Ireland and Germany, from Scotland and France, from Holland and Eastern Europe, what made them set out on the terrible voyage, often traveling for months on foot to get to the harbors of Hamburg and Rotterdam, what gave them strength to persevere, was a hope of life.* Nothing sophisticated, nothing but the trembling awareness that for once the process of history was on the side of the humble! They wagered their lives upon the progress of a life of decency and independence.

This is the fundamental ethic of America, overgrown as it often is by greed and ignorance. It is true that while plenty was a

---

*Among the references used in this chapter are: James Loewenburg, *Power and American Ideals,* The Standard: N.Y. 1950; Oscar Handlin, *The Uprooted.*

potential in this country, the immigrant more often than not found poverty the reality; that liberty meant to some the liberty to exploit others for the opportunities of a few. Nevertheless what did not die was the idea and the forceful teaching that freedom was for something, not against something.* Freedom was to benefit the people, it was not just a weapon to use against the aristocracy. Yet we have to discern beyond the innocence of origin the realities of present political and economic power. Power is not evil in itself. It must be controlled, so that human resources can be used for the centrality of freedom. This necessitates a consideration of ourselves especially in times of national turmoil and war. Is dissent in times of national crisis disloyal? Is it permissible in such times to acknowledge the aims and purposes of one's adversaries?

Where does one draw the line? What is the difference between dissent and disloyalty? This surely is a crucial issue. Nothing bears so much upon the national posture as an understanding of the relationship of the individual to the state. In a dictatorship, whether fascist or bolshevist, national security is aimed at the preservation of the totalitarian state power.

But in a free society, in a democracy, national security has but one quite different aim: to protect and to expand freedom. There is no doubt that since the McCarthy period, for whatever reasons, many in this country have come to accept encroachments upon personal freedom in the name of national security and loyalty. Many Americans frightened by the complexities of the world and the hostility of those who oppose us, have come to consider liberty, the right to speak one's mind and to dissent, as a liability. Thus loyalty is often confused with conformity or uniformity of thought. Variety of opinion is felt as a confusion somehow inflicted upon the loyal populace by fuzzy-minded, slightly disloyal intellectuals. Still, we know that the only loyalty that means anything is that given without

*Loewenburg, *op. cit.*

request, given freely and generously. Husbands and wives, brothers and sisters do not swear loyalty oaths to one another.

In the same vein, the loyalty within a national community comes about because there is a general acceptance of certain values. If one stands for the idea that liberty can never be a liability, then we assume the duty to dissent and to speak up when we feel that certain underlying values are threatened. This is the meaning of government by the consent of the governed. Such consent is based upon diversity, it is "the loyalty of free men" who can disagree, on vital issues, and maturely agree to disagree and still maintain unity without fear of each other. It is not disloyal to criticize any facet in government. Quite to the contrary, by the dynamic process of asking questions and of getting answers, one can overcome the distrust that so easily arises between people. It is distrust which leads to the destruction of freedom, and to nihilism.

Every community needs protection against the power of the hateful, the emotionally immature, the character assassins. Where such character traits lead to the undermining of the work of the community or worse to treason or frontal attack upon the survival of the group, steps have to be undertaken to decontaminate the community. No entity can survive when private hostilities have become more crucial than group purpose. But safeguards are greatly needed since those zealously convinced of their own righteousness may be especially uncharitable in judging others on ideological, theological or personal grounds.

This was recognized early in our history. James Madison, in *The Federalist* (Number 43), his brilliant interpretation of the Constitution, wrote the following: "As treason may be committed against the United States, the authority of the United States ought to be able to punish it. But as new-fangled and artificial treasons have been the great engines by which violent factions . . . have usually wreaked their alternate malignity on each other, the Constitutional Conventions have with great judgment opposed a barrier to this peculiar danger by inserting the proof necessary for conviction of it . . ." And what was that definition? We find it in Article Three, Section Three of the Constitution: "treason against these United States shall consist only in levying war against them . . . in adhering to their enemies, giving them aid and comfort." Now let it be clear that there are no other acts—acts, mind you, not ideas—than those specified in the Constitution that can be considered as treasonable. What psychological and ethical insight on the part of Madison! How applicable this understanding is for our day when the country abounds with millions of rightwing extremists who would use precisely those "new-fangled and artificial forms of treason" to "wreak their alternate malignity on each other." This is the danger, the disloyalty, which subverts the very principles of a free country.

Thus, dissent and loyalty are in no way mutually exclusive even though we know full well that in times of international tensions there is a great temptation to lump them together and to smear and denounce all those of different persuasions. The excitement of a nation at war can turn many otherwise tolerant and gentle people into fierce persecutors of any opposition. Yet this does not make it less incumbent upon those who disagree to speak their minds. The more the war accelerates and the longer the casualty lists become, the greater the danger of artificial uniformity.*

Who is the true patriot then? Who then is truly loyal to the best interests of a free world?

A great many decent persons live in silent terror of possible extermination by nuclear war and therefore, even among the conscious citizens, there are many who are tempted to close their eyes to reality. They, too, learn of cruelty, torture and death and then go back to their business, or work, or vacation.

*The Loyalty of Free Men, Alan Barth, N.Y. 1951.

THE END OF INNOCENCE

This is the mortal danger to freedom, because the ones who protest are increasingly seen as freaks, "troublemakers" or "way-out" intellectuals. It thus is imperative that this trend be reversed. Under super-patriotic fervor which so frequently is nurtured by anti-Negro, anti-Semitic and anti-alien sentiments, lurks the insecurity of anxiety-ridden personalities. The super-patriot is not so sure beneath it all, not so sure that he wants a government of liberty and democracy. What he seeks is power, authority and uniformity.

True patriotism and loyalty consist in the work of men and women who would never shout their patriotism from rooftops, but who believe, work and raise their children within the supportive ideals of a free society: the workers of the Peace Corps, the businessmen, postal workers, housewives, book-keepers, engineers, the volunteer workers of the many associations devoted to peace and world brotherhood, tolerance and humanism, they are the young students who risk their lives to work the hot summer months in Alabama or Mississippi and also the young soldiers who, because it is their duty, will go to distant inhospitable lands and face the possibility of death. Of course I do not plead for American military intervention as a sort of Holy Grail. What has happened in Vietnam is a national tragedy. I refer here to Americans as soldiers of peace, as part of a system of international law.

Our hope is in the down-to-earth efforts of common people, provided that they demand to be informed, that they educate themselves and each other and stand for humanity, hope and the capacities of love. I do not agree with everything James Baldwin has written. However, he has something important to tell us about ourselves. Of course, his primary concern is with the position of the Negro but his remarks have a more general significance. In his opinion, the 1954 Supreme Court decision concerning desegregation of the public schools was inspired neither by love, nor by justice, but by the pressures of the Cold War. The decision would have come earlier had it been born out of justice or love, he argues. But even if the Negro cannot expect to come to power in the U.S., he is "very well placed indeed," says Baldwin, "to ring down the curtain on the American dream."

Baldwin thinks that racial tensions are involved only symbolically with color. They originate in the same depths as love. His thesis is therefore that Negro boys and girls facing hostile mobs today "come out of a long line of improbable aristocrats— the only genuine aristocrats this country has produced."*

This aristocracy and this individuality is indeed the American ethic at its strongest. It is to be realized now and for all time on this continent and its powerful attraction can diminish only if we fail to set it as an attainable goal in each person's private existence. We have not come this far as a nation, as a community, to be stopped or to be destroyed by the self-destructiveness of the worst among us, the forces of reaction instead of loyalty and progress. It is not the abstractions of politics with which we are concerned but with human progress so that we can quicken in each other the hidden excellences and thus form an entity, immensely varied and differentiated, yet bound together by the vision of progressive goals.

We have here a profound affirmation of the revolutionary essence of national purpose. Each has not only a right and a duty to become himself, but he is so destined because he is human, because his nature is, in principle, a moral nature. Identity is the result of life suffered and struggled with, of realities faced and dealt with in a growing sense of human capacity. Status is the neurotic overemphasis of the insecure person who needs the symbols of status, whether money or his white skin, to feel that he is alive. Stature is an achievement of maturation.

*James Baldwin, *The Fire Next Time*, N.Y. 1962.

Only an educated populace, alert to the possibilities of the encroachment of political or economic power, will be able to keep on pressing for changes, for loyalty to the principle of history-as-process.

We have a duty to see the reality of freedom, loyalty and progress in America as part of what happens to us as individuals. We cannot sidestep some of the major contradictions in our American civilization that make change for moral progress and maturity exceedingly difficult, if not impossible. We have to know, in order to change. Our economy is still based upon individual competition,* not necessarily for excellence, but for survival, for a slice of the cake. Fundamentally, therefore, individuals have to fight with other individuals in order to surpass and, very often, to push them aside.

We see this murderous competition around us daily. It results in a permanent, omnipresent, diffuse, hostile tension between individuals, men as well as women. Everyone is a potential competitor. This invades all relationships, it determines whom we ask to our homes, whom we are afraid of, whom we hope we can trust. This is also apparent in family life, in friendships. Yet, as Freud has shown us, the rivalry in families is not caused by our biological traits but by our cultures. The perpetual tension between potential competitors results in fear, especially of the potential hostility of others, and a fear in oneself of the possible retaliation of others because of one's own competitive acts. Thus there is also the eternal shadow of failure. Many persons measure themselves only by the way they think others value them. The person who thinks he is not succeeding frequently feels as if he were entirely worthless.

A man I knew of tried to commit suicide a few years ago because he thought a detailed report recommending changes in his business organization had been turned down by his employer. After weeks of anxious waiting, he decided that he had

*Karen Horney, M.D., *The Neurotic Personality of Our Time*, N.Y. 1937.

been rejected and tried to take his life. Life had lost its meaning, he had become worthless and ridiculous. Later, it was revealed that the employer never got the report and that it had been held up by another junior executive, afraid for his own position. Reckless, frightened competition is a major threat to mental health.

In terms of the culture in which we live, we often create impossible tensions by preaching brotherhood and humility but, at the same time, insisting upon standards of success which foster latent hostility and anxious competition. We have to educate so that there is an understanding of the limitation of achievement as well as an understanding of outstanding performance. Both are necessary to keep our community a functional entity.

Again, as in the case of power, competition of and by itself need not be rejected. Competition of performance is not evil and breeds none of the latent hostilities and frustrations mentioned earlier. The question is obvious: power for what, competition for what? The fear of failure is a normal one, because the chances of failing from time to time are so much greater than of continually succeeding in what we set out to do. It is only when the loser in the competitive struggle is threatened with economic annihilation and disaster that we deal with a moral wrong. Loss of a sense of security or prestige, in whatever one does for a living, is a hard blow and a humane civilization will not add to that the further punishment of economic misery.

Societal and cultural circumstances can create human individuals devoid of conscience, of all ethics. A community is responsible for its goals which must be an organic part of specific attainable ideals. Only then does it make sense to speak of hope and aspiration without the danger of using hollow words. To insist that the unlimited opportunities for money and position are open in America and, at the same time, to have an economy which creates ever greater dependence upon the large corporate structures, is to throw a person into despair about values, goals and happiness. It will leave a deep sense of helplessness and frustration.

There are many American illusions that have to be challenged. Prof. Charles Frankel* of Columbia University called them:

a) The illusion of words, that is, being stuck with a phrase like "the international Communist conspiracy," while in fact, communism has many different aspects in Poland, Yugoslavia, China, Cuba or the U.S.S.R.

b) The illusion of stability, to assure that the main task in life is to keep things stable and unchanged, thus seeing as our natural enemies those who strive for change or revolution.

c) The illusion of a classless society when there are clearly tremendous differences between those who *have* and those who have very *little*, thus making it impossible to understand the meaning of social revolution.

The occurrence of these illusions may well be tied in with the concept of America as an innocent nation, but this is hardly tenable in a realistic sense. For the time of innocence disappeared when we became a world power.

Our community will be secure so long as freedom is an instinctive reaction and progress an unspoken, self-evident reality. It is this instinct for freedom which will, in the long run, determine whether or not we bring off the American experiment. For there will always be those who distrust the people, who want to set class against class, race against race, religion against religion. But they will not carry the day so long as freedom is rooted in private courage, as long as loyalty is loyalty to the revolutionary origins. "The banner of freedom," a poet wrote, "may be torn but it will stream at its strongest against the wind."

*Charles Frankel, *N. Y. Times*, Sept. 22, 1963.

CHANGE OR CHEERFUL STAGNATION?

Who can fail to love Paris? It was my good fortune to return there on Bastille Day, the day the French commemorate the storming of Louis XIV's most important prison, the anniversary of the day which was, in fact, the beginning of the French Revolution and of the proud proclamation, "Liberté, Egalité, Fraternité," the beginning of a noble attempt ending in the miserable military dictatorship of Napoleon.

The evening I arrived, all of Paris was in the streets and particularly visible were the young men of the Army, some in the khaki of modern paratroopers; others in colorful uniforms of years gone by, in caps with white feathers and trousers with red stripes. The same red stripes which the Germans liked so well in World War I since it made the French "poilu" an easy target . . . It took the general staff three years to abolish those stripes!

As the soldiers marched past my hotel I could see behind them, on the walls of the street, little tablets in bronze indicating where similarly young and patriotic men had been executed by the Germans during World War II. One had to look carefully for those commemorative plaques and in the bustle of Paris, the festivities, the military bands, it was hard to find anyone paying attention to those fallen so recently.

It was in sharing the elation of a national holiday which set an ideal for humanity and realizing the futility of so much sacrifice—that the desperate urgency for human change presented itself once more.

The marching soldiers and the citizens applauding them, represented all those forces of stagnation which bind humanity to eternal self-destructiveness. Yet, that very activity passed for praise-worthy patriotism and one would be less than welcome in criticizing the banners, the proud marching, the invigorating music. Doubtless, these young men seemed to the onlookers the pride and the hope of the nation. No word is taken in vain as frequently as "hope."

What is it that continually prevents a more mature world order? One crucial factor is the immense global expenditure for arms. Is the desire for peace more than wishful prattle; is the human species at all capable of rising above its infantile aggressions based upon territorial jealousies? Nations simply are no longer absolutely sovereign and we cannot be satisfied with the smokescreens of propaganda. "Nobody," wrote columnist I. F. Stone, "seems to be willing to risk anything for peace—anything, that is, but the human race." These tendencies are not due to the schemes of misguided leadership but result from complex cultural motivations. Blundering inertia allows conflict to deteriorate society as if we still lived in the era of swords and cavalry charges. Yet, H-bombs cannot be turned into plowshares. One central barrier to progress then is the tendency to think that the way in which we have organized our particular society is the "inevitable" way and that therefore, all other possibilities are chaotic. Social anthropologists have pointed out that this is not due to some innate defect but to the propensity of human beings to perform their tasks, as they think they have to. Since the society in which they live is the only society that has true meaning for them they want to serve it trustingly. Thus the wish to leave things as they are is molded by the expectations of environment.

When changes take place they are usually resisted and the realization of change almost invariably is accompanied by upheaval. There are two fundamental factors involved which were meaningfully stated by Erich Fromm, in his book *May Man Prevail?*

First, most leaders of nations have been incapable of peacefully adapting themselves to new conditions. Changes, by and large, are allowed to "happen" and are only infrequently anticipated. Second, most leaders of nations deify their particular ways of life. They are willing to die rather than to change—fundamental change often appears to them worse than death.

Nevertheless, as Heilbronner stresses in *The Future of History* the main challenge of any epoch is always this: are leaders and citizens capable of using their historical understanding in such a way as to further concrete political action? If they are not, they will cling fanatically to the status quo and seek by denial mechanisms and scapegoats to avoid dealing with changed reality situations. An example of constructive adaptation to change can be seen in the rise of the working class in capitalist countries. Unions once uniting those who were the objects of exploitation are now partners in the economy. Compare this adaptation with the attitudes of religious institutions in Europe, which were balanced only after the bloodbath of the Thirty Years' War and the inane, sanctified killings of the Inquisition. (In World War II, although the Nazi defeat was certain in 1944, the Germans had to be pursued into the buildings and subway corridors of Berlin before they capitulated.) This is how mental inertia distorts the appreciation of reality factors.

To avoid shallow exclamations against violence and war, it is necessary to find the key to the ingredients of the human character. There is much that will not become conscious, and political events are but rarely understood in terms of the crucial subconscious layers of experience. And so we carry into our social and political relations attitudes which only have an appearance of rationality. It is this which makes collective inertia and brutalization possible. All the indignant rhetoric in the world will not change convictions based upon supposed realities which are, in fact, the superstitions of collectivities or the projections of their aggression. The Judeo-Christian tradition has had a retarding role in that it glorifies man's suffering as a way to sanctify life. Yet, the unmistakable fact is that enslavement and death have in no way purified the human race. Quite to the contrary, they have triggered more violence and more recriminatory hostility. Because of our role in the collectivities we have therefore become accustomed to see our lives, even our loves, as a means towards the end of the aggregate. As Moravia has pointed out in his "defense of humanism," we think of a cheerful life as the opposite of suffering. Yet suffering when not idolized, and when not bathed in holy unction can be a way of discovering that we are an end unto ourselves. The immobility of society, the inertia of the mind are the result of man being used for ends other than his own happiness, Moravia maintains.

It is a vicious circle in which mass destruction becomes a rational proposition! In fact, this utter rationality stands out in what is happening in the modern acquiescence to butchery. Our problem is that we do not have an active, functional value base to oppose this. We suffer from too damned much objectivity! We are teachers, or businessmen, or soldiers, nursed by the values of collectivities which carry with them the elements of our destruction. We are taught complacency and apathy, not how to overcome the bondage, the enslavement to suffering.*

National collectivism cannot be concerned in terms of personal love but only in terms of justification of the use of power. It cannot care in terms of personal justice but only in terms of the right to sacrifice private existences to the savageries of abstract principles.

At last religion therefore will have to start to teach—and by religion I mean all the ethic-creating channels of society—that in co-responsibility and the private pursuit of happiness there is as much catharsis as the Greeks, Hebrews and Christians found in the tragic. Life as tragedy, life as suffering is the nefarious ideology by which war after war is foisted upon unsuspecting victims steeped in defeatism, who meet their execu-

*Alberto Moravia, *Man As An End*, N.Y. 1966.

tioners and pretend bravely it is their Maker! Moravia is correct that the future of man demands an inventiveness and a self-reliance in which joy of living can be the catharsis rather than all that which lurks eternally "in the cave of Caliban."

The foremost task then is to avoid drifting towards the old violences by readiness to anticipate change. This means sifting fact from fiction so that we can end the confusion of national interest with fanaticism. It also means suggesting doggedly that there are alternatives to destruction.

Progress in politics depends upon the faith that policies can effectuate change and therefore must emanate from people capable of self-reliance and of comprehending reality.

For while nations as well as individuals may pay lip service to "reason," their understanding is often blocked by irrationality. Freud called such blocks "resistance"—resistance which does not come from lack of information but from a lack of emotional freedom. Mass insanity results from thinking pathologically about oneself and the world. Remember the story of the proud immigrant mother who went to see her son march in the Fourth of July parade and who came home aglow, saying: "Yankel, how beautifully you marched! You were the only one in step!"

We all recognize a paranoid personality, a person who thinks that everybody is "after him," or out to "get him." Such a person inhabits a world all his own into which eventually he will withdraw. Sane people discover that there are a variety of ways of dealing with threat and danger and by considering alternatives, they create new possibilities. They persist not as means of "historic forces" but as co-creators of their history. They remain ends within themselves.

Another psychological trait in this context is the world-wide practice of "projection." One encounters this frequently in marriage counselling. Many partners succeed in being so entirely submerged in the problems of the other that they find therein justification not to face their own. This then creates the impression of the one being the embodiment of innocence and health and the other the personification of sickness. Projective thinking is manipulative thinking in which the other is used as a tool for our needs.

Americans behave this way towards communism and Communists do the same with regard to ourselves. It is seductive thinking and hard to take issue with for most persons who think projectively sound convincing. They "burn with ice" as Freud put it. They are fanatic and tend to what George Orwell called "doublethink" in his book *1984*. Opposition to the manipulation of consciousness is needed not because one fancies oneself superior but because idolization of the projective "reality" leads *linea recta* to dehumanization.

Such selective "reality" becomes apparent when we speak about "the free world" while blandly including dictators in our alliances, or when the Russians speak about "people's democracies." Projective intoxication camouflages the obvious reality that communist governments do not rule with the consent of the people. "Doublethink," as Fromm* points out, is not an innocent gimmick for confusing one's opponent. As a way of life it leads to the so-called "realism" where one's own propaganda becomes gospel. It leads to what the late C. Wright Mills called "crackpot realism"—the "tough" and "hardboiled" positions based neither upon reflection nor upon understanding.

If man is to advance beyond the misconceptions of the past, it will be essential to expose the paranoid, accusatory, mechanisms since they invite self-destructiveness. Brotherhood, seen as the workable solidarity and interaction of nations may not lead to utopian harmony but at least towards considering conflict as an asset.

Global man is a changed human being. He is not the cave dweller with a club. He can be the product of enlightenment

*Fromm. *op. cit.*

if only he learns to nourish that part of his personality which hungers for purposeful living.

INNER DESTITUTION AND HUMAN DESIGN

Let it be bluntly stated then: War is the murder of children. War is: children left alone crying on the roads of devastated cities. War is: children searching for something edible in the ashes and dust of what once were homes.

There is no international law against the killing of children. There are nature preserves for birds and animals, wrote George Bernard Shaw, but not for children . . .

Yet something deep and angry within revolts against the cavalier approach to human life. Where are the voices of the millions of children silenced while History was "marching on . . ."?

Human communities are secured by the operational approaches to social, political and human problems. Sane nations emerge not by state theories but by human functionality. But—alas—our culture is rapidly being militarized.

Greater security, it is believed, will result from more weapons. There must be—we are told—a balance of terror. What is proposed is permanent mobilization.

Perpetual mobilization however demands the psychology of warriors, it demands psychological warfare, which will frighten the potential enemy. It also demands keeping alive, in one's own population, the feeling of being threatened. Perpetual mobilization demands, in short, the stimulation of collective hostility, collective fear and the delusionary wealth of a war economy.

The average citizen is not inclined by nature to be a hero, nor is he obsessed by the desire to write history with his own blood. But if Mr. John Q. Public, who wants his job, his home, his vacation and a little bit of comfort, is to become and remain a mobilized entity in a mobilized civilization, he will have to learn to subordinate his "pedestrian" private life. This means rupture of his private life, interference with his pursuit of happiness as he sees it and the breakdown of the little pleasures he wants, a family, a boat ride, time with the children. By making the echos of war our response to the world, we perpetuate totalitarian hostility and fear. Have weapons and alliances stopped the ideological advance of bolshevism? They have not, because communism addresses itself not to the solution of military problems but to social and economic questions which find ready response in three-fourths of the underdeveloped world!

The sicknesses of the human community can never be overcome by more and bigger fears; war psychosis has never yet prevented war.

As one who did his duty in wartime under the continual threat of death, amidst the devastation of broken human bodies and the cries of the dying; as one who loves democracy, I am not driven to speak because I embrace absolute pacifism. I hate war but I have fought the enemies of democracy, fought them philosophically, ideologically and as a soldier. Yet, our future depends on finding different operational approaches.

Uprootedness in a world community beset by increased militarization and perpetual mobilization has its repercussions in the lives of individuals. Yet, we all need a sense of to what we belong, and where we are going. Rootedness is really another word for connectedness. When such connectedness is disturbed, adjustments must be made which often shake the core of a person or community.

The father raises his son and thinks: "One day I will tell him what stirred me, what moved me to go on." But the son grows up with ambitions alien to the father. In his eyes there is no recognition of what it is that the aging man is trying to express. The father must adjust to the emerging identity of his son.

That which is dear in life has always been under great pressure; tenderness is forever bound to what is grievous and desperate. What is precious to us is of necessity bound to hurt. When a death occurs we feel the outcry against the wound ripped in our flesh and yet do we know how not to waste our sorrow?

Of course, there is also the larger historical experience. Why do we always draw back into ourselves when another person wants us to enter into his deepest need? We have preached for centuries to each other, "Love thy neighbor as thyself" but the naked truth is that our neighbor is not like ourselves. What is needed is the exploration of the unlikeness in people, not the romantic quest for similarity. Partnership is not built upon likenesses but upon the quickening of the differing essence of each. An adult cannot feel as a child does, a man cannot feel like a woman. Yet we are in need of each other and ways of explaining ourselves to ourselves. By exploring the unlike qualities, that is: by work and compassion, we can avoid drawing back when confronted with the needs of another existence. Maybe, at last, as Philip Rieff says in his *The Triumph of the Therapeutic*—we can learn to ask "What will cure me?" rather than "Who will cure me?"

In the old Testament, the rebel-prophet Amos cries out, "Then I said unto the Lord, 'Lord, how long?' and He answered 'Until the cities be wasted without inhabitants and the houses with men and the land be utterly desolate.'" We do not have to wait for such emotional devastation; more immediate consolations are at hand. The misery of living is not alleviated by prognostications of disaster. In our reciprocal hungers, in the ecology of our being, as much as in our biological ecology, we find the elements for saner intercourse, saner "purposing" as William James called it.

We are threatened then not by an innate darkness, but by ignorance of what keeps our roots alive. Einstein demonstrated that the universe consists of non-simultaneous events and that one could therefore not conceive of "the end" of the cosmos. The design is one of sequence rather than of suddenness. Can we not think of human growth in the same fashion? May it not be assumed that there is, at least, an "anticipatory design"* of an interfunctioning reality for the aims and efforts of all men? Simone Weill pronounced a profound truth when she suggested that we are pulled down by the gravity of our ignorance, not because of "original sin" but because our wings are still too weak.

It has been said that life is frequently "an exercise in unreason." Yet, I do not think that it is rationality we lack so much as valid norms that make the burning of the candle worthwhile. After all, there may be a great deal to life which remains beyond comprehension and which is real to us nevertheless. Life, as such, has never appeared to me as tragic in the existential sense. Is a flower tragic because, being a flower, it will wither after a while? To be tragic one must have magnitude, said Aristotle, and to me that means simply the "magnitude" of effort. Our disappointments and heartbreak are the result of what is wanting in the relationships with those to whom we are close. Heidegger's obscure notions of being "thrown" (geworfen) into life have no tragic meaning.

I do not want to be mystical, but from what I understand of the theory of relativity and biochemistry, there is no longer any doubt that everything on this earth and in the cosmos is in a continuous process of regeneration. If that is correctly reasoned why would it be so outlandish to assume that the design of man is as much an "anticipated" model as that of the gasses which emanate from the plants and which help us breathe? We may be unconscious of it, most of the time, but we too contribute to the earth's survival. The connectedness of man is now a reasonable proposition, not some poetic daydream.

*Suggested by R. Buckminster Fuller in "Vision '65," *The American Scholar.* Spring 1966.

Human life, viewed as a narrow, never-ending trial; as a draining interlude between birth and death, invites attitudes of a provisional character only. "Provisional" means the attitude which hopes merely to "squeeze through." Life is a privileged interlude. "We are travelers between two stations," as Boris Pasternak put it. Not from outside but from within comes our replenishment. Our private world is created in the environment of our nature and that of others. It is selected, perceived and organized; it is thought about and felt according to what we have learned in life. And the roots of life can be understood not only biologically, genetically, but also in terms of moral origin. We can trace them back. The traditional teachings of our culture offer us, by and large, an image of self-defeat and distrust of the world. Yet we cannot replenish vitality with insufficient tools. Perhaps this is the underlying tragedy of the helplessness of organizations such as the United Nations. Individuals and nations not only create their own problems, they perpetuate them by regressive orientation.

How great our liberation if by embracing our inner environment we can discern the ongoing strengths rather than the short-circuits of another individual or nation!

We are not superhuman, yet we can bring about an immense relief by modifying what we think. What sense can history, monuments, books, bibles, and rituals make if they exist apart from man? What passes for our past is but a faint reproduction of what men are about for there is greatness behind the shadows played upon the screen of our foibles.

Earlier in this book I stressed Albert Camus' insistence upon man's basic innocence. It is because of this innocence (which the old and wise Erasmus called the "praise of folly") that man is able to overcome the blows of life. When an individual is vicious, that viciousness is the result of a dislocation of personality. The essence of man remains innocent.

This is an important theme also in Karl Menninger's essay on

*Men, Women and Hate.** What we blame on fate, heredity or misfortune, can usually be traced to destructive forces within. Menninger writes: "Men drink themselves to death, antagonize their friends, stumble into sickness or accidents as if they wished to suffer the failure . . . Whether one kills himself suddenly or slowly . . . the suicidal impulses . . . are psychologically the same." To Menninger, the causes lie in the thwarted capacity for innocence.

He believes that at fundamental stages of life, hostility is built into "the inner environment." Thus, the love we are taught is often little else but a way of dealing with resentment. This also applies to socially demanded gratitude. What can be more regressive than to be coerced into being grateful to people one may detest? In the same vein, marriages are frequently entered into by women who want at all cost to break with their mothers and by men who mistake sexual appetites for affection. All the exhortations of teachers, preachers, moralists, authorities and the law, that we must love one another, do not deal with the flow of inner resentment. What is intended to enforce love often stimulates exactly the opposite!

Something deeper is at stake, therefore, than what Erich Fromm called "the art of love." It is dealing frankly and honestly with what corrodes the roots of life. It is said that American Indians were terribly shocked when they saw frontier fathers whip their unruly sons. To scalp an enemy in war is one thing, but to hit a helpless child seemed incredible to the Indians. If the files of all psychiatrists, counselors and ministers could be opened, we would be aghast at the secret cruelties of men towards women, women towards men, parents towards children.

At the roots of our social violence is the profaned human personality. This is particularly apparent in stunted marital relationships. There are couples that live in relative harmony but

*Karl Menninger, *A Psychiatrist's World*, N.Y. 1959.

such marriages are possible only when men and women have learned to avoid retaliatory destructiveness. "Behind the wars of nations stand the wars between men and women," as Menninger puts it.

Whatever the ideologies, whatever the slogans, the scars of intimate battle must first be healed. Just as hostility and aggressiveness have an accumulative character, so has their opposite. A deepened concept of the "innocence" of origin can create a new security, stronger than the archaic beliefs drenched in a philosophy of suffering.

It is in that context that the perpetual mobilization of the last fifty years must be seen as surrender to a pessimism which promotes totalitarianism. By becoming part of the totalitarian infatuation with power, which demands control over the individual and by accepting the ethos of war, moral alternatives to military conflict are gradually negated. Yet democracies dare not cede the initiative to dictatorships and need to come forward with imaginative efforts of inclusion to help lessen the anxieties which trigger military infantilism. Pronounced hostility is always a symptom, never a cause. So also, the wars within us, which breed resentment against culture, can only be overcome by the coordinated strength of those who will be neither "victim nor executioner." The innocent in the world community must at last become available, willing to risk as much as the destroyers. They must get beyond the nineteenth century materialism and the cult of objectivity in order to recover an inner environment which will reject nothing in life, nothing of life.

We must overcome what Merton called the "inward destitution" by nurturing a matrix beyond the merely temporary.

If the innocent learn this, they can become sanctuaries in the world, gripped by the strength and practice of their ideals. The world needs not victims but men of innocence.

CHAPTER 5

THE CONSENT TO LIVE

Life experience does not of necessity yield self-perception. The haunting realities of existence may occupy us so entirely that a larger perspective remains unattainable. Immediate pressures, immediate responses required by life-situations demand so much of our strength that it becomes difficult to sustain a focus. Yet personal confidence is only discovered by involvement with the life-giving tensions of confrontation which, at the most critical moments, may regenerate our recuperative powers.

A balanced life contains a sense of permanence and is the fruit of existence within the context of lasting human relationships. The more balanced person deals with discouragement, reverses, and sorrows by being neither isolated nor overcome by self-pity. He distills a certain continuity of confidence from his dealing with these perplexities, and thereby overcomes the temptation of fatalism.

Apathy is one of our great detractors. It suggests that "plusque ça change, plusque ça reste la même chose." It is the product of how we see ourselves and what we expect of ourselves. Complacency suggests that, finally, blind fate tips the scales and that self-destructiveness will always dominate the life-loving tendencies. Kochendoerfer called this the "captive audience" psychology.

Complacency is broken by exploring alternatives and renewal of private perspectives. Thoreau's comment to a cynical visitor still holds true: "I never yet knew the sun to be knocked down and rolled through a mud-puddle; he comes out honor bright each time from behind every storm. Let us take sides with the sun." Some life experiences entail being rolled through mud-puddles but only excessive pessimism would conclude that we must remain there.

The concept of time plays an important part in developing a perspective. We are painstakingly aware of the progress of time, but only faintly of the moments of change. This limited sense of time makes it particularly hard to perceive more fundamental evolution. Our strength is expended on the obvious while crucial transformation may pass us by.

In 1964, an entire mountain was created by an underwater volcano near Iceland. We think of mountains as permanent but it needs to be realized that they too change. In the course of billions of years, the cosmos expands or shrinks; some stellar systems are born and others die out. Some change is slow and some rapid. But nothing is permanent.

So do we change. It is true that we are the same as we were last year, but we are not "the same." We have changed. Some things that seemed utterly desirable just a few years ago are not so today. Some expectations we had were modified either by circumstances or by our own shifting view of life. When I was in the West Indian island of Curaçao a few years ago, I was told that the island had been formed by billions upon billions of little shell-fish, one layer upon the other had built up. The shell itself had remained the same although the life within the shell was no longer there.

Life is motion. Through it courses one solid streak: endurance. Within the range of evolution and recurrence one thing is certain: the enduring regeneration of life in all of its forms. Man, as Buckminster Fuller wrote somewhere, has for two million years been on a self-contained space-ship.

In our own body we continue elements of earlier existence of which we have no conscious memory. What influence then can a single human being have upon his own life direction?

The determining factor is that human beings can interfere in that silent succession by interaction with others and with nature. Our experience depends both upon what happens around us and on what we make happen. We are not born merely to die. We bring something of an intervening substance to what happens and in so doing, we are free in a sense that the shellfish was not. Man adds something to evolution, or as Julian Huxley put it, "Man is evolution become conscious of itself." Yet, while no existence is identical there remain deepseated superstitions concerning the supposedly cyclical nature of reality.

It is assumed that every twenty to twenty-five years a major war will be waged. A new generation has grown up, one that did not directly experience the previous slaughter. Yet, man can choose whether or not to intercept the persistency of such patterns.

Musicologists tell that the German composer Gustav Mahler had a superstition about the number of symphonies he produced. Since Beethoven and Bruckner both had died after having composed nine symphonies, Mahler changed the title of his Ninth to: "Das Lied Von der Erde." (He died of heart failure after completing two movements of his Tenth Symphony.)

We are aware of the brevity of our life and how swiftly we pass through it and yet there is also one crucial factor: that we are able, to a certain degree, to transform our existence. Growth depends on the degree of interception and its direction.

While physical growth occurs, mental growth depends upon

the transaction of emotion between people. Our concept of *the* universe may be an abstraction but each human person is a tangible, emotional experience. The deeper we probe our unity with all creative and re-creative forces, the more we learn to understand what caring means. We are in fact directed towards each other. What we expect of ourselves, in transaction with others, is therefore crucial to what will happen to us. An example of the confusion about this was demonstrated when the Austrian government at last apprehended the police officer who arrested young Anne Frank and sent her to her death in Bergen Belsen in 1944. After the former Gestapo-man was arrested, his wife told a Dutch newspaperman: "I don't know why they don't leave my Karl in peace. The Frank family was a family like thousands of others. Who could have known that Anne Frank would become famous?"

To this woman there was no moral perception involved. Her husband had done his job: arresting Dutch children. Her range of perception was limited by a warped universe of collective non-conscience. She could only perceive her husband's "bad luck" in being caught and exclaim: "Why don't they leave my Karl alone . . .?" (Actually Karl was released soon afterwards!)

Maybe the tensions of choice are too great and apathy is a defense mechanism. In Biblical times a man could say, "I will lift up mine eyes unto the hills from whence cometh my strength." We cannot truthfully affirm that. Strength has to be constructed in ourselves; we need not be victims of life. We can walk through anguish and come out with hope. But to attain such affirmation, we have to substitute the confirmation of alternatives for helplessness because renewal is possible only out of life's depths.

Therefore, Man first has to know who he is and such knowledge must be reconciled with the complexity of what he is in an existential sense. Knowledge separated from life makes possible "objective" attitudes by which nations can prepare death

in spotless laboratories with a clear conscience. No decent society emerges without decent men.

We have acquired greatly expanded knowledge about ourselves and the processes of life, but we are simultaneously at
the border of insanity. It is possible to have immense psychological and sociological knowledge about human beings without understanding them, without meaningful perception. Sane
life depends on expansion of knowledge matched by relatedness. The question is not just what happens, but what we bring
to what is happening. Many a scoundrel is, after all, disguised
as an apostle. Relationships entered into in bad faith lead to
isolation and harm. All the exclamations of how well one meant
really amount to very little. To be sound, human relationships
must create reciprocity in perception as well as in aspiration.
We will see that a person who has achieved sound expectations
of himself does not need to browbeat others. Neither does the
person of balanced expectations need to repeatedly apologize
for himself. He does not need to say continually how sorry he
is for his mistakes or for whatever he failed to do or say. A person with a balanced perspective of himself and his fellowmen
seeks to express gratitude and appreciation. We can measure
our development towards such balance of expectation by the
way in which we learn to control our behavior. This simply
means: "I will try to do better next time . . ." We will do better
when we get another opportunity. If we have failed, we will
try some more, because we know that we are human. So also,
if we cannot see eye-to-eye with somebody else, we will use our
self-perception and expectation to soften disagreement. We will
make it clear that we disagree, but in such a way as to leave
the other in one piece. We will not "take him apart" or make
him look like a fool. We will act in such a way as to exercise our
ability for self-control and thereby strengthen the self-respect
of the other.

This is what reciprocity means. We can help the world become more of a whole place by the restraint of reciprocity; by insisting on seeing ourselves and the other as an instrument for making both of us, if possible, a bit happier. I would consider this an essential tenet: never to exploit any human being emotionally or physically, even if truthful relationships may sometimes involve pain. What we are and what we do is inseparably one. If what we do is indecent, no talk can make it decent. If what we do is destructive, no proclamations about "human dignity" will change the destructive effect. What we do and what we are belong together. Man's reality is, of course, ambiguous. Our ambitions can lead us to great promise as well as to great disaster. We are, therefore, neither good nor evil. But surely our choices, whatever the ambiguous grounds, offer us some kind of control. We can know which side of the scales we will help to tip, the scale of trust and love, or the scale of violence.

Therefore, the person of sound expectations accepts his existence as a becoming and attempts to leave something of his presence behind. A life of reciprocity helps to achieve inner familiarity with others and thereby lessens the fear of the chasm of death. Any worthwhile life philosophy must prepare us for death while leaving the love for life intact.

There is a beautiful parable on this subject. A gardener was at work in his employer's rose garden when he suddenly spied Death across the way, standing there, smiling, as he watched the man work. The gardener, deeply shocked, ran into the house and told his employer that he had seen Death and must flee. He went as quickly as he could to a busy city. Surely among the hundreds of thousands in this metropolis, Death would not find him. But as he turned the corner of a street, there stood Death who smiled at him again and gestured for him to come. The man said, "Why did you have to come to the rose garden where I was happily engaged in my work, and why did you follow me here?" Death answered, "Yes, that was a strange coincidence in the rose garden, wasn't it? As a matter of fact, I was on my way to meet you here, tonight, in the City!"

In the brevity of existence is our solidarity; the perception of its nature can help us to know, as well as to understand. Death always creates an intermission, a moment when something hopeful may break through in people. Suffering challenges us profoundly if we have identified with it. Alas, the opposite is possible too.

It was reported that the typists in the police barracks in Capetown, South Africa, protested one day to the Police Commissioner that beatings administered to Negro prisoners provoked such agonizing cries of the victims that it was impossible for the girls to concentrate on their typing! One employee said, "I sympathize with the police but I wish we didn't have to listen to it." The Commissioner was greatly impressed and ordered henceforth the beatings to take place only in the basement where nobody could hear the cries of the prisoners.*

Much of traditional morality is like the typists' protest. It tries to muffle the sound of the beatings in this world. Yet, an ethic that does not spur men and women on to better lives might as well be discarded. This is why I place practical ethics above theology.

We must expect as much of each other as we do of ourselves. For however stunted it may be, each one possesses the potential for deeper sensitivity. I see in this assumption the conditional validity of a humanist hope.

We can overcome inner destitution by seeing whatever we are capable of doing in the light of the possible. Life in its ongoing unity embodies, in all its various forms and moments, the capacity for love. The expression of that embodiment may be the heart of our capacity to endure. Yet, Man's image is often grotesquely distorted. Incredible cruelty as exemplified by the bombings and lynchings in recent years in Birmingham, Ala-

*As told to Ronald Gittelson in *Man's Best Hope.*

bama and Meridian, Mississippi reveals this distortion in all its nakedness. We are surrounded by hateful voices. At the same time, our organs for sensitive response are often inadequate to register the outcries for help of the thousands trampled upon.

A queer form of anger was experienced by two Americans visiting a new African Republic. One of the men spoke native Swahili. Proudly taken on a guided tour by a government official, he stopped to listen to a sweet rhythmic melody some villagers were singing as they worked in the fields. When he came closer and could understand what was being sung, he found that what had seemed a peaceful work song was in fact a chant of outrage. The villagers were singing:

> Jesus Christ, do I hate the white man
>   from the pit of my stomach
>   to the tip of my tongue
> Jesus Christ, do I hate the white man!

Perhaps as we grope for understanding of ourselves, we should not only consider literature, the arts, science, religion, psychology, but also what brews in the depths of doubt and fear. Those emotions are no less authentic than the more complex cultural reality.

WHAT IS NEEDED FOR OUR DAYS?

Ever since the Renaissance, Western civilization has stressed the unique value of the individual. Out of that philosophy of individuation were born the great scientific thoughts that tore off the mask of theological and metaphysical obfuscation. But this very development led to a technology which herded modern man back into the collective consciousness from which, after the Middle Ages, he had just escaped.

A medieval soldier, sword in hand, a scarf of his beloved lady around his neck, could seek out his opponent in a gallant contest. The modern warrior pushes buttons that will deliver death to an enemy he has never seen. How true Don Quixote's lament about "this cursed age of artillery . . ."

For hundreds of years a child would be sent to the fields to cut some cabbage, dig some potatoes, or milk a cow. The mother would prepare the family meal in the presence of the family. Today, the mother thaws out frozen meats and vegetables. Or again, the child instead of being served at home, may put a coin in a slot in an automat and be served by a mechanical source of plenty while the mother is still performing her labor at a place distant from home.

The tendency then is toward loss of close relationships. Hand in hand with this go the socio-political conformist trends that make it possible for many—as Meerloo points out—to experience only by proxy; to love by proxy, and to be easily manipulated. "We are", Sir Isaac Newton said, "as children playing on the beaches, building our unstable castles of sand while the great ocean of truth is right before our eyes."

The optimism of the Enlightenment has been replaced by a deepseated philosophical and psychological pessimism. At the heart of this is the loss of a sense of unity, for the family as well as for the world. Scepticism as to the validity of any unifying purposes permeates the great urban masses of our epoch. In its wake follows a confusion of life values which is in part exploited commercially in order to stimulate and overstimulate our appetite for commodities. Actually this stimulation has become a prerequisite for the survival of the national entity. National pride and cohesion are tied up with productivity and ever-expanding absorption of commodities. To survive as an economically viable community, Man, in the modern technology must forever be a happy producer and consumer of things.

It was Toynbee, I think, who remarked that the soldier of the Roman Legions was not outstanding militarily but he was sustained by a tremendous pride and confidence in the virtues and invincibility of the Roman Empire. His strength came from convictions of the society he felt he represented. But what convictions are central enough for our time?

No community can persist on the basis of institutionalized absence of private direction. If anything, the growing suicide rate among us—even of children—should be a clear indication of an increase of social aimlessness.

This is not a philosophical statement but reflects a reality. Many lives are warped because of lack of significant communication. Obviously, communication depends upon an *a priori* acceptance of the worthwhileness of the other. Without this assumption there is only frustrated monologue. Think of the thousands of babies in shelters who remain in hospitals not to be cured but because there is no one to call "father" or "mother"; children whose mentality is steadily undermined and who become victims of a lovelessness so great, a human distortion so painful, that it is almost inconceivable.

Is the task hopeless then? Can any culture provide sustaining aims that will lessen such suffering? How persistent can be the effort of even the best among us?

Two world wars have made us generations filled with bitter tears. Still, neither was Man steeped in gentility in other epochs nor did earlier faith come more easily. It also was maintained with a grim "and still", and was held onto despite disastrous madness.

What specific effort is needed for our days? One central need stands out: to speed up social evolution so that within the next ten years we can cope with the tremendous unleashing of economic and political power all over the world. Whether from India or Venezuela, England, Nigeria, France or Germany, this one message is conveyed: democratic civilization at its best must adapt itself to a new kind of world structure. Impatient millions want equity now—social planning now. Newly emerged nations are in urgent need of a philosophical base.

They are groping for workable patterns of values which are not tied to stunting ideologies, but rather concerned with human fulfillment. There is a focus slowly but surely moving in the direction of social revolution. As yet it is a hesitating, uncertain focus, but it scans the horizon for a valid outlook and for hope. It seeks functional solutions which will enhance national cohesion for entities which are as yet without unifying identity. A practical ethic of communal mutuality, not a "Western" or "Eastern" blueprint, is needed.

Take specifically the question of population planning. The leaders of India do not have time to help the Roman Catholic Church outgrow its senseless and medieval attitude towards family planning. Nor do they have the patience to do so. They have to tackle a socio-ethical problem right now and they are going to do it on a humanist basis. The same applies to the situation in parts of South America. Eager and socially aroused new leadership has neither patience nor time to wait until the United States Senate has understood the difference between social democracy and communism. We live in a time of gigantic social change and the question is only whether we will be involved in the acceleration of the social evolution or stay behind.

A central issue is, therefore: "Can we be sure of an upward social evolution?" This question was exhaustively discussed by Dr. Gerald Wendt,* a high functionary with UNESCO. Wendt drew the comparison between biological epi-organisms and social epi-organisms.

Epi-organisms are those systems of organization in nature by which smaller organisms fulfill their role in the make-up of larger ones. Thus protons and electrons are organized into atomic structures, atoms into molecules, molecules into crystals, or cells, in the case of living things. Each epi-organism has its existence which is superimposed upon its constituent organ-

*Gerald Wendt, *Prospects for our Changing Culture*, N.Y. 1963.

isms. As long as the epi-organisms are adapted to their environment and evolve, they will flourish. When they stop doing so, they perish. Is it possible to imagine the same process concerning social organisms? How long did Hitler's 1000-year Reich last? Twelve years! How long the Holy Roman Empire, or the Czars or the modern institutions of human slavery? How long will Christianity last, how long the U.S.S.R., how long the Roman Catholic Church, how long democracy? Could not the answer be: as long as they adapt themselves to and play a role in the acceleration of social evolution? For there is social "mutation" as well as biological mutation.* It has been Julian Huxley's main thesis that we can control and speed up social and human evolution. In that context he called for a new religion which must practice "the art of spiritual health". There is a desperate need for facilitating "mutations" of a social character, whether in regard to world mental health, the planning and distribution of food or the creation of a decent economic equity. Human fate is not a mysterious or metaphysical affair. It is determined by what we decide.

There is, however, one peculiar problem involved. When a scientist has developed a new method proven by research, his work is accepted immediately all over the world. Not so with social mutations. Social innovations are usually resisted; more often than not their spokesmen hanged, villified or ignored. Whatever upsets that which is established is felt to be suspect and is treated as such. Obvious lack of social maturity stagnates adults everywhere in life-long patterns of inertia. The resistance to social evolution is the result of emotional backwardness in social and political leadership. Everywhere we run into fixations of character that upset any forward movement and thus many a debate whether in Congress or in a learned society is,

---

*Mutation is obviously not synonymous with "betterment." Modern biochemistry seems to suggest that biological mutation can be "directed" and controlled. Could not the same apply to social mutation?

in fact, the debate of emotional adolescents. Inertia can be a fatal reason why new epi-organisms are not recognized and no evolution takes place in crucial areas of human endeavor. Think for example of the resistance in the United States to signing the treaty against genocide, the idiocy of talking about water fluoridation as a "Communist plot", or of the TVA as "creeping socialism"! What all that means is resistance against coming to terms with reality.

Just as the neurotic adult continues to deal with life problems in an infantile way, so nations can be emotionally immature. Very often reluctance to "grow up" is the result of unresolved inner conflict. I know a man in his early fifties who still tries to get his way by temper tantrums, browbeating people who work with him, bawling out his children, spreading malicious gossip about everybody he dislikes. He is, in fact, still playing the role of the "nasty kid on the block" and enjoying every minute of it! His anger and regression, he has found out, terrorize others into lethargy!

Others, again, express their immaturity by direct aggression, or by living in fantasies of grandeur, discrediting everyone else as "stupid" or dishonest. If we can learn to understand the difference between psychological and chronological ages for individuals, we can also learn to enlarge our social intelligence in order to accelerate the societal structure. The obstacles to social development are no different from those which block individuals. If there is one absolute prerequisite for modern man, it is to find out and to act upon the knowledge of what stimulates sane life. Progress is determined by comprehension, motivation, and health and it requires outgrowing what we experience as harmful for mental growth.

To grow up as a culture, to grow up as an individual is to learn how to use one's powers, how to realize one's immediate influence in the lives of others. Only by an integration of knowledge and rejection of social regression can we find the hope that comes with life affirmation. The individual's capacity for maturation is fatefully intertwined with the world he creates.

One of the crucial ideas of social anthropology therefore is that sound societies nurture the influence for wholeness which individuals can stimulate in one another. There is a radiation of our essence in the lives we touch. John Dewey was often reproached for supposedly having taught that we "learn by doing". He corrected that misconception repeatedly, saying that "we learn the right thing by doing right, and the wrong thing by doing wrong." It is not just any experience that counts, but only those motivated for some betterment of quality in relationships.

Take as an example the relationship to aged parents. Will it just be charity? Will it be irritation, and the projection of anxiety? Will it be grim duty extracted by the Law, or will it be the older and younger generations nurturing each other's influence? Do we not need each other? Why should age be a calamity? Since we are never out of the influence of the other and are, in fact, decisively determined genetically and socially by other lives, why not devise social integration of the generations?

The "good" life is one in which such influences are stimulated by a process of concern. If this assumption is a religious one, I accept it, for its aim can be nurtured without dependence on anything outside of man. What people believe or do not believe is not very important; these are private choices. But a dynamic ideal for living is more valid than any doctrinal exhortation. We can transmute pain and suffering by deliberate effort for one's faith, or lack of it, may save, as it may break, another person's life.

I was told by an eyewitness about racial clashes in Alabama and about the way some State troopers treated the young Negroes. One boy, Lester Cobb, a student at Meadville Theological School, learned that a woman had been wounded and was greatly in need of medicine. He ran out of the crowd to get help. When he rushed back to where the woman was, he found his path blocked by a cordon of state officers. One of them grabbed his hand and, ordering him to close his eyes, put the barrel of his gun against Lester Cobb's right eye and told him he would shoot if he did not "disappear within 10 seconds."

The excitement was such that Cobb could expect an "accident" to happen and so he talked to the trooper, begging him to let him through with the medicine. He knew that if he ran away, he might be shot in the back. Cobb was willing to sacrifice himself for the cause of human rights, but not to die foolishly. All this flashed through his mind. Then he walked slowly backwards, fearful that at any moment he might be shot . . . and suddenly, out of nowhere, two older Negro women, brooms in their hands, moved in between him and the troopers. There was no dirt on the street but they began to sweep furiously, forming a shield around the young man. This is how he got away with his life! What we do actualizes our influence in the lives of others, not what we profess! In Dante's *Divina Comedia* he speaks to one of his confessors in Purgatory and concludes by saying, "My converse with thee lifted me up until I was more than myself." Were not these women "more" than themselves? Without their particular quality our world would be surrendered to the brutes.

I propose that we link our vision of the future to that which can be observed and therefore at least in part, controlled. There is a great deal which will remain beyond our control: illness, natural catastrophe, death. But our choices, the way in which we influence other lives and thereby direct our own, these are fundamental projections well within our grasp.

Deep pessimism can be overcome by an increase in individual commitment over against conformism and collectivism.

A humanist vision is therefore a concrete vision of Man in the turmoil of emotional effort. Its essence is the activation of unifying attainable purpose, not the divisiveness of ideology or creed. Vision can be related to concrete effort.

There is in human beings something to be revealed, to be cultivated, not because of a sentimental involvement with "all men" but because we can affirm with Emerson that every man is a "divinity in disguise." Hostility and fanaticism are merely Man's disguises.

THE SUSTENANCE OF LOVE REKINDLED

The essence of love is that, while it may be obscured and almost deadened, it can also be stirred from its arrest, by the simplicity of a word or a glimpse of hope. Yet, frequently, love remains a distant goal and is lost in the play between light and shadow. When it is rekindled, when we comprehend the need of another human being, the vague, the wavering, regain focus; the incomprehensible becomes clear. When we love there is a concise reality to our hungers and our pains; to endure life has become to endure-for-a-reason. We recapture a personal center by which we can acknowledge the potential of ourselves and others in a personal, direct way. This makes it possible to accept the realization that there is an elusiveness to all human experience and that all we have discovered, nurtured and loved, may be taken from us. Love enables us to live on when life is ruptured, it invokes a strength which remains even when one whom we love has died. No one escapes the shattering of what we hold most dear.

To "bless" the other for his or her love, as Elizabeth Browning put it, and at the same time to learn how to renounce that love, if necessary, is that not the core of what experience should prepare us for? These depths of emotion have to be tasted and finally suffered. And still, even love has a twin component: doubt and sometimes hostility.

Popular psychology has propagated the idea that doubt and

hostility can be overcome by positive feelings of love. It is not that simple. As the dismal failure of Christianity's main dynamic concerning love has shown, love as doctrine is not the solution to hostility. Love is the basis of all social ethics and therefore its libidinous element must not be denied. Love is neither esoteric, nor impersonal nor external. It is determined by the encounter of living souls in the process of self-actualization.

I would call love hope transposed but hope not as a lofty abstraction or a "cosmic feeling". For the world we perceive hangs together because of us, and when it comes apart, it is because something in specific persons has come apart. Hope is what can be discovered even though we are linked to all the external realities—our physical makeup, our appetites, our bearing up under all things inescapable and the reality of our death.

Hope as love transposed is the quality by which we find freedom for action while not denying our fundamental, natural confinement. This is what human beings are given to do. As with love, so also with hope: if we do not pursue it in emotional freedom, we are confused by appearances. Some people will say: "I don't see it, it doesn't make sense! One is hopeful when things go one's way; one loves when fulfilled!" But is this true?

I remember a man in an important civic group who had had one specific expectation when he joined the group. Since he was a man of means, he made generous contributions to the work. But one day when he felt that things were not going the way he thought they should, he withdrew his support. Because this act endangered much of the work, a trustee was asked to talk with him and argued that the sudden lack of support would jeopardize all the work that had gone before, but to no avail. The man frankly said that he had meant his retraction of support as a punitive step. He once had had a vision but the vision was gone, and now, symbolically, he tried to destroy what he had wanted to love completely. His suffering and hostility were the result of an upset of the balance between self-love and self-rejection. Every facet of a man's being, all the different kinds of love (including rejection) enter into every choice. How many persons attain sufficient maturity for love as life-renewal whatever the disappointments? Nevertheless, sound personal ambition is tied to both love and hope, and thereby linked to all human aspiration. This does not refer to generalized pieties such as "love of humanity" but rather to the tangible communion between people, the participation in one another's life as Buber's "I-Thou" rather than "I-It" relationship. There is nothing abstract about love, even though sometimes only a symbol, a sigh, may make it part of ourselves again.

Take a small object owned by someone who died. A cup, a book, a letter, even a signature becomes a symbol for a particular quality to be rekindled. "I don't understand you", the cynic exclaims, "you are talking about spirits!" But we, who loved and hoped with the person now dead, we know the object's reality for it is a bridge from despair to courage. A loving attitude is not an escape hatch from realities; it is a pathway back to ourselves. We may be confined, but we are not imprisoned by the fact that we must die. Hope is not for the hereafter but for significance now. The tragic, the doubts, are as real as the affirmations. What is essential is that we need to avoid being crushed. Hope should not be thought of as akin to wishful thinking; quite on the contrary, hope can be used for evaluating past and present. We do our share in preparing the future which we will not live to see. Therefore, nurtured love makes us recipients of deepened experience. While it is true that certain things remain uniform for all—we are born, we work, we love, we die—it is nevertheless true that love breaks in upon the uniformity of destiny. By our loves, by our reasoned hopes, we contradict the heavy orthodoxy of whatever we must accept as "given" in the human situation. Someone compared this with a mountain stream: it assumes a new character when it crashes against rocks, as it carves out a new bed. What ran down as a stream of uniform character is broken up in many contrary whirlpools. By losing the fear of contrary aims within, it is possible to see those around us—those also tested—not as soldiers in mortal battle, but as co-explorers who found the present to be what the present is—neither good nor evil but simply to be engaged. To participate in this "immense journey" means to discover purpose. Man is greater than his fate, because he can love and because he can harbor reasonable hopes. That is the urgent message the generations bequeath each other. The uniformity of our ultimate destiny is far less interesting than the many variations which individual lives create. Those who went before expressed something to be deciphered and across centuries of silence, an ambition is handed on. It may not be much to shout about, nor is it much to weep about either; it is just ours, for today.

So love and hope intensify the consciousness about ourselves and even illiterate men and women become poets when they love. Between them they kindle a consciousness that lifts them beyond their immediacy. They cease being prisoners and emerge as distinct Selves. Sexual fulfillment is part of this process, as an added source of tender vitality. At the core of love and any love-act, is a mental activation and motivation. It is not true that we "fall in love", that we are "caught" off-guard and passively "swept off our feet". When we love, the activated mind becomes a giving mind, for a heightened awareness spreads a specific joy. When we give, we are replenished because we are entrusted with the precious reality of another soul.

The man referred to earlier who had to become punitive towards what he once loved, was not a man filled with joy. When he gave, he received; when he withheld, he was lonely and starved. This is the mystery of love and obligation, even in nature. The mother who nurses her child is not depleted but builds emotional and biological replenishment.

Much is distorted in this connection in our culture. Delusions of masculinity are responsible for the idiotic pedestal on which woman was placed in the romantic past, or for virginity fantasies, holy or otherwise. Add to that the modern commercialization of the "polarity" between man and woman. There is so much sickening artificiality and perversion of plain, natural, human identity. It is often frightening to consider how many young people are thus pre-conditioned for unhappiness and love-starved existences. Twenty-five percent of our marriages end in divorce. Immoral alimony rulings distort both men and women who once loved each other. Is it not time to realize the cause of so much misery? The damage goes deeply and has grave consequences for civilization as a whole. We teach our children to say "I", not "we", when they seek a partner. The giving capacity of love is passed over for a competitive sensuality; that which should be desired becomes merely tantalizing; the natural hunger for giving, a suspicious calculation, often carried on, automatically, into marriage. The polarization between men and women can easily become a separateness from all of life; the woman feeling that she is the brunt of all family burdens; the man frustrated in his socio-economic ambitions and thus feeling less than a man. These prototypes are not natural, they are determined by the culture.

Instead of guiding children towards love as encounter: love as that which is bestowed both by him who loves and by the beloved; instead of preparing children for that meeting in depth which becomes possible because of the humble awe and hesitation with which another life bestirs ours; instead of all that which can liberate a profoundest knowledge of life, we condition our young to see the pursuit of love as one among many pursuits. We do not teach children that the essence of love is the intense discovery beyond what we can "have and hold". We do not teach them that by the most unique unfolding of ourselves as we speak our love to another, we also place ourselves in harmony with the generations. We do not teach them that by such loving mutuality we merge ourselves with whomever shares with us the essence of our joining, as partners of a universal reality.

Yet, by not conveying to our young this substance of love, we lock away their best selves and condemn them to a narrowing of their hearts, a doling out of their feelings, instead of a celebration of their inner abundance.

How shall they discover, amidst the shallow sensualism and the possessive rationalizations of our culture, that by loving another human being they may enter into communion with that shelteredness surrounding all of existence? All those in the fields of social work or mental health are able to testify about the numerous cases of people merely "wanting" each other, instead of wanting to be entrusted by the other. This is mistaking the transitory for what is permanent in principle and leads to an uncertainty of self-respect which makes respect for the other almost impossible. Sexual union by itself, while often confused with "freedom", leaves men and women strangers, as far apart as continents. Sometimes it makes them ashamed of each other, hostile and feeling consequently that they are only a means, never an end. In the socio-political realm this is what has been the undoing of all slave societies. When the masters have lost their recognition of a common fate with the slaves, social mutuality becomes impossible and both the exploited and the exploiter are distorted by inner poverty. It is happening today in South Africa, as well as in quite a few parts of our South. It is what is behind the massacres of our time. Hate and death are the result of life unloved and therefore unlived. The concept of mankind as a communion of trust is not merely symbolic.

Therefore, as Erich Fromm suggests, to love someone is a

decision, a judgment, a promise. What then is the promise men and women, groups and nations can rekindle in themselves? It is this above all: that for which we activate our being, in its essential passion, is that which we can love.

When we see another primarily as the object for our needs, yes, even when we honestly want to help another, we may still remain outside of any significant meeting in depth with that person. Love, in that case, atrophies. Of course we all harbor both tendencies, the one that is willing to risk the more completing entrustment and the other, which retreats from such encounter. The yearning to "belong" and the yearning to withdraw. The question is what in the long run will dominate as life attitudes since obviously we cannot be involved in depth with everyone we meet. There is no doubt that a limited perspective of the kind of love in which we forget that we need to live in the emergence of the other's recognition of us, deprives us of a much needed source of strength. Extreme self-love, which seeks to use the other—sometimes out of one's honest needs—is not infrequently based upon self-doubt or self-rejection. For example, the perfectionistic expectations of one's partner or fellowman in general may be the result of a deadened capacity for self-respect and as a result our moral progress remains suspended.

What I have tried to stress is that happiness and fulfillment must be rooted in a desire to care for that aspect of the other which concerns his being rather than his needs. For example, an overbearing mother can drown her child in "loving" hostility because her child remains a means, a vehicle, for her own needs. This applies equally to the father who impresses rigid authority or ambition upon his son. In such cases, what appears to be deep concern is a camouflaged lack of a capacity to love the essence of the other. The collectivist "love" for the citizen in a totalitarian state is of the same kind, demanding and deadly.

The essence of love is that in it can reside the continuation

as well as—in the case of its distortion—the repudiation of all
that makes life worth living. We give because of the joy of
bringing something to life in the other. Suffering occurs when
we are deprived of that joy and have to fight muteness in
ourselves. Abstractions, philosophical or mystical, are of little
help in alleviating such suffering. I can find no substantial
sustenance in vague projections outside of myself. I can have
faith in the potentialities of others when I have observed and
experienced those potentialities in down-to-earth living. This
is what is meant by "reactivating" or rekindling love. It is the
weakness of the Father-oriented religions that they stress
power, and faith in power. But power is not the crucial question. Stronger and more potent is the courage to activate love
as obligated giving which brings something to life. In existentialist terms: faith in the unawakened makes love possible.

Erich Fromm in *The Art of Love* puts it succinctly: "Love
is an act of faith and whoever is of little faith is also of
little love."

My hope is that a rebirth beyond the nihilism of our age is
possible. It is true that we are going through much darkness.
But there is no denying that both in Western and Eastern
civilization many are yearning for dedication beyond the illusionary facets of Man's emotional infancy. Psychological warfare, as Meerloo has shown in *The Rape of the Mind* is a
powerful, political manipulation by the State, to prevent Man's
hunger for self-disclosure.

When love is reclaimed in us we may seem to be the same
person, and in a sense, of course, we are. But we have also
become more ourselves than we ever were before. That applies
to nations as well as to individuals. And as a species we have
only begun to exist. As Thomas Merton wrote in his *Seeds of
Contemplation,* when we love and free that inner necessity,

> ". . . All that went before was a fumbling preparation . . . the
> doors fly open into an infinite freedom . . . there is now the

fullness of liberty . . . these depths in the midst of you . . . form a citadel."

It is this "citadel" that matters, not a passive "peace of mind". These are its ingredients: activation of the inner life, commitment to the unawakened in others, freedom towards ourselves and, therefore, a universal human partnership.

THE STRUGGLE FOR SELF-RESPECT

We live in a time of exaggerations. Proportioned judgments on questions of life and death are frequently reduced to catchphrases, meant to frighten or to lull one to sleep. Political candidates suggest that one must choose between war or surrender, prosperity or depression, youth or experience. But such polarizations are alien to reality. The tensions we experience have created philosophies that either look gloomily upon Man as wholly insignificant or Man as the scientific manipulator of all things. We seem to stumble between the wonderful people we are supposed to be and the lamentations about what we so glaringly are not.

Colin Wilson, in *The Stature of Man*, rejects such laments and instead decries those who habitually exaggerate our conditions without offering alternatives. What kind of physician is he who freely offers a diagnosis but attempts no cure?

If this were where Wilson had stopped, one could well agree with his indictment. But he then proceeds to prescribe a "new existentialism", by which individuals will be so strongly "innerdirected" that they can afford to become "outer-directed", a modern, messianistic expectation that Man will be able to be God again. What Wilson and today's neo-orthodoxists forget is that those who are supposedly alienated do not therefore become insignificant or meaningless. The problematic also goes into the making of Man. There is no need to write off any one section of consciousness.

A more helpful way to reflect on the life of common people, their ambivalences, frustrations, and their struggle for self-respect was offered in the 'twenties and 'thirties by the pariah-hero portrayed by Chaplin. What he meant to his audiences was stressed in a study by Prof. Hannah Arendt in *The Reconstructionist*.* It is her thesis that Chaplin's popularity did not wane because of his left-wing leanings, but because people stopped seeking release from their frustrations in levity and lost the capacity to find relief by laughing at themselves. Today we do not want to identify ourselves with the powerless little man but rather with the adequate, "adjusted" person. Chaplin never tried to be a superman. He portrayed a character fundamentally at odds with the world in a thousand ways and long before the words "displaced persons" meant anything, he was a man without a passport . . . Consequently, millions all over the world could identify with him and love him.

He aroused sympathy because when he landed in incredible situations it was the way all "little" men everywhere always became entangled. Chaplin was a tramp who did not try to appear virtuous. He and his heroes were full of little failings and frustrations. He always ran afoul of the law. One could see that his punishment was out of all proportion to his trivial trespasses. He was often caught for things he had not done, although most of the time he managed to get out of the clutches of the law. Basically, he was an innocent man. He showed that there is a huge discrepancy concerning the price common people pay for their few happinesses. Justice is always out of focus for the weak. Millions could recognize their own situation, their fears and their familiarity with danger, for they too were pressured beyond words and had learned to look upon life with irony. What people also understood was that if one is small, one may get hit hard but one may have a chance to hide somewhere, in a hole, or in a garbage can where "they" cannot get

*Published by Society for Advancement of Judaism, N.Y. (May 1960).

at one. The unobtrusive citizen must neither excite the heroic statesmen who are making history, nor policemen with delusions of grandeur! The unobtrusive citizen has enough trouble just living and surviving.

Chaplin, as Franz Kafka, portrayed man in incredible situations. Mr. K., in Kafka's *The Trial*, much as Chaplin, does not understand how all this can be happening to him. He is accused and ultimately condemned without ever knowing what wrong he supposedly committed. He is under indictment simply because he is alive and so his days are full of inexplicable dangers from which we know that he will not be able to extricate himself. It is as if his sense of Self and self-respect are continually destroyed and the reader, or the audience in Chaplin's case, knows that he too is caught by contradictions and fate. It is all simultaneously logical and mad. Perhaps there is no more for Man to hope for and yet by the common decencies of living and by our work we overcome within ourselves the helpless despair of that madness. It is too easy to rest our case with either declarations of love or despair.

When we outgrow the sense of the uselessness of effort we attain at least the liberty to continue trying, even though defeat may not be prevented. That effort is more trustworthy than the assurances of harmony.

Our struggle for self-respect demands that we wrestle with our ambivalences. The contrasts in our reality have not been our undoing. Their manifestations, an inner antimony, were already recognized in ancient Rome by worship of the double-faced God, Janus.

Janus, to whom Dr. Joost Meerloo has devoted a recent study,* was the guardian of gates and doors, of coming and going. This is why the first month of the year was dedicated to him. The Romans liked to picture this god with two faces look-

---

* J. A. M. Meerloo, *The Two Faces of Man*, N.Y. Also, "Janus, the Integration of Man's Inner Antimonies"—Int'l Record of Medicine, Vol. 73, #3.

ing in two different directions. The origin of all things was ascribed to him; the change of seasons as well as the fluctuations of fortune, life and death.

The Romans did not invent this deity whose worship expressed a deepseated psychological need. The same paradoxical figure symbolizing youth as well as old age appears in almost all tribal mythology. The Hebrew Jonah, and the Viking Haakon are derived from his name. His is a polarity to be traced in the Chinese concept of Yang and Yin; in the two figures of the Assyrian religions, Ormuzd and Ahriman. It is the polarity of light and darkness, of male and female. This same polarity was stressed by Freud in reference to the dualistic instincts in man towards life and death (Eros versus Thanatos or Libido versus Destrudo).

There is a polarity built into man which is probably shaped at the moment of birth. The physical separation from the mother leads to a persistent yearning for an "oceanic" homecoming. But in our sanitary culture, ambivalence is largely repressed.

Why must we use such denial-mechanisms? How much of our social violence is the result of hidden tensions about morals that have been accepted at the price of repression? Obviously, no solution for inner clashes is found by camouflage.

When a delegate rises at the United Nations and says, "My esteemed colleague, the Foreign Minister," he need not tell us that he is posing, that he may be hiding contempt or hostility. He does not mean that he esteems the man. In fact, he may think the other a scoundrel. Such polite camouflage is obviously no substitute for decent relationships. Thus also, when private ambivalences remain hidden, they easily develop into hostility or contempt which in the end are directed against oneself. As children we learn to mask such drives by being taught automatic cleanliness and politeness, the purpose of which may be to avoid the risks of real emotion. This method voids the possibility of dealing with ambivalent impulses as a way of liberating emotion for loving. Thus many of our young are taught words instead of realities, given stones instead of bread, handed down ambivalences as an uncomprehended prologue to defeat. This is primarily based on illusions of perfection which suggest that one must renounce because one is incomplete. Our psychology is steeped in this as are our religions and education. Still ambivalence is a 'given', without which there is no evolution from the biological to the ethical. We can deal with ambivalence and frustration, by considering life-experience never as finalistic but as continual effort, with room to improve, for in the course of life we change a thousand times! No certainty of fulfillment is needed in order to engage and persevere. By including ambivalence, energy can be freed for emotional growth which will make it unnecessary to renounce or negate. As Spinoza wrote: "Omne determinatio est negatio" (to define everything is to negate everything). Emotional progress is possible when doubt is accepted, and contrasting forces and influences and reasonable compromises are incorporated. We do not need ethical "supermen" but common men who will not feel trapped either by perfectionistic delusions or by overpowering self-doubt.

Whatever we know about destiny has to be dealt with in these few years of our existence. We are granted only brief enjoyments and cannot sidestep our griefs. Our indifferences which result from a defense against never-ending pressures are always in danger of overwhelming our moments of tender consciousness.

So, we are pulled both ways and must meet repeatedly the suffering created by these ambivalences. Strangely enough, the realization of our potential occurs frequently only when we stretch our expectations beyond what might have been reasonably deduced from our personal experiences. Who can be sure that his ability to rise again is not fatefully impaired until, by the immense effort of going on, he discovers a revitalized hope?

I knew someone who said that every day when she arose she felt that tomorrow would be her birthday, tomorrow would be a celebration. This thought kept her going, she said, for tomorrow would be better. Yet even cheerful self-deception is in fact negation. The key lies elsewhere. The key is that whatever the way of acting upon ambivalences, at the beginning of life is the certainty that the courage we may gain will be bought at the price of conflict. The result is not one magnificent, all-encompassing self-image, but rather the realization that we are made of many partial egos.

In that connection, a motion picture entitled "Hiroshima Mon Amour" comes to mind. It is a love story about a European woman and a Japanese architect, both of whose lives were broken off at a vital moment during World War II. They find each other in that most symbolic city, Hiroshima. The movie expresses a philosophy which holds that only primary vitality can provide consolation. They spend their nights intimately together even though they barely know each other and desire no deeper sense of obligation. They both need consolation and a transient relationship is suggested as a solution, since the obligations of permanence would negate their solace. No one who has known loneliness would deny the blessing of even a passing friendship. "Snoring is the most beautiful music in the world", wrote one psychoanalyst, "just ask any widow or widower." And yet, transient sexual experience creates further detachment from reality. The truth between two people is fundamentally betrayed when they cannot count on at least being wanted for more than the surface of their presence. Hope is not destroyed by facing difficulties and uncertainties. All these can be probed and accepted as long as there is a rockbottom loyalty of each to the dignity of the other. What sustains people, even when their sexual vitality is waning, is relatedness and shared aspirations. Whatever tense conflicts have to be worked through, it is such care that makes us stand in awe before a love that is irreplaceable. Our culture suggests that the fundamental issue between men and women is one of their sexual bi-polarity. Nevertheless, the bond of shared human destiny is infinitely more important than that which sets us apart. True, when no trust is developed, no ambivalences need to be dealt with. But confident living is not gained this way. Where no fundamental trust is nourished, man remains a wounded, lonely animal. Trust, confidence, affection are products of tenderness gained by suffering; they are not axiomatic.

To love means to love within the reality of ambivalences, to struggle for a mutuality of self-respect. It is all too easy to have contempt for ourselves, our stupidities and inadequacies. When individuals make choices within the reality of life situations, a "harmony of contrasts" becomes possible, for the heart of all completion is that from time to time the tensions of the parts can be resolved.

I remember a young woman complaining that her husband's feeling towards her had cooled because he felt that she was demanding and distracted him from his medical studies. Somehow "woman" meant polarity to him. "Woman" meant emotion and tears and wanting to have children and involvement in discussions about feelings. His ambivalence towards his wife was briefly overshadowed but later it recurred with full force. Marriage now appeared to be a trap. He did not know how to fit reasonable expectations within a context of workable compromise. His focus on entering the marriage had been blurred and he could make no adjustment to his changed reality.

This would have demanded emotional self-education and an orientation towards an unstirred capacity within himself. Such self-discovery cannot be achieved in a vacuum and partners cannot be expected to stretch themselves beyond what they can "afford" in terms of emotion.

Therefore, a postulate about motivation makes sense only if

it fits within the specifics of the life situation of that particular human being. This illuminates the question not only of private conscience but of what we accept as ethically "normal" in society. Much social cruelty is built into the social order and is passed off as moral behavior. Society as well as the individual has its ambivalent tendencies.

Hence, the moral stature anyone may claim can have a normative significance only in particular situations and not by a generalized principle. Whatever is universally valid must be locally true first; whatever principles of social ethics one accepts, they need to be based upon real relationships. Ideology or theology can wait.

Many of us are weighed down, however, by perfectionist expectations and supposed leaders of men are consequently elevated to pedestals upon which they do not belong. Idolatry of any person obviates the need for probing relationship. Yet many find it easier to deify and then to tear down when disappointed, than to suffer through the labor of realistic encounter. It would be so much healthier not to obliterate ambivalences of feeling. After all, the most any man can do is to have integrity about his life and his work.

Life is not found in universal principles but in the shadow and frustrations of the particular: the particular of youth's turning into age; the inevitable passing of our hopes into the slower channels of dogged work. To yearn for perfection is but another way of not bothering with one's real capacity. How difficult not to succumb to the pride of one's own false expectations! There is a melancholy edge to life because even the most fervent effort does not guarantee progress. Everything has to be distilled out of doubt and failure. Man's self-respect is contained in seeing that which is tragic as a way of discovering the object at stake in each.

Our polarities are not the battlefield of Olympic gods. They fit within the limited context of precarious lives. If we can stop complaining about what we are not, we may be able to comprehend what we were meant for.

BELEAGUERED EGO AND SOLIDARITY

Earlier, I maintained that the word "hope" is too easily misused. By that I meant that many facets of life which pass for hopeful are, in fact, hollow despair. The Judeo-Christian hope of "good tidings" appears such because it prevents Man from taking stock of the human condition, in which God is neither love nor mercy. Whatever is meant by God is not encountered by superficial adoration. The reasons for hope emerge from the reality of pain. Values for living have no metaphysical basis.

It is most unfortunate therefore that the concept of hope has been monopolized by traditional religions which prophesied millennial deliverance. The "true" believers nurtured a sense of urgent yearning about something superb to come. The more disaster befell human life, the more intense became their hope for salvation; that is, the delusion that they might escape the human condition and death. Thus, we find in many religions the idea that a "golden" age will precede the final, terrible judgment, when only the righteous ones will be "saved". This notion negates the necessity of coming to grips with the reality of death and thus serves as a subterfuge, a promise of "sweet" death and eternity, when all we have is this wounded day.

As a result life is suspended between the poles of despair and hope and the expectation is promulgated that this suspension, in the "vale of tears", can be overcome only by the revelation of grace. Whatever its philosophical meaning for early evangelical Christianity, this state of grace, when the adversaries of light and darkness are to be reconciled, has maintained a powerful grip upon Western imagination. Life is: to be exposed to temptation and danger. Death is: to be relieved of the burdens of contradiction. In the furtherance of the Protestant ethic after the Reformation, this meant that the human order demanded a high degree of individual enterprise and action. Each man needed to rely upon his own increased competence to find his salvation. Because of this requirement he had to develop his competitive instinct. Those who could not muster this drive were looked upon as weak, as moral "underachievers". While this accent upon self-reliance helped in formulating an idea of man as courageous, venturesome and imbued with a fierce sense of independence, it also helped to foster a psychology which Tennyson called "red in tooth and claw". Compassion was not cancelled but it was clearly understood that an excess of empathy might endanger one's own standing and strength. Propelled by the genius of his productivity, Western man—and I include modern Russia—saw in self-preservation his primary tool for reaching a state of self-sufficiency, status and ultimate grace. Yet social anthropology today possesses an impressive body of knowledge which maintains that egocentricity is far from a natural state of affairs and that it is largely the result of childhood conditioning in particular types of civilization.

Ashley Montagu, for one, has pointed out that the ego-directed personality which has emerged from this cultural development is the result of coercion and emotional deprivation. His suggestion is that a world order, which will abolish collective hostility, will have to start with a radically different method of child rearing in which Spartan competitiveness is replaced by a concept of co-relation and co-responsibility.

This may also necessitate a rethinking of the function of the family as an institution. Where at one time the kinship structure was a socio-economic prerequisite for survival, this may no longer hold true for an industrial age. Since an uncanny number of marriages end in divorce the question is raised whether fathers and mothers are indeed the best agents for the transmission of intranutritive values to the children. Could specialized agencies, in which the neurotic interaction of parents would be neutralized, play a role? Can the projection of parental unhappiness upon the children be prevented? Can a more supportive and cooperative social order be envisaged by lessening the influence of the modern atomized family structure?

If child rearing is the key, what can we learn from other societies in which war, competitiveness, and profit as a work motive have been historically absent? In short, is a socialization process possible based upon cooperation, compassion and interdependence? My good Danish friend, the late Peter Freuchen, fell so completely under the spell of the cooperative sense among the Eskimos that he stayed with them for many years and married an Eskimo girl. Children in these cultures have sunny personalities, they are happy children. They are not insatiable in their need for attention because they are not separate, self-directed units. Instead of "me" they think and feel "we", and therefore the frustration of these children is very low. As a result, they do not grow up as demanding, authority-dependent individuals.

Compare that with the degree of frustration imposed upon our young. In cooperative societies, the arrangements of living are made in such fashion that the personality can be sure of the non-frustrative, cooperative support of others. This sounds fantastic to us. Yet we have knowledge that life may have been meant to be lived rather that way than in our present fashion.

Dr. Montagu, in his book *On Being Human*, writes that we are "out of line" with our evolutionary destiny which is geared upon "cooperation, not disoperation". Compassion which grows out of supportive and cooperative behavior is probably as "natural" to man as is his need for food and air. But somehow in the conditioning process our thought and action patterns were determined differently.

Is it not strange that everyone will readily agree that in some far-off future, eons from now, man will be able to live with warmth, social feeling and cooperation, while as for today, we must accept muddling through separation and hostility? Is it really so "visionary" to want improved relationships now? We accept beauty of music as universal. Why not a more stable world culture?

In MacLeish's play "JB", the author has one of Job's comforters cry out again and again, "Without the Fall, we're madmen all!" That means that without a concept of Sin, and innate evil, men would live like madmen. The realization of sinfulness and guilt supposedly keeps us on the "right" track and fear of punishment inhibits and controls us! That is—alas—part of our theological heritage. But is it not time to accept, as anthropologists, child-psychiatrists and educators already do, that the concept that the child is born egocentric is a projection of our own conditioning as adults? The facts are that the newborn infant's organism is already an actively cooperating entity. Prof. Charlotte Buehler found in her magnificent studies that our young ones are basically cooperative. Hostility in children tends to increase as they grow older, for aggression is the response to deprivation of tenderness.

We learn to love by having been loved. Actually, compassionate feelings are the basis of every coherent society. A civilization in which individuals not only stick together for mutual protection or self-interest, but in which they share specific ideals and purpose, is a civilization of love in which hostility and fear of the future have been replaced by supportive aims. There is no doubt that such a world community is possible and may be probable. The crucial question is when?

We do not have to go to the Australian aborigines to find examples of what a cooperative society might mean. The late Professor May Edel writing about *Anthropology and Ethics*, gave a good example of certain American Indians, young men of the Pueblo tribe, who served in the United States Army. They remained loyal to their primitive religion and its moral rules of mutual aid. After the war, these men fitted organically into their own communities without the adjustment conflicts so many G.I.s experienced.

The important issue here is that the Pueblo tribe is a supportive, cooperative community in which our concept of competition is unknown. Actually, the Hopi language does not contain the word "competition"! These Indian societies fit within Ashley Montagu's analysis that compassion and love are organically necessary, that they are biologically determined factors of sound organisms. The tribes are composed of farmers working the dry prairie lands and of families which have to work together closely as organic entities to survive. Dr. Edel pointed out that each stalk of corn planted in the soil of the Pueblo Bad Lands had to be protected individually and grown with great care. This attitude carried over in the dealings of members of the tribe with each other. A sense of the precious value of each person therefore remained dominant. It was a pragmatic not an ideological arrangement so that love and concern were ways by which to work better together. By so doing, a "right" kind of living was established, pleasing to the tribal gods. Thus communal action became the guarantee for individual security from an economic as well as an emotional point of view. Since money and property were not values by themselves, an entirely different moral perspective for children was created. Care and compassion were not taught as "luxury" emotions. No, friction and conflict were looked upon as "abnormal". Thus there came to exist a social, emotional, and religious matrix grown out of the precepts of a supportive society.

Yet for us, too, compassion and love are in their very essence social phenomena, values to be aspired to as definitely "good", since they tie the self in with the preservative needs of all. We need to learn how to live and teach them anew. For, as Montagu points out, man's need to form societies and his need for love are one and the same thing. Only in the competitive

order are substitutes for love sought in often violent combative-
ness, which then passes as the "unshakeable" reality of things.

The point to consider above all is that man is not at the mercy
of hostile drives. Nature is not in a conspiracy against man, nor
is the cosmos hostile.

Sexual needs, so often feared and degraded, offer an important insight. They need to be fulfilled and because of this
organic necessity, lasting relationships can be developed, out
of what started out as merely impulse. When evolved into love,
these drives yield security, are security, and remain basic. Thus
is the biological basis strengthened by that which our organic
design implies: integration of personality and hope. The question is never sexual only, but the evolution of the sexual which
helps mold the entire person. Such concepts of love have been
discovered everywhere in the world, whatever their cultures.

Thomas Hobbes, who greatly influenced the thinking of
Western civilization, declared that in his natural state, Man is
entirely egotistic. Since we live in continual fear of danger and
violent death, life is "solitary, poor, nasty, brutish and short." *
Only by iron laws could social life be made tolerable and
"tolerable" was about the maximum of happiness Hobbes could
envisage. Being incurably asocial, Hobbes said, men cannot
possibly have disinterested emotions. When they feel compassion, it is because they are afraid that one day the calamities
they witness may be visited upon themselves. Such concepts are
ingrained in the thought processes of our civilization and, yet,
examples of a supportive nature are numerous even though
minimally stressed.

In his *Profiles of Courage*, the late President John F. Kennedy
offered as an example of moral heroism, Senator Edmund G.
Ross of Kansas, "the man who saved a President". Ross' one
vote could have impeached President Andrew Johnson but he
refused to join the punitive bandwagon. Ross had disagreed

* From Hobbes' "*Leviathan.*"

with much the President had done and belonged to the opposite political party. Tremendous pressures were brought to
bear upon him and it was clearly indicated to him that he
would commit political suicide by voting "not guilty". Ross
described the final session as follows:

> "Friendship, position, fortune, everything that makes life desir-
> able to an ambitious man were about to be swept away by the
> breath of my mouth, perhaps forever. Then came my answer in
> a voice that could not be misunderstood—full, final, definite,
> unhesitating and unmistakably: 'Not guilty.'"

Senator Ross had decided to be able to live with himself
rather than follow Hobbes' precepts. We make ourselves grow
when we become members of one another. This nuclear generation has the utterly decisive task to use gathered insight to
change the intent of world culture. Love, solidarity, have to be
made operational means.

The problem is how to effectuate changed behavior on a
world-wide scale. What is it that makes us anxious, often
ferocious and brutal? What else but conditioning which en-
slaves us and compels us to march mutely in a gigantic pro-
cession of self-destruction! It is difficult to understand that
silent power and its seemingly compelling inclination.

Still, although we can be most uncompassionate ourselves,
one day we will beg for compassion too. Our basic obligation to
ourselves is to help the "better" person to unfold, especially at
such moments when the most unlovable characteristics within
become apparent.

When are we our happiest? It is at the moments when we are
our reciprocal selves, when we laugh, work, eat together by
passing food around, not hoarding it for ourselves. By our
mutuality we calm, we heal, we build up. Life is about these
things. A surgeon who is an egocentric bully is not a good
surgeon, whatever the skills of his hands. A parent is not a good
parent when he increases the separateness of his children, even

though he may be a magnificent provider. We must have the courage to return to patterns of reciprocity. When we give and allow ourselves to feel compassion, we experience the awesome wonder of growth.

LIFE'S BROKENNESS

Death in our literature is frequently spoken of with disdain. Samuel Beckett, in his play "Endgame," has the death of the central character occur upon a garbage heap. The author obviously wants to impress upon his audience that human existence is devoid of meaning, that everything climaxes in nothingness, and that life, whatever its enchanted moments, ends as so much debris. This may be valid literature, but it does not enter into the blinding pain caused by the sudden death of one much loved—or the wasting away of someone to whom we are close. No one can enter into that realization until he too has experienced such pain and found how little permanence there is.

Not all suffering is of this magnitude though. Much of it is created by the drainage of daily setbacks.

When faced with the greater crises of life, we usually find some way of dealing with them, for from resources hitherto unknown is frequently distilled the determination to go on. What affects us most are the common recurring frustrations, the callousness of the environment, the struggle to deal with willfully inflicted hurt. Suffer we do, with the trivia of living, the frayed nerves, the fears, and the narrowing horizons of hopes and ambitions. In daily life much of what appears to be tragic is, in fact, the accumulation of such smaller aggravations.

In a drama, "Mother Courage,"* Bertold Brecht, the German playwright, tells the story of a woman, Mother Courage, who

*Seven Plays, Bertold Brecht, Grove Press (1961).

in the Thirty Years' War functioned as a "vivandiere", a peddler, following the armies. In that prolonged period of violence, Mother Courage sees her two sons and only daughter destroyed. Yet, she remains a "rock of strength", she is "indestructible" and in the end, when even her horse has fallen victim to the hostilities, she harnesses herself to the wagon and carries on.

Brecht, far from wanting to glorify Mother Courage, pointed out that her very perseverance furthered the causes of war and also promoted the destruction of her own children. Her daughter Katrin, a deaf-mute, is molested by soldiers and her face disfigured, but Mother Courage stubbornly counts her money. Brecht identifies the daughter with the mute suffering of humanity which so frequently kills what it loves. In the last scene of the play, Katrin sacrifices herself by awakening a town that is to be attacked. Standing on a roof where she can be seen from afar, she beats a drum until a soldier shoots her down. While Mother Courage mourns her children, she will not disturb the "order" of things. Her daughter could not accept a world which compromises with death but the mother has learned to endure suffering, how to become part of it.

In our time, stress has become so much a mass emotion and is so colored by the anticipation of incredible disasters, that many, like Mother Courage, have learned to hang on without a sense of personal involvement.

This, I am afraid, is the totalitarian infection of this epoch, the collectivization of even the most private of emotions. We are not left to ourselves but made part of depersonalized responses. We do not allow ourselves to scream out our private despair and are caught up in rituals of reality-denial even at intimate moments of suffering.

Is there anything more degrading than the mortuary business of this country; the morgues called "funeral homes", the graveyards "gardens for the living"—that entire ritual of deception built to keep away the experience of death? Every ounce of nobility is drained from the profoundest trauma of life by commercialization, necrophilia and show of hypocritical "concern". We are not allowed solitude when nevertheless our entire being wants to withdraw within ourselves. The need for isolation is trampled upon and replaced by a fascination with the mechanics of death and burial. Quietude is violated by the fraud in the funeral parlor.

Of course, when one cares deeply for someone, it is almost impossible just to stand by and see him go through heartbreak. Yet, I am convinced that the course of greater wisdom is to respect the need for isolation. The collectivized emotion must be counteracted not by the Mother Courage type of stoic "carrying on", but by reiteration of the private character of grief.

We do not mourn in uniform ways. Some can express grief, others cannot. Yet, in our culture, as in many others, there are ritualistic—almost prescribed—expectations concerning bereavement. Thus the essential experience of an individual is frequently exchanged for a show, a display of mourning by which no genuine feelings are engendered. Also, far too often, the sympathy of friends becomes meddlesome interference when the bereaved person wants to be left alone. How easily do the tongues of our comforters turn to gossip when grief is not expressed in a fashion moralistically considered "right"? There is mourning and postponed mourning, and the impact of death never ends; it reposes within our consciousness as long as we live.

Nevertheless, regaining a perspective of life after a traumatic loss is a most individually conditioned matter. There is no doubt that a life, nurtured by the need to be of sustenance within the life of another, yields strength to break away from isolation and depression. Out of suffering can be born a consent to live. Not an apathetic acceptance of whatever happens, but a dealing with, a living through utter pain and suffering.

How untenable, then, philosophies which teach that pain

does not really exist and is but the result of man's separation from God! Such delusions belong to the world of "Mother Courage". They are a fatalistic acceptance of adjustment to what should be rejected. The outcries of the heart are needed as well as more reasoned processes of consolation, for to be consoled means to have accepted a direction for the future. The consent to live cannot be based upon anesthesia; on the contrary, it depends upon nurturing the tissue of human outreach.

The complexity of this issue was illustrated at a meeting of the American Cancer Society in April 1962, where Dr. David A. Karnofsky of the Sloan Kettering Institute of Cancer Research took a strong stand against abandoning treatment in "terminal" cases.

Said Dr. Karnofsky: "Many objective observers contemplating the dismal scene (of a dying patient) plead with the doctors to let the patient go swiftly, with dignity and without pain. Withholding treatment can be urged by efficiency experts, social workers, theologians, economists and humanitarians. For here is one means of ensuring an efficient, productive, orderly and painfree society, by sweeping out each day the inevitable debris of life."

Karnofsky answered the question: "When should a physican stop treating a patient?" by saying, "I believe that he must carry on until the issue is taken out of his hands."

There are arguments in favor of euthanasia of course, but is not Dr. Karnofsky, as Brecht did in his play, indicting the collectivist invasion of suffering? Is there not, in those in good health, a tendency to turn away from that which is decomposing? Is there not great difficulty in identifying with what seems to be surely dying helplessly and thereby has become remote or even repugnant? Visit any home for the aged and see the many who are begging for death, calling upon the physicians to help speed nature along and whose final, universal complaint is that their children and relatives have forgotten them.

We are so much inclined to think in terms of the vital person that it may become increasingly harder to be involved with suffering. Have you not known someone who is ashamed of being in pain, of being a nuisance and helpless or embarrassed at not being able to function adequately? We live under the mass suggestion of a happy, healthy society in which it is somehow unfortunate that some people do not seem to be able to start functioning again. Could it not be that under the spell of such suggestions, patients are considered beyond treatment earlier than necessary? Karnofsky seemed to feel so! His was a purely medicopsychological argument, yet he touched upon a question of vital ethical importance: can we still recognize each other's essential humanity at times of great suffering? Human beings are not only made up of conscious motivations; many subconscious elements play a role, especially in our dealings with the weak, the ill and the dying.

In his *Children of the Ashes*,* the Swiss writer Jungk reported that in Hiroshima the lingering victims of the atomic bomb were treated as "dangerous and tiresome pariahs". Those with scar tissue were not allowed to use public swimming pools. Japanese doctors tried to prevent free medical service and the American Atomic Bomb Commission was described as treating the victims "purely as guinea pigs". The author stressed that it was explained to him that the official policy was that "no air of atonement is to be suggested in any way by the Commission".

This phenomenon is serious enough to dwell upon, because we see universally a diminishing consciousness about what is actually evil. Thereby we invite the alienation of knowledge from ethics. When humanists and scientists no longer sustain a dialogue, great danger results and some of this becomes apparent when one is in need of surgery. The most traumatic element is not the pain which is part of the therapeutic process. It is not even the feeling of separation which one invariably suffers

*Jungk, *Children of the Ashes,* London (1962).

in the secluded society of a hospital nor yet the sense of help-lessness as the patient realizes how far removed he is from the swiftly moving doctors and nurses who assume an air of cheer-ful unconcern. The deepest trauma results from other factors.

In the first place, by a mere, technical device—anesthesia—all consciousness can be taken from the brain in but a few seconds. It is a blissful relief from the pain of incision, but it is also a frightening realization of one's utter dependence. We are taken "out of ths world" by anesthetists whose names we do not even know!

Then there are the moans at night when the corridors are empty, the visitors gone and when men and women by the hundreds, in dreams and nightmares, sigh their hopes and pains, revealing the sadness and loneliness of life. What a strange universe we harbor within, which breaks out of us when we contemplate death—what hidden tears are sobbed at night, what expectations whispered never to be heard by those for whom they were meant; what solitude is housed within our veins! Life, that must be upheld as Karnofsky put it, "until the issue is taken out of our hands", is a mysterious affair, held together by the most tenuous sinews of mentality and physique.

It is out of such solitude that we may discover that all sus-tenance is contained in our relatedness to others. Especially at times of great suffering, what can keep us hopeful is that we know that others expect certain attitudes, actions, and words from us. Is it not true that we have a right to certain expecta-tions of each other? For in these hopes about each other is hidden the tenderness of love; the tenderness that leads us to consent to life, whatever its suffering. The core of living with hope is the recognition that we maintain our sense of self only because of others.

It is evident that there are those who have given up and to whom the expectation of being wanted for something besides themselves has disappeared. The tragic part is that many, plagued by feelings of rejection, no longer try to establish bonds of concern. Relatedness is hard to perceive, especially when we are desperately ill and incapacitated. It is then that we can nevertheless find some measure of connectedness with an adult or a child. Every person can find at least one such bond of concern provided the need is accepted. No one is an "island entirely to oneself". Consent to live means to be willing to direct ourselves towards this potential for tenderness.

We remain alive as long as we have not surrendered the dormant capacity to love again. Only then will grief or suffering not suffocate us.

There is a period especially after the death of a beloved person when it seems that all reason for living is gone. I believe that it is necessary for a person to go to the bottom of that pit, that one must not be hurried back into the circle of friends, but given the opportunity to discover strength in silence and to deal with one's self-doubts. What we can and must do for each other is to keep the lifelines open. Slowly, more complex dependencies can be developed which can form the basis for a subsequent renewed independence. To preserve ourselves we need to preserve a belief in love. This is exceedingly difficult in times of loneliness when the tendency is to see oneself as unwanted and unworthy. It is hard not to be needlessly overcritical of ourselves at such times, for one assumes so often that "I should be able to react better to pain". Consent to live means to accept the limitations of what we are and can be, as well as seeing ourselves related to what we are potentially. Emerson once wrote that religion is "the centuries speaking to the hours", and so is suffering eternity speaking to the seconds. The trivia fall away when we can perceive hurt as a tool, not as a metaphysical visitation. We are more than our tormented parts; we are more than a sick body; we are, because of what we choose to be, more than the seconds that pass hastily, we are part of a regenerative power, which but few of us know how to use.

It is therefore not enough to admonish each other to be strong and faithful, for essential meaning results from quest. The human predicament is that we cannot discover this without suffering. It follows then that suffering means working through the multiple facets of identity, of knowing who we are, and why, and at the same time knowing the separation suffering creates. There is no other way.

When a specialist seeks a diagnosis, he does not start out with the entire concept of the patient. He does not have the entirety before he knows the parts and he must combine his knowledge of the entity with his knowledge of the functional. He needs intuition as well as experience and microscopes.

This also applies to a sense of persistence within us. It is derived from separation and isolation as well as from identity and resourcefulness. Integration and disintegration occur simultaneously and only in the uniqueness of our own experiences, can we build a life. Man lives with the intimate stabilizing factors of relatedness as well as with the unsettledness of a mortal being. It is a paradox but not without dignity.

In a book* on the Triangle Fire which shook New York in 1911 (146 young immigrant women died in a terrible sweatshop blaze) the author tells us about one of the victims who desperately tried to escape the flames. She was Sally Weintraub, one of the last girls to jump from the inferno which was caused by exploitative negligence. Standing on the window ledge, flames behind her, and the uncertain earth below hidden by smoke: "For a minute she held her hands rigid, her face upward . . . . before she jumped she began to make gestures, as if she was addressing a crowd above her . . ." What silent question was she posing for that crowd *above* as she leaped? What promise did she wring from a cosmos unconcerned with her fate? What sweetness did she remember as she fell towards the pavement? Her separateness was beyond repair, but for this

*The Triangle Fire, Leo Stein, Lippincott (1962).

one result: out of her suffering and the disaster of the other 145 victims, grew social consciousness which today gives dignity to millions of workers. Maybe all that life leaves us with, finally, is the courage to be.

Such consent is the opposite of resignation. In it is an element of gratitude, and the hope that by our loves we can overcome life's brokenness. Such love is as real as pain.

ARE PAIN AND AFFLICTION THE HUMAN APPRENTICESHIP?

All of us—sooner or later—learn to "walk humbly". John Gunther in his book, *Death Be Not Proud,* gives a moving account of the life and death of his son Johnny. The despair which beset the parents was described as follows: "Johnny died at 11:02 p.m. . . . little by little the life color left his face . . . What is life? It departs covertly. Like a thief, Death took him." Rereading those words, I could not help thinking of King David and his son Absalom. Absalom rebelled against his father. When a crucial battle had been lost, he tried to escape but his hair—in which he took great pride—became entangled in the branches of a tree and he was slain by David's general, Joab. David knew that because he had caused so much bloodshed and because he had married Bathsheba after sending her husband to certain death in battle, he would not be allowed to build the temple in Jerusalem. Yet, he had his son. But his son turned against him and was killed. Through the centuries we can hear David's lament: "Oh, Absalom my son, my son Absalom! Would God I had died for thee . . ." Death here too came "as a thief."

What is left to man but the opportunity to salvage his courage, to believe in the possibility of beginning again?

We all start out from a fathomless loneliness and as we break through illusion after illusion we find this loneliness still awaiting us. The acceptance of great pain is a realistic involvement with the world. We cannot hope to shed our fears, but we can try to continue to be engaged with each other. In spite of everything, in spite of David's eternal outcry and accusation of life's endless betrayals, in spite of all this, there is growth measured as much by fleeting rewards as by suffering.

Such growth entails the willingness to leave something of the old behind and to venture into the unknown. The risks are enormous. The life of growth is a life of effort and difficulty, a life, as the Frenchman Condorcet wrote in the eighteenth century, of "quand même," "and yet . . ." Commitment to that "and yet" demands, from time to time at least, an almost unshakable insistence that even that has reality which has not yet emerged in actuality. The psychiatrist Maslow called it "seeing with care" and the poet O'Neill called it "thinking feelingly." This means, above all, a reorientation concerning pain. We cannot remake ourselves as long as pain is seen only as intrusion. Suffering imposed upon us by others is not the result of some innate evil in those who transgress, but is rather the result of their thwarted potential for decency.

Much cruelty is the consequence of fanatic attempts at perfection, when often all we may hope for is the soft expression on the face of one we love, the quietude of a walk along the oceanside, the way a baby holds on to our hand.

Those who cannot believe that the human effort makes sense, cannot see the meaning of pain either. Their only standard is who dominates whom and the future does not entice them out of their closed circuit of unhappiness in which nothing echoes but their own solitary voice. The cosmos is neutral about human suffering, but our potential greatness is in that even while we have no proof of destiny, we are willing to pay the price of living and of loyalty to the world. Man only borrows strength from the ages but without that strength there is no meaning.

Any notion of future depends upon trusting Man's reciprocal capacity, for without such trust there is despair. Neither equality, nor liberty are therefore merely political goals. They are instruments—means towards the purpose of a more human order. Behind them is the realization that while immense personal tragedies cannot be forestalled, at least death need not be "proud."

Thousands of years ago, in Northern Israel, the prophet Micah lambasted the inequities he witnessed and denounced the rulers because of their misuse of power. Predicting their destruction, he cried out: "and what doth the Lord require of thee but to do justly and love mercy and walk humbly . . ."

It was a time when the forlorn people of Israel, resuming the sacrifice of children to God Moloch, lived in perpetual fear of having offended the Gods; Micah's teaching was simple: he preached righteousness, not sacrifice; justice, not ritual; mutuality, not spineless privilege. He indicted those homes where "a man's enemies are the men of his own house" and stressed the need to perceive the sacred in every man. Love mercy! Not merely to be accommodating, but to be just.

In this era too, there is a great need to strengthen the capacity for life. The knowledge that another is in need of one ought to trigger the desire to respect him the more. To use one's emotional resources to keep the dignity of others alive, to help avoid tragedy for someone else, to practice forgiveness, these are the elements of a world worth living for.

After all, "dignity" remains only a word until it becomes an operative principle. This may never be felt as sharply as when we remember a beloved person who has died, or when the bonds that tied heart to heart are broken. What shall we make of such almost impassable separation?

Edna St. Vincent Millay wrote about such experience: "this and no more of pain" as her stark resolution of courage. Hers was a quality of love given because she could not help but bestow it and which expressed not only her own need but also her concern for the preservation of the other.

It is the kind of love towards which one aspires, a form of "higher" life, a direction. Such direction is found when men and women, loving together, hoping, and sorrowing together, remain capable of struggling with their inadequacies. Notwithstanding all shortcomings, there remains an opportunity to nurture in one another the ability to rise "high among the run of men . . .", as Millay also expressed it. Such recognition of the essential dignity of the other is obviously full of pitfalls. Yet, there is little else to life but the passionate urge for the quiet "and still." If realized between nations, it might yet reverse the drift towards sanctimonious mass extermination.

As in Micah's time, idealists today need to become realists. I will not, therefore, lament the weaknesses of society. It is too easy. Exasperation is the first step towards suicide. It is nowhere written that this must be a generation beaten by the times in which it lives, alienated from its essence by lack of direction. There is a basis for love, decency and justice in the world. It can be evoked by common people, in their common effort. Courage and perseverance are not the monopolies of saints or heroes!

To care for an inner freedom of multiple alternatives is to dare to love life enough. This brings to mind Mr. Otto Frank, the father of Anne Frank whose *Diary of a Young Girl* may be the most moving human document of our era. After the war, his wife and children destroyed, Otto Frank decided with superb nobility, to let the world share the tenderness that was in the heart of his young daughter even as she was shipped off to the extermination center of Bergen Belsen. Here is an example of the higher facet of human character transcending unspeakable pain. A world numbed by human suffering could not turn away from Anne Frank's "and yet," spoken with simple dignity at the portal of death.

It is in seeking such affirmations of human greatness that one must confront the question whether there is purpose to pain and whether suffering is a condition for inner growth.

Shakespeare's "Hamlet" is a man in quest of the meaning of his suffering and he wants, at any price, to obtain truth about his deepest motives.

"My fate cries out!" he screams at Polonius. He needs to get to the root of what besets him and make it understandable. What does his affliction mean as it makes him contemplate murder? Hamlet believes that nothing but complete revelation can liberate him, for he is vaguely aware of his fateful ties to his mother. When his friend Horatio wants to die with him, Hamlet tells him:

> Oh, good Horatio, what a *wounded* name,
> Things standing thus unknown, shall live behind me!
> If thou didst ever hold me in thy heart,
> Absent thee from felicity awhile
> And in this harsh world draw thy breath in *pain*,
> To tell my story.

Hamlet must get at things unknown. "Tell my story, draw thy breath in pain"—and finally, "The readiness is all". . . .

The "readiness is all"—the readiness to understand that pain and affliction do not exist in a vacuum but are a crucial aspect of human development.*

The ancient Greeks thought that if a man offended destiny by unravelling its secrets, he would have to suffer death. The punishment of Prometheus was a terrible one. Oedipus was blinded when the truth about himself was revealed. Yet Hamlet exemplifies that the insistence to understand, even at the abyss of experience, is the only pathway to sanity. And so do all of us want to know "the truth" about our affliction. Deep down, we know that truth will not destroy us but that escapism will. When a life aim helps us lift the veils of suffering, we can take experience in stride. The world may finally exclude us, yet we cannot afford abandonment. The grace of submission can be

---

*Karl Jaspers, *Tragedy Is Not Enough*.

replaced by the jolting justifications gained from insight.

All of us suffer pain in one form or another and unless it is unrelenting animal pain, one of the unexpected results is introspection. Such self-contemplation makes us ask not just "why" affliction but rather: "How shall I live with it? Shall it be as a stranger surprised that I too must suffer; shall I be ignorant of the meaning of my sorrows?" Pain forces us to consider our helplessness.

Physical pain is not, of course, the only pain. In this era of complex anxieties there may well be a perpetual pain pervading all of our lives. I am not just thinking about wars, but about the nagging realization of how little we can do.

Of course, everyone pretends to have a remedy for pain, whether for a toothache or for loneliness! As an experience it is constantly devaluated. He who suffers pain can but rarely be silent; he must talk about his suffering. There are some to whom sicknesses and pains become the main preoccupation of their lives. Thus, sickness can become a camouflage behind which one hides.

Someone once said: "That which gives light first endured burning". Burning, in short, is part of transformation. True, torches light the scene for a while only and then are burned out. While life too is of such fragmentary presence, man nevertheless resembles a sculptor, as Victor Frankl remarked in his book *The Doctor and the Soul*. Man works with unshaped stone. He seeks purpose, he hammers out his values in his own "blood, sweat and tears". But in the process of living, he is transformed, much as radium, which also has a limited life-span. The energy created by using radium can never again be reconverted into the same material: an irreversible process. So is there just so much exposure for any one given life and then the film ends. Nevertheless, I believe that that which is transformed is enough to live by. Each of us revives every day, by our work and our loves, gentle affirmations more lasting than all pyramids.

TO DEFY THE NIGHT

Yet human beings inflict such hellish suffering upon one another—disguised as salvation! Beyond physical pain, therefore, we need to consider many types of affliction which affect us more deeply. When we feel threatened we experience a constriction, a biological reaction. Nevertheless, pain that is physical can frequently be absorbed relatively well. One may have a small surgical act performed with local anesthesia and when it is done, one forgets about it. It is only when suffering is prolonged, or too often repeated, that affliction sets in. Life is uprooted by persistent pain for it is an irresistible, brutal intrusion from which one cannot turn away. Such pain can tie down all our feelings, all our thinking. It is the kind of pain with which we associate anxiety. We are afraid of being overwhelmed.

Certain types of physical and psychological deprivation cause pain quite beyond the endurable. Persons tortured by Nazis or Japanese have been known to experience inexplicable sobbing years later, after an initial defense of the psyche against the saturation by sorrow. Affliction in our lives, therefore, is not caused by illness per se, but by something that has fundamentally taken a psychological hold over us. A person can do little about the pain of loneliness after the death of a beloved partner. The issue is to help prevent his pain from becoming an all-enveloping affliction.

Yet, even affliction can be a doorway to life regained. This may be the greatest "enigma of life" as Simone Weil put it. Affliction which could have led to a mutilation of personality, something beyond the comprehension of anyone else, and which seemingly could not be healed, may suddenly result in transformed self-perception. When we narcissistically cling to our afflictions, we find irreversible despair. This is why totalitarian governments, by a careful process of dehumanization, impose upon persecuted minorities an irrational sense of hopelessness which destroys their will to resist. Step by step, the victims begin to see themselves only as objects for further infliction of pain. In the end, the final blow is felt as relief! This is the secret of the success of the executioners of history. They fashion out of the sense of total affliction a psychological weapon.

During World War II, I heard a French patriot say, discussing the apathy of the Nazi targets: "But, mon vieux, there are wolves and sheep in the world. And wolves must eat too, you know." He was not at all a fascist, he often risked his life to save other people. But the passive manner in which the victims offered themselves had slowly convinced him that the "wolves," whom he detested fiercely, were successful because of some innate cowardice on the part of the victims and this aroused his hostility. In fact, the victims were mesmerized by the unspeakable, inconceivable reality of mass destruction. No one taught them how to resist, they felt abandoned and alone. This is the pinnacle of evil because it destroys even the capacity to stand up against the ultimate violation of one's person. It is—alas—a contagious group-affliction, in which, sometimes, the would-be rescuers become infected by the totalitarian plague so that they, too, lose identification with the victims.

I know no word for that particular suffering which results from feeling utterly deprived of one's moorings. Perhaps Emile Durkheim's concept of "anomie," the total deadening of the sense of self, applies here. Whatever it is, our pains have become very complicated. One may go to a doctor and present him with a very simple complaint: a lower backache, headaches, palpitations. But beneath the simple complaint hide the complex anxieties of an age in which a great many are daily immersed in thoughts of death and destruction. This continual preoccupation with catastrophe and possible catastrophe overshadows countless lives of men and women in our time, and, therefore, is an invitation to a return to primitive fatalism.

Traditional religion has always been aware of this, insisting that suffering, conflict and death are "the wages of sin," thus creating an impossible tension between the very human experience of evil and a "pure" harmony attainable by faith. As a result, guilt or shame are seen not as normal and natural emotions, but as the forerunners of "final judgment" and doom. I am convinced that guilt, thus misconstrued and used for the sake of indoctrination, has been—and is—the major source of anxiety in Western civilization. Self-doubt becomes not an instrument for trying harder, for transforming one's motives and actions, but rather a sign of weakness which stifles self-development. Compulsive preoccupation with personal sin has killed off the capacity for growth and resulted in the pessimism and fatalism which are responsible for much of the pain, alienation and discontent of our culture. In turn, this fatalism has made it possible to portray human suffering in unreal and metaphysical terms.

Yet, men and women are not symbols. The human condition is a private condition. It is not true that in the face of tribulation no courage remains. In spite of the urge for oversimplified consolations, we can still insist upon the capacity to reconstruct private agonies into affirmations of life.

Obviously, then, pain serves a psychological function, it is more than the response to an irritation. It is not without meaning that many of our most severe pains are often felt at night, and that we feel better when morning dawns. We especially dread the night when in pain for, as Meerloo pointed out, it threatens to separate us farther from the world. Such psychic "pain" is the result of recognizing the precariousness both within and without. There can be no painless life, for there is no cure without trauma.

A few years ago, a remarkable book was published in France, entitled *The Last of the Just,* by Schwarz Bart. It is a novel based on a seventeenth century myth, according to which there are always 36 righteous men in the world who are unaware of their saintliness. One appears in each generation, according to a tradition dating from 1185 when a congregation in York, England, chose to take its life rather than be sacked by Richard the Lionhearted.

It is said that the Righteous One often does not know that he is to be a just person until Heaven warns him by some affliction or suffering. His pains remain forever inconsolable and the legend says that the tears of the Righteous Ones become rivers running towards the heart of God. Therefore, when the lives of the Righteous Ones are recounted by pious scholars, they end each recitation with "one tear for him . . ."

The Righteous One must fulfill his mission in the world and since he is an Innocent Man who does not know how to commit injustice, he stands outside the universe of violence and has no adequate reaction to it. He must transform the suffering of the world and in this is his mission. Human separation, sadness and affliction are recreated by him into an active love of what is right. Of course, the Just One may doubt: "Does God really want to see His own children die?" Yet he can never deny God because in that case all suffering would become senseless. He must warn men that they must not kill. Why should they be in such a hurry to die? The Just One does not understand that those who are innocent are usually met with cynical laughter or trampled upon by heavy boots. He does not understand the meaning of sin.

The myth states that while the world deals cruelly with those who are just, they themselves will remain innocent. This again raises the question of what personal suffering means.

When the last Just One, Ernie, is young, he lives in a German town. One day his playmates want him to play the "Jew who crucified Jesus". A little girl will portray Jesus. The children decide among themselves that Ernie must demand that the girl be crucified. They say, "You are the Jews, you must say that Christ must die." But Ernie, the Righteous One, cannot do it. The children then descend upon him. In the fight that ensues, Ernie falls, and now that the Just One seems dead, the circle is once more complete. The cross has become the symbol of death for the innocent! The children dare not look at the real Ernie who lies bleeding on the ground and they run away. This is the function of the Just One: to show men that their worst affliction is what they impose upon themselves. The Just in this world die when human ambition has been killed and the soul perishes.

The legend of the Righteous Ones ends with the death of the "last of the Just" during World War II. Ernie and his family are arrested in France by the Gestapo and deported to a death camp. The inner destitution of those who violate life leads to the destruction of those who are innocent.

Amidst the horror of the gaschamber, Ernie's wife asks, "Shall I ever see you again?" And the Righteous One answers, "Soon, my love, soon, I promise you. . . ."

This is an allegory concerning a pain peculiar to our time. The main characters in this work do not compromise their dignity and will not be torn from their beloved ones. By their tender relationships they transmit a truth about Man: No life is ever wasted. The innocents, even in death, maintain for eternity the value of life. But what of their transgressors? They exemplify that denial of this value condemns human beings to act like animals. When a bird is hurt in a fight, others may attack it with their beaks as a natural reaction to physical weakness.

In human society, too, the sick and the weak are frequently despised, the victims often hated more than the executioners. Who ever loved refugees? Life remains consciously human only for those who will not allow affliction to extinguish their love. Those who suffer have a hard task: not to turn pain and doubt against themselves.

In her book, *Waiting For God*, Simone Weil expresses some

significant thoughts on this very question. While seeking to accept Christian faith (she was never in fact converted), she wrote, speaking to a priest: "Christ has been made a curse for us. In the same way, every innocent being, in his or her affliction, feels accursed." Men can become accomplices of their affliction, instead of seeing them as stepping-stones. The stress upon Christ's expiation corrupts his message of love.

Those so saturated by their affliction create an ever-widening distance between themselves and others. Yet, at the same time, they wish for a perpetual nearness, a lasting condition of being sheltered. I see both affliction and love as mere hints of destination; we all work out our private destinies—part blessed, part accursed.

Yet again, we are not dealing with symbols. If we separate ourselves it is from someone we could potentially love. There is a precious inner obedience for human beings, the same obedience—I think—as that of the waves that topple over as they reach the shore. It is true: some ships are shipwrecked in attempting to reach port, but I choose to see pain and affliction as apprenticeships. In time most of us find that the vibration of whatever is sacred to us registers identically for pain and joy, for both are needed for our transformation. None of us only progresses upward and we therefore need to consent to life without regret. All growth is pain and so is all transformation.

Martin Buber said that we do not create love but that love is waiting to be awakened. It is waiting for our consent expressed by our ways of living, as is the strength that is beyond mere defiance. Persons are not fixed like stars; love and affliction are the expressions of an implicit wholeness, something anticipated within.

We have to engage upon what is potentially painful so that we can enlarge the consciousness of what we may become.

BECAUSE OF A CHILD

Consider in this context one of the paradoxes of human existence: we need as much to be with others as we need privacy and solitude. Human beings cannot be without the voice or sight of other human beings for long periods of time. Prisoners of war, kept in solitary confinement, reported afterwards that their greatest doubt had been whether they were still capable of independent feelings and thoughts. Recent tests undertaken to determine psychological effects upon astronauts indicate that loneliness will almost inevitably lead to hallucinations or fantasies.

Yet, in order to remain sane we also need privacy; we need the opportunity to daydream, to be away from the eyes and tongues of others. We need times when the presence of others will not bear down upon us, when we can regain perspective without outside intrusion.

Part of our problem is that not only are seclusion and intimacy practically impossible, but that a great many no longer feel this need. There are many persons who never have experienced the exhilaration of solitude.

In addition, many seem to have lost the need or desire for *privacy.* Relationships between men and women are often entered upon with a minimum of knowledge about the other. They meet and are both in need of a partner—and, as much of our literature suggests, such encounters have to end in bed.

Our civilizations seem to suggest that we need not retreat within ourselves if we can only keep up with appearances, for the point is not how to achieve inner quietude but how to be acceptable.

Thus—as McIver points out—have we also learned to live in a perpetual din.* There is noise all around us, noise that invades our consciousness by day and our slumber at night. We are sur-

*Prof. R. M. McIver, *The Pursuit of Happiness,* New York, 1959.

rounded by commercial prattle, by the hoarse threats of politicians and mass exterminators and by soothsaying evangelists.
Whether we are in the dentist's chair or at a funeral chapel, our
emotions are drowned in the regurgitation of sentimental tunes.
For our recreation we go to movie theatres where the volume
of sound is so great that it bursts upon us almost like a physical
threat, and it is indeed meant to overwhelm us. Children walk
the streets with transistor radios clasped close to their ears and
we ourselves rarely find time to question whether or not what
we think we need is perhaps what others suggest we want. We
find it increasingly difficult to live without intrusion. Still, a
sense of reality depends upon the willingness to be alone with
ourselves, at least from time to time.

Does an appeal such as Thoreau's still make sense? Does the
notion of "inner life" have meaning for our age? Must we not,
in order to survive, be largely invisible in the crowd; must we
not, in order to make a living, in order to help our children "adjust" to their world, become part of the din, of "the dusty city of
externalized living"?

Of what does "inner life" consist? Nothing in it stands out as
much as the fact that we are separate from anything but ourselves.* This seems to be an essential part of our nature and
therefore the solitary feeling is deeply ingrained. Our own path
is always a lonely one and we are conscious of that loneliness.

Now arises the paradox that while we are deeply aware of
being unto ourselves, at the same time we seek to overcome
this separateness, and to have our own pathway merge with
those of others. It is the knowledge of loneliness which forces
us to do so. We have our being in a good many of such paradoxes.

This means that to discover quietude, we must know the
world as a source of both anxiety and fulfilment and that these
may be experienced at the same time! All we can hope to dis-

---

*Dr. Benjamin Miller, *Time To Be Alone*, New York, 1960.

cover are approaches to life situations; "solutions" are never given in their entirety. Solutions are part of a functional approach to realistic choices in marriage, in work and in the world at large. Still, many can see no such direction.

How then can we speak about guidelines for happiness by which to overcome our separateness?

To be human entails living with the tensions of paradoxes. Yet, the person who loves deeply may think all paradoxes resolved, may feel a great oneness and belief that a new identity is merging two separate personalities. Much of our religious and secular literature is filled with accounts of the effect of such "all-encompassing love".

But this cannot be. We cannot in fact step out of our own personality and become "one" with the other.* This may be tragic but it is true. All-pervading love does not resolve frequent separateness, even though only in relatedness to others do we discover a measure of our strength and purpose. It is the very character of such relatedness that it is limited by the essence of what each one of us is.

On one occasion I listened for many hours to a young woman who had lost her husband in a shocking accident. They had been a devoted couple who, in five years of marriage, had developed deep involvement with each other's hopes and pains. The man's death seemed an insufferable blow to the woman who fell into a deep depression, desiring nothing more than death for herself. She would hardly leave her apartment and when she did go out, would hurry back to sit through long hours of mourning in her darkened living room. In order to survive, she had to be helped to break her preoccupation with the dead, to extricate herself from the all too tangible absence of her husband. It was difficult to say to her, ". . . . you have mourned and grieved enough; now see your separateness as part of reality. Your marriage was not meant to enslave you, but

*Miller, *op. cit.*

rather to build you as a person. You have a right to cry your heart out; you have a right to speak again and again of the kindness of your dead partner, but make your bereavement bearable for yourself and others by accepting, nevertheless, the fact that all of us are by ourselves."

Our entire resourcefulness must be mobilized if self-pity is to be replaced by renewed goals for living.

The realization of separateness after great hurt can be balanced by a growing understanding of our capacity to rebuild life content. Human capacity includes the possibility of redirection of resources. The fact that we are alone at the crossroads; and the truth of solitary existence, can evoke in us a renewed ability to share of ourselves.

When such response is stimulated we can use the memory of the past to relate to the world again. By relating, I mean working relationships with others evoking tenderness, and responsibility. These are our tools.

Think of those who face surgery. One can accompany one's parent, one's husband or wife, one's child up to the operating room. But then the figure of a beloved person, wrapped in a blanket, is wheeled into a room full of strangers, and the doors close! One does not know what will take place in there and one does not know how the other person is going to come out. One may get word from time to time from a recovery room but one does not know, really. We are alone, with all our premonitions, and so is the other alone.

We long for connectedness of life, but the fact is that much of our attitudes is the result of solitary struggle. It is with this that human beings have to keep their sense of Self together.

Therefore, the need for "inwardness" exists not only at critical moments of life when pain, affliction or death strike. No, the fruits of inner life are at least as necessary at moments of deep inner conflict.

For example, we like to think of ourselves as thoughtful and humane. Still, everyone has known moments of lashing out towards another or using the weakness of that person to make a point, to lodge a complaint, or to draw attention to oneself. Sometimes we may even raise our hand in blind anger. Then there is disruption in the connectedness with the other and we feel drained by the effort to maintain our sense of self-respect. Recovery of inner life is paid for but it is a price we pay for the possibility of returning to each other, rediscovering each other and facing conflict.

Healing cannot always be achieved by reaching out. Human growth depends also on moments when, while we may desire involvement we cannot, in fact, *be* involved.

To love is to have achieved the humility which can lead to forgiveness, to solidarity and willingness to sustain and heal rather than to be submerged in the failures of another. Partners can learn to nurture this quietude which is not the silence of isolated individuals but a silence-together which leads to a self-evident impulse to strengthen the other, to uphold and honor, rather than to judge and to humiliate. It means to trust because one is entrusted by the other. Not to trust because we, in our magnanimity, condescend to let the other come close, but to trust out of a fullness, regardless of the flaws. This is to consent to life and to sidestep illusionary perfectionism. Such partnerships are rare, but they do exist.

Marriages such as these also create the resources to face the aloneness of death. Nothing may be more difficult than to comprehend such shared knowledge which, however, liberates us from fear.

"Silence together" means awareness of mutuality; it is disciplined because we want a greater good than self-aggrandizement, something more worthwhile than an inflated sense of self-righteousness.

What then are some of the guidelines for happiness which may be distilled? I mentioned the consciousness, that we live in separateness for which we have no solution, but that such solitariness does not exclude intimacy and trust of life. We can— as part of our nature—discover solidarity with others.

Man is a product of nature, bound to this earth. Nevertheless, by his work and intensity of effort, he can transcend many of his ambivalences and direct his energy to achievable goals. The fad of anti-hero, anti-philosophy, of knowing reality only by negation, is a dead-end to thought. It is true that there is no foundation for easy optimism. It is true that a world of science can simultaneously be a world of absurd values. But that does not negate all scientific effort.

It is necessary to exorcise the phoniness surrounding us. The inroads of sanity and of life direction are possible if we do not give in to an anarchism of the mind. Because of the kiss of a child, life is worth living; because of a caress of solace, love is worth being given and received.

We need to guard ourselves against cynicism which corrodes all hopeful effort with a sense of nothingness. In the long run, we learn that life is part failure, part success, and that we can practice compassion as a positive act of mental health. Inner quietude is a fruit of life lived without persistent delusion or recrimination. If there is anything distinctive about human beings, it is their capacity to rebuild after defeat.

TENDERNESS

What is it that stands out when a man tries to total up the balance of his life? What is a man to himself, what more is he than an ocean of loneliness? If we would try to say "everything" about ourselves, what would we really select to say?

Dylan Thomas, the young poet who destroyed himself with alcohol after coming to New York from his native Wales, wrote about that essential reckoning with oneself:

> "Do not go gentle into that good night. . . .
> Rage, rage against the dying of the light."

Frequently we try to dispose of emotions by analyzing them, but we cannot dispose of the emotion conveyed in Thomas's words. For it is all the world's dying light to which the poet refers, all the dying light of our days; the dying light also of tenderness withheld.

What shakes us more fundamentally than the knowledge of our personal vulnerability? We need trust on all levels of life as a condition for survival and when that trust is threatened, the expectations about ourselves and the world may disappear. When trust in us is cancelled, we are humiliated to the deepest core of our being. It is a humiliation which never dies and which can only be overcome by renewed tenderness. Tenderness is that openness of experience which helps us repudiate the kind of humiliation threatening the will to live.

The Russian novelists of the nineteenth century were extremely effective in getting to the heart of that humiliation. Tenderness, destroyed in the often inexplicable estrangement of people from each other, was their deepest concern. Turgenyev, in one of his novels, tells about an aging pianist who tried to express his love for a young woman in a very feeling composition. However, when it was played by the woman, the music did not convey his deepest emotions. Turgenyev wrote:

> "Alas, the music turned out to be complicated and painfully strained. It was clear that the composer had striven to express something passionate and deep, but that nothing had come of it. Without uttering a single word, he put his song back into his pocket and replying to the girl's proposal that she play it again, he only shook his head and said, 'no, enough' and shrinking into himself, he turned away."*

Such "shrinking away" is something most of us experience one time or another, it is a chasm between the world and ourselves; a sudden sense that all meaning has vanished from one's life.

*As quoted by Lynd in *Shame and Identity*.

A most remarkable piece of literature entitled *The Children of Sanchez* by Oscar Lewis also touches upon this experience. The book is a documentary based on tape-recordings made in the home of a pauperized Mexican family of five. This family, as 60% of all Mexican families do, dwells in one windowless room in which birth takes place, children fight for space and food, husband and wife cohabit, and loved ones die. The children fly out of that frightful room as birds "seeking the rain and stars, and they hop back, whimpering, their feathers soiled and their wings broken," said a reviewer of this book.

Still there is tenderness in that outwardly demeaning life. The family of Jesus Sanchez suffer want and insecurity, but its members do not lose a sense of what is important. The mother of the family died shortly after the last girl was born and one of the boys remembered how his father had to shout: " 'Get up, you bastards. Your mother is dying and you are lying there!' Then I got up and I was very scared."

This child understood that his father was cursing not because of anger but because the tenderness of life's trust was breaking in him. His source of affection was taken away from him and this betrayal of life moved the father to utter his curses. Nevertheless somehow trust persisted amidst the brokenness of that family's life. Sister Consuela, the oldest girl, said about her brother Roberto,

> "He reminded me of a person walking backwards in darkness. His gaze was fixed upon little stars shining . . . He tried to catch them . . . He never looked to either side or downwards because if he did he would see the dark abyss beneath him."

The remarkable poetry of that statement from a young girl living in a hovel shows the far-reaching strength of tenderness. Can we safeguard tenderness even though we must rage against the "dying" light? The Sanchez family somehow managed to and showed that suffering is as mute as it is universal. So much of life is caught in statements about man as an abstraction, about man as an animal in the collectivity. Most of the history we read is a lie because it deals with man in the collectivity, whereas in reality, our lives unfold on the deeply personal level of the "dying" light.

In the response of others to our pain, we sometimes discover ourselves and become more human and less of a passive victim. When we can listen to the call of others in our suffering, we may rediscover our own voice. As the land calls out to the farmer, the child to the parent, so does another being call out to us in his groping. The man about whom Turgenyev spoke as "shrinking into himself and turning away", and the boy whom Consuela described in *The Children of Sanchez* have this in common—that they reached for something sublime: the one—a beautiful way of expressing his love for a woman, the other a powerful reaching for the glitter of a star, and both were turned away by a suspension of tenderness.

We live, alas, in a culture in which this kind of withdrawal is greatly enhanced by the character of our environment. Archibald MacLeish pointed out that our extravagant perversions of life are but the symptoms of the present human crisis, and that to most of us, the crisis of our time is a crisis in the sense that a fire is a fire, something which can be put out.

It is obvious that this is impossible. The exploration of tenderness and mutual love suffers greatly from such oversimplification. Instead of seeking causes, we are preoccupied with symptoms. No passion can be sustained, if it is not nourished by a large degree of tenderness. After all, the hesitating heart is replaced all too easily by calculated self-interest which, of necessity, leads to loneliness instead of shelteredness.

In a society of mass production, sexual life, too, is perpetually in danger of becoming a commodity; it is to many what one author described as: "The last frontier to which man looks to see whether he is still alive. . ."

Tenderness is the capacity to discover others in terms of their independent existence. He who truly is beloved can rise above narcissism and mere self-serving relationships.

Tenderness is the continued full appreciation of another being even after death; it is re-experienced in little acts like arranging a flower or by our hesitation before the discovery of another person. It is in this elation of extension, in this stepping forth in innocence even into the "dying of the light", that we find unknown resources of strength. We are in such a hurry, we want so much to understand and possess immediately. But all true knowing, with tenderness, is step-by-step; when we approach too hastily we may never communicate.

At times of crisis, I so often see people pressing to penetrate the distance between the living and the dead—a chasm we cannot overcome and need not fear. At one such occasion I admired a widow who, after a memorial service at the graveside, spoke to her husband in all simplicity: "I loved you so, your hands, your voice and what you wanted. I will tell the children. I have no tears left." Then she walked away, somehow sheltered in the solitude of that shattered moment by a matured tenderness, a remarkable discipline which kept her intact.

Total peace will forever escape us; at best, life is a "becoming" even in the most fulfilling moments. Our courage consists of not retreating from a fundamental expectation, which through tenderness-of-being can help us face the unknown. Thus one remains open to fullness of experience whatever the frailty of our existence. Tenderness is in fact the emotion that makes self-reliance and self-esteem possible, for it assures us that we are respected for our being, not just for our achievements; it means being loved not because we have "made the grade", but because of self-growth. This kind of tender being-within-life leads to a mutual enhancement and the support we need. It means creating a capacity for entrusting one's life to others. Our civilization—alas—gives little support to such tenderness for there is more respect for the "tough" than for the tender-minded person. We assume that a mother gives love to a child because she is its mother, rather than because she is loving of the child. We assume that relationships between men and women can endure only if their needs are met, instead of their accepting the incompletenesses in one another.

This is one of our great tasks: to create the support of tenderness which strengthens the identity of the person. So many seek identity, without willingness to take the risk of entrusting themselves; what they seek is a sounding board, not an equal. Thus tenderness is replaced by performance and that in essence is a denial of the more trusting expectation.

Yet, such sham relief only throws one back into greater loneliness and isolation, because for so many of us, anticipation of tenderness has ceased after childhood, after the first big blows and disappointments. Instead of anticipation of tenderness has come the anticipation of danger and destruction by which the limited character of one's life becomes accentuated. This is anxiety enthroned; anxiety frequently stimulated and manipulated for the purpose of commercial or political domination.

Tenderness is a capacity to venture, an innocence which involves us in the possibilities and intuitions which lie beyond rationalizations. It is being able to be conscious without being self-conscious; knowing the lovable in life and not being overwhelmed by evil. This innocence of involvement is trampled upon so often that we shy away from the conflicts that go with that freedom. There is always the temptation, instead of reaching for the significant in life, to adjust to what is anything but fundamental. The result is a decreased vitality or, even worse, emotional anemia. For just as we can withdraw from being able to be free, so can we become fearful of what we really want. The "good life" is meeting conflict and anxiety, moving through both without withdrawal, without adjustment to what is absent in quality or intensity. I say, then, that to discover tenderness is to be open to our goals even if we cannot entirely comprehend what lies at the other end of much of our expectations.

I hesitate to use the word "creative" here because it has been misused so much, but renouncing our capacity for tenderness is renouncing our creative potential. There is a relationship between tenderness and art. Art, not as a question of production or performance only, but more importantly, of entering into a joy of being able, the entrusted state of mind in which we claim and express a synthesis of capacity. Art is what we revive in ourselves; it is the dialogue between a necessity within and that which calls to us from without. Art is a way "by which man interrogates the stars" as André Malraux put it. Still, to many, art is primarily a decoration, a luxury. But I see art as a vital expression of life itself. A Van Gogh is therefore as completely engaged as a scientist. The ferment that surrounds art and great discoveries is derived from a passion to make life intelligible, and from the hope of establishing human identity amidst the indifference of the cosmos. That is why I find it difficult to accept some of today's art. The unbridled emotion of a flowing form, or color or just plain rhythm do not make life more intelligible! Much of what passes for "free expression" spells chaos and emptiness and, in turn, promotes the urge of death rather than a hunger for life. Compare the torn, disfigured bodies and broken faces of Picasso's painting of "Three Women" with Rembrandt's portrait of his mother! So, also, are relationships true only if they foster judgment and a capacity to place the pain of life in a framework of expectations. For above all we need to keep open the windows upon new experience if life is to be salvaged from its continual confrontation with the deeper shadows.

Here again, certain social conditions are as if in connivance for the destruction of tenderness. The public wishes to be titillated and is enthusiastic in its approval of playwrights and novelists whose major theme is hatred of women, or deviation.

In an important article on this topic "Love and Death", a Dr. G. Legman dealt with the question of literary sadism in America.* It was his opinion that the motif of much of our literature shows a complete anomaly of norms. Sex and death are almost continually mentioned together. Our first atomic bomb was called "Gilda" (the title of a Rita Hayworth movie!) just as the abbreviated bathing suit is called the "Bikini" for the island on which the first hydrogen bomb explosion occurred.

Our civilization accepts sex, sadism, and violence in one "luscious" package and of course this leads to a negation of sound sexual feelings. Death, yes; love, no! Thus audiences swallow the stock formula of a Tennessee Williams in endlessly similar plays in which females are "enthralling but shared pleasure", a "pleasure" which results in the prompt death of one or both partners! Over Broadway hovers a brooding violence that *The New York Times* called "a captive agony".

Of course, an author has a right to say what he wants, but mature audiences have a right to take issue with abnormality.

It may be the tragic fate of Man that he often becomes aware of matters that he cannot successfully control. But what are we without that awareness? What are we without the risks of awareness? The possibility of tragedy in our lives is the price we pay.

If we take our limitations into account we can, by our love, discover an urgency of life without which the entire concept of self-fulfillment collapses.

Every day, each man and woman has to avoid the nether-world of destructive impulses and is confronted with the question of why?

As Epictetus wrote: "What harm is there while you are kissing your child to say ever so softly to yourself, 'My love, my love, tomorrow you may die.'" Love as tenderness is grounded

*Harper's Magazine, November (1960).

in our passing essence. This emotion captured me one night watching my son asleep:

JOB

All through the day,
I see his smile,
His little hand in gentle sway,
His nodding head—
To rest a while.

And from the rising of the sun,
Until the dusk of every night
His eyes fill painfully with light.
Ah, the frail heartbeat of my son.

But what will shelter his dear breath?
If but my life could die for his,
Now he will know but furtiveness
As silent nature moves in death.

Was there a night I did not know
Receding light that touched his head?
Could I but lift his little bed
And halt his breaking passions so . . .

He doesn't know yet he is bound
To part the curtains of despair
I warn him of this shrinking air,
He laughs and bends towards the ground.

CHAPTER **6**

THE WOUNDED LOVE

My aim throughout this book has been to explore the landscape
of our yearnings rather than to analyze the details of circumstance.

This was done because I have come to see that much of what
is significant remains submerged and can be awakened only by
seeing ourselves as born into and part of a community. To take
possession of our lives, we need to overcome the assumption of
mystery and see that all being is surrounded by and involved
with sharing. Our moments of happiness as well as our moments
of suffering are shared within that larger landscape. When we
overcome our separateness by guiding each other towards a
recognition of love and tenderness, we are also brought into
touch with ourselves.

Perhaps it is our fate as human beings to long for the impossible, but I have found that this at least cannot be alienated
from us: the capacity to be one with all that draws us toward
an inner obedience, toward a direction-setting relatedness.
Amidst the worst periods of loneliness and physical and mental
torture, I have found that all experience is merely threshold,
an indication and direction, not a finished product. By this dis-

278]

covery, it has become increasingly possible to obey the obligation of being a son, a husband, a father, a citizen, out of a secure
reservoir of deeper obligation. To be so engaged has meant to
be seized by an urgency to fit within the utter readiness I discovered in all of creation and this could not be estranged from
me. An illumination of personal experience can be translated
into fruitful action that enhances life within the human community, for others too express this unspoken demand to be
loved and reached and awakened. It is therefore never a matter
of choice but of finding the means to overcome the muteness
or blindness that separates us from each other.

It is in this context that I see the impulse towards ethical
growth as a fundamental revolt against despair and meaninglessness.

Therefore, there remains this question to be traced: how is
the will to persist grown in us, how do we cultivate courage to
face the never-ending sequence of devastating experiences?
What is the fortitude which carries us through illness, through
the doubts that come with disillusionment?

Is that quality of heart at all communicable; can one describe
it, locate it, and share of it with others?

Can anyone know himself deeply enough to reveal to another
what holds him together when he is tested to the pit of endurance?

Stephen Spender's poem "What I Expected" goes to the heart
of these questions:

> "What I expected was
> Thunder, fighting. . . .
> What I had not foreseen
> Was. . . .
> The wearing of time,
> The pulverous grief. . . .
> These I could not foresee."*

*Selected Poems, N.Y. 1964.

The "wearing of time" is revealed by the unforeseen. We all travel through time, and sooner or later face questions that in the past could have been referred to the gods but which modern men have to face for themselves. How we meet such stress helps determine the character of the family, the community and the world.

When the Swiss psychiatrist, Carl Jung died in 1961, he had nearly finished his autobiography entitled *Memories, Dreams, Reflections.* He wrote: "The decisive question for Man is, is he related to something infinite or not? That is the telling question of his life." That question is particularly significant for those of us who live amidst perpetual crisis and radical change. One way of looking at this is to concentrate on everything that is breaking down. But another way is to see a dying age and to discern that new norms are being ushered in. Those afflicted by perpetual melancholy see only decay and death because their vision is limited by their own assumptions, fears, and prejudices. I do not deny that this generation has known darkness and terror beyond all imagination. I do deny that there is nothing but crisis. The crucial challenge is to love life enough.

We must ask what has numbed the millions of persons to whom the newspapers are the horizon of consciousness and who sit back after supper to be brainwashed by endless repetition concerning war, accidents, and disaster? Blurred vision, which is the result of living with the surface rather than with infinite connection, eventually distorts personal perspective. To preserve life we have to fight for life, for ultimately we have to face death and this is not done by slipping into a morass of negativism. Our response must be more than crisis-psychology.

Since humanists seek for answers here on earth, they should have something very concrete to propose. More important than the question of our historical identity, more important than the "isms" of ideology, is the centrality of a secular idealism. The strength of such idealism can be that it aims for a socially based wholeness. For too long have we meandered under the illusion that completion of personal life can be achieved by faith, when it is so obvious that those who believe can very well close their eyes to a multitude of evils and pretend that they are not related to those who do not "walk in righteousness . . ." No, there must be tangible relatedness to others, tangible attempts at economic justice, human rights, an end to capital punishment, and the lunatic proposition that the increase of weapons for mass destruction can ever result in security. Personal wholeness makes sense only if it results in awe for the existence of every creature.

When I speak about Mankind, therefore, I think of concrete human lives which, individually, are accountable for a community whose reach is more than its parts. We have to expect a great deal from each other so that any good we have been granted in life, any advantage of health or intelligence or property, will in part, at least, be reinvested to lessen the pain and the suffering of all. In that way, our trying and doing and gathering and suffering will have a deeper significance and will help to effectuate a devotion to the progress of a livable ethic.

This, then, is what I mean by a humanist attempt at social wholeness, not collectivization but heightened personal consecration. Such idealism expresses Man's desire for a tangible immortality, for a triumph over nature. Whether it is the engineers who build water reservoirs, or whether it is the paintings of Rembrandt or the philosophies of Spinoza or Einstein or Gandhi, whatever was attempted in such creative effort, I see these as the expressions of true social forces that helped Man not just to win the raw battle against nature but to triumph over much of the melancholy within himself. All such idealism, in fact, is an attempt to deepen the love that is in us, not just for ourselves, but toward each other. It is a "wounded love".* It is a love that is bruised daily but it is there; its expressions are the result of

*Dr. S. Tas, *The Illusion of Decline*, Amsterdam, 1947.

a process. It is a love within the "wearing of time", mortal but infinite as long as there is human life and striving.

Human beings, as they journey through time, want to heal, to sustain. Perhaps in that desire they write their protest against the reality that all living also edges us toward life's conclusion. Religion of old has used that impulse of protest against death and prepared the flight of man from reality. However, an affirmative humanist ideal nurtures hope by directing energies towards a better life here on earth through practical labor. Thus, there is a link between the ideal and reality, continually urged on by a "holy" dissatisfaction. Again, I do not wish to oversimplify. None of this is a perpetual climb towards "bigger and better" idealism. But any peace of mind is the result of a desire to make more out of life than just a preparation for death. There is no such attempt without a consciousness of the tragic. Yet out of necessary change, crisis, and sometimes devastating suffering, can emerge an essence of strength. For we belong to the community of Man, whatever our tragic or wounded love. The better the men in it, the better the community. We owe it to each other; we have a right to ask of each other that we try to make this a better life. For the way in which we deal with the tragic, as well as with our achievements, has an effect upon other people. We are what we are, but we are also what we are potentially at any given moment. We can prepare each other for a supportive love of life.

It is a mistake, therefore, that we do not educate our children to deal with shock, failure, and loss. In our culture, those who mourn or suffer a loss, or who have failed, are somehow treated like pariahs, as if they do not really belong. Still, I believe that from childhood our young need to be prepared to accept loss and failure as inevitabilities, as part of the life process. Looked upon as inevitable, it will be possible to help others, and by accepting suffering in others, we can become more capable of accepting it in ourselves.

Of course, we all try to avoid suffering or pain. I agree that we should do this as much as we can. I am not propagating suffering. But human beings have been equipped by nature with means to overcome shock and great mental and physical stress. Therefore, all experiences are valuable to us. Why should a man in turmoil pretend well-being? Mature persons are entitled to grief, and to show grief, and in the end to absorb it as a true experience. By "accepting" and "inevitable" I simply mean that there are cycles to human experience: as there is a beginning to sorrow, so there is an end to it; as there is a beginning to defeat, so there is its termination.

To gain a certain peace of mind does not mean then that we are sure that we will always have enough confidence for the future. But it means at least having the confidence to continue. To be alive so as to know peace of mind means to have considered our motives, our conflicts, and then to live—whatever the day will bring. A very touching example was offered by a British couple—Bet and Paul Cherrington—in *Practical Humanism.** The Sherringtons lost a three-year-old child. Bet Cherrington wrote:

". . . I was almost unable to use my arms which had so recently held the dying child; I felt guilt, as I had had drugs to ease the birth which the baby barely survived. I had failed totally in a mother's first duty—to keep her child alive—and my cowardice, I thought, was probably the prime cause of his death."

And Paul Cherrington too was overcome by guilt, first for wanting yet another child when they had already had four youngsters —secondly, because he had insisted that the confinement take place in the home.

These two people suffered greatly before finding any inner peace. Paul put it this way:

". . . (This experience) led me to the final step out of Christi-

*Practical Humanism—A Symposium, Blackham, edit. London 1964.

anity . . . The explanation that it was part of God's purpose that our little son had to die just would not do. Very gradually, and bit by bit, we could accept our place in the natural order . . . that life is worthwhile in spite of the risks involved . . . I do not say that we accepted these ideas at once, and were therefore happy, no—we worked through many hours of sorrow, in discussion and argument, trying to come to terms with the death of our small son. Yet if we enjoy the benefits of life, we must accept the whole of life . . . If other people suffered as we had, we must be ready to suffer too . . . we *could* not claim exemption and *do* not claim it."

INNER PRESENCE

This last insight is an especially crucial one: not to claim "exemption", to remain related, to fight for life by practical labor. It helped this couple see that what had befallen them was not punishment for earlier actions and that in the end they too had to "accept their place in the natural order". They found strength so that more than words of comfort could reach them, so that they themselves could reach out to the world and again enjoy fellowship of common purpose. Thus, out of an open wound, a heightened vitality and involvement was born to protect the beauty and vulnerability of all the young of the world. Time—plays a role, time helps. However, time is not a panacea, it merely creates distance.

I speak of our life attempts as a journey because I want to accentuate the concept of process. Since we are born and die, we are inclined to think of our emotions as being fixed. Thus, peace of mind appears to many a desirable goal because it promises stability. But this is deceptive. Life is process, and our individual insight and peace of mind is part of and is discovered within the journey.

It is not a static peace. It is not the deceptive bliss of ancient faiths "forever and ever". It is a peace of mind notwithstanding the world, notwithstanding the wounded love.

Inner balance is the result of being committed to life, of having put aside self-deception, of probing for the roots of our conflicts without being lost in their analysis. All of us leave some kind of trace, some kind of footprint. Some of us will leave traces of vanity, of hurt, or a need to dominate. Some of us will leave traces that will be remembered with a smile and with a sense of affection and nostalgia. Not to have lived in vain is an ambition for the future.* It is the exact opposite of the feeling "I missed all my chances." We do not seek consolation as such, but consolation that opens up possibilities, deeds, acts; not a self-elevation but a threshold towards fulfillment. The life I stress is a life of compassion.

Of course, some people are better than their community and many are worse. If we want to give ourselves, there must be an emotional core that is stronger than the temptation of shared frustrations. Do not forget this: no evil, no hatred, neither wars nor crusades ever lacked volunteers! More difficult is the idealism expressed in practical social labor. That is a way in which fear is gradually taken from us and we find strength to merge past and future. Our journey through time should, in the long run, help us to achieve a lessened fear of dying. If we truly believe that Man is a product of nature, then in the long run, we must have the courage to say that death will be beyond our scope, we need not fear it.

It is extremely hard to discover this because we only know death by what happens to others; we see others die and we maintain only a reminiscence of their presence. Yet even in the absence of a person there is much that suggests their reality. That silent presence of those to whom we are loyal can also make it possible for us to accept our own death. Again, not just consolation, not just death as a passive observation, but understood as a process, as a rock-bottom truth. The Greek, Hebrew, and Christian vision of time is a different one. What emotional

*Tas, *op. cit.*

energy is wasted in self-torture concerning death! When we have overcome this, what liberation and strength comes to us as we give a quiet example of facing death without fear of dying! That kind of courage works as a liberating emotion in those who stay behind—it is again a source of strength, an aim for the journey through life.

Thus, in the last analysis, by the strength of our mind, we learn to accept, to be at peace. Of course, even that being-at-peace is not absolute! We have a right to tears amidst all the strong resolve; these tears may be as important as intellectual strength. What we arrive at, what we conclude about ourselves is a token, just as courage is a token, and each act of decency is a token which in the aggregate creates some measure of goodness in the world.

I can only hope that these thoughts suggest a certain cohesion to the reader. For myself, I have found a pathway to hope amidst the unspeakable sorrow of my generation.

We must respond to man's fundamental hunger to affirm himself amidst the ideologies of inhumanity and horrible destruction. My faith that human transformation is possible is based largely upon what I understand to be the persistent quality of our biological nature: in essence, organic life is supportive, cooperative, sustaining and endlessly creative. This essence suggests that a truer social nature is well within our grasp.

There is no universal evil, there is only the evil of individual man; there is never "collective guilt." The issue then is to build the characteristics of "Fundamental Man."

Martin Luther King admonished his followers in one of his letters from jail that

> ". . . in our generation we do not only have to repent for those who committed (such) evil acts, but also for the millions of good people who did nothing or next to nothing to stop it. The battleground is with the good and innocent people; the decent people."

It is not enough to have social or political movements, important as they are. What is needed is an education on how to translate principle into social fact, for no social action is successful unless it translates its faith into fact for individuals. The strain of life comes to all of us and in fairly equal measure, but what matters is what we have done with that strain, what our response has been.

Are we not brothers in despair? Can we not therefore learn to become brothers in hope? At the heart of hope is the impulse to keep on because of what is required of us.

The question of whether or not one should be hopeful is not crucial. I am interested in maturation, not comfort, and I see the curative aspect of human experience as the basis of faith. To be able to pursue reality, not myth, to be able to fight life's struggles with increased capability and thereby to lessen our inner misery—these are my goals. In order to reach up to these goals, I know that I must constantly work for a receptivity towards all those emotional and intellectual resources from which my nourishment may come. The freedom to call upon those resources seems to me the highest fulfillment of humanist aspiration and evokes a religious earnestness which vanquishes disenchantment and opens new doors towards happiness. It is the only response I know against the happy warriors of the atomic epoch; it is the only meaningful pathway I have found to resist resignation and paralysis.

In trying to unthink and unlearn the inroads of mythology and ideology, I have discovered a modest hope, but it would be preposterous to offer such hope as a "message" to others. As Thomas Roethke wrote in his poem, "The Waking":

> "I wake to sleep and take my waking slow . . . .
> I learn by going, where I have to go . . . ."

One of the greatest hindrances in maintaining faith in any human capacity is the tendency to slide into the fearful because of ignorance. When the mechanisms of hostility prevail, we lower our own status. When we join hostility's pathology, and relate ourselves to its evil, we in fact embrace self-destruction. For as we respond with our own anxiety, we create a central void and by compromising instead of drawing the line, we create more fear. That is the ultimate victory of destructiveness which threatens the whole of mankind today. Yet, these mechanisms can be intercepted by a resolve to seek within ourselves for the explanations of what happens to us and our world.

At times we see very little, but at other times there can be awareness that keeps our kindness, our tenderness, and supportive qualities unspoiled.

It means resistance against the easy mechanisms of hostility —private and collective—it means activating generosity.

To find any completeness necessary for a better life-capacity, we have to be in touch not just with ourselves, but with a more encompassing reality. Our whole outlook on life is a growing toward greater complexity and it takes willful effort and much labor to attain fulfillment at any one moment. Norms of human responsibility can help us discover this from time to time, but it is enormously difficult and without any guarantee of accomplishment. Perhaps much of our human effort brings forth only minimal results, but if we can make what we achieve complete enough within ourselves, life remains worth living.

Coming into reach of one's self is very different from living happily. Our moments of strength may occur to us when our acts are not necessarily spectacular. Our character, for better or for worse, is shaped by the way in which we interpret experience. This is a language we must learn to understand.

The spiritual aspects of life are often thought of as separate from daily experience. But this is a tragic mistake. No one is all together denied cognizance of them for they are part of our nature.

Understanding our lives means that the inexplicable is indeed so and that we must live with it; that there may be development and individual growth, but that nobody really knows whether there is any kind of meaningful totality.

We may sometimes regret that we have lost the secure ancient poetic universality. Yet, to see a further dimension to Man, makes it possible to believe in his dignity and capacity for self-respect. The new world of scientific knowledge guarantees us very little other than that we ourselves are responsible for our goals and values of living or our lack of them.

To live does not mean just to snatch a bit of happiness here and a bit of pleasure or money there. It means to have our reach extended so that an ideal of life becomes an inner possibility. Life is, above all, possibility. Whatever the realities of existence and death, while life is with us we must live it now. These few years, these precious hours are all there will be! We must engage upon them passionately; not just because we are hungry to live, but because if there is any quality for which to live, if there are any finer hours to gain, any values to be built, *we* must gain them, *we* must build them, nobody else will or can do it for us. There is no home for us anywhere but the incomplete home we make ourselves, the home of a renewed perception of what we are. Man probably would be happier without such awareness of himself and yet, since we are capable of it, it is our only weapon against the spiral of fear that tears us apart.

To some, I am sure, this may seem a flimsy foundation, a base too uncertain on which to build one's life.

I have not said that the task of being human can be performed without loneliness and danger. Much disillusion and bitterness will come our way. And yet, I have experienced that a sense of shelteredness becomes possible when we rise above our jealousies and feelings of being deprived by factors outside of ourselves. Life can consume us if we cannot learn how to overcome bitterness and monumental egotism. To find a way of life is therefore not just to discover methods for controlling our passions and anxieties. The most controlled individuals are not necessarily the happiest or the most mature persons. To find a way of life, we need to educate ourselves away from the excitement of death, the terrible ecstacy of destructiveness. We stand in the midst of each other's existence and when we fully face what oppresses life, we can become the spokesmen of all happiness, the consolers of all pain by removing that which imprisons us.

I hold deeply that each life is a gift which the centuries bestow upon the continuity of existence.

A Passio Humana, a passion for Man, is what will negate totalitarianism and oppression, it will open the jail-doors of history, provided our mutuality and love outpace our tools. All of us are constantly close to death and yet we are also in touch with the perpetuation of life through what we create and build.

The sense of future derived from this position has resulted for me in an infusion of insight, which even at moments during my captivity, when death seemed certain and sealed, did not desert me.

Therefore I trust that infusion, for it has made it possible to see each man's life as firmly tied to an outreach beyond frustration.

On this evidence then I base my faith in Man's inner presence which all of us can experience as a watershed for increasingly clearer vision.

This vision may yet liberate us from despair and make us turn to our reluctant brother to say: "Yes, because of you I will dare to live, yes, because of you I will dare to dream. . . ."

About The Author

Matthew Ies Spetter is "an extraordinary man who has led an extraordinary life . . . one that gives evidence of great courage and strength of character of uncompromising dedication to the ideals of human happiness and human dignity and fearless resistance to all forces that seek to destroy these or thwart their attainment." (Thus the Netherlands' Ambassador to the United States recently speaking of his former countryman.) For Dr. Spetter, educated in the Netherlands, England and New York, served during World War II as liaison officer between sections of the Dutch and French Resistance in Nazi-occupied Europe. Captured by the Nazis, he was condemned to death by a German Naval Court in Bordeaux, France in 1943 but escaped execution through a fortuitous mistake, only to be held prisoner at the Auschwitz and Buchenwald concentration camps.

Following his liberation, he functioned as a witness for the United States Prosecution at the Nuremburg War Criminal Tribune and served as Interrogation Officer with the Dutch Security Division of G2-G3 at the Seine Headquarters of the United States Army in Paris. Returning to the Netherlands at War's end, Dr. Spetter continued his studies in social psychology and

291

philosophy and his interrupted career as author, lecturer, foreign affairs commentator.

A citizen of the United States for many years, Dr. Spetter earned his doctorate at the New School and is a member of the Social Psychology Section of the American Sociological Association, the American Association of Marriage Counselors and the Academy for Religion and Mental Health. He is also a Fellow of the American Association for Humanistic Psychology.

As a Leader in the American Ethical Union and for twelve years of the Riverdale Society for Ethical Culture, Dr. Spetter has become a spokesman for liberal religion and a militant civil rights worker. He is co-author of the Arms Control Project. In 1960 he founded the Riverdale Mental Health Clinic in New York City and also initiated the Riverdale Committee for the Defense of Human Rights.

A highly respected teacher (he is Chairman of the Department of Ethics of the Fieldston School in New York), he has also served on the faculties of the Encampment for Citizenship, the John L. Elliott Institute for Human Relations, the Community Forum and the Bard College State Department Program.

Dr. Spetter is married and has a large family.

A 1 6v niqual
15
1 3 6v wl niqual

16'½ -30

cu 30: 1
Rooke 3 cv
15 -30
cu 30:1

AMERICAN ETHICAL UNION
79th National Assembly

DR. MATTHEW IES SPETTER

We, the **79th National Assembly** of the

AMERICAN ETHICAL UNION

Meeting in Riverdale, New York, on the
18th day of June, 1987,
are pleased and honored to present the

ELLIOTT-BLACK AWARD

For unwavering devotion to ethical principles, both
before and during his thirty-five years of
Leadership in the Ethical Culture Movement, to

DR. MATTHEW IES SPETTER

His efforts locally, nationally and internationally
to help heal and rescue the human spirit; his
example in counteracting cynicism and resignation
by practical action; and his determination in
promoting a vigorous interfaith humanism committed
to the worth and dignity of every person, have
enriched our lives. He gives us courage.

The **ELLIOTT-BLACK AWARD** was established in 1971 to
honor two long-term and highly esteemed Leaders of
the New York Society:

DR. JOHN LOVEJOY ELLIOTT

and

ALGERNON D. BLACK

It is granted by the American Ethical Union as a
recognition and tribute to individuals in the
larger community who have made a significant
ethical contribution to American or world society.

Previous recipients are:

Aubrey M. Daniel III	1972
Peter Bridge & Earl Caldwell	1973
Henry Durham	1974
Jerrold terHorst	1975
Joan Claybrook	1976
Dr. Luis Recque	1977
Father Bruce Ritter	1978
Karen Silkwood (posthumously)	1979
Michael Pertschuk	1980
Robert Eckhardt	1981
Eugene Babb & Stephen Joseph	1982
Joann Bell	1983
Hon. Robert E. White	1984
Mary Sinclair	1985
Helen Caldicott, MD	1986

PROGRAM

Welcome   Marian S. Irwin
                                 President,
                                 Riverdale-Yonkers Society

Greetings   Sophie Meyer
                                 President,
                                 American Ethical Union

Musical Interlude   Joel Martin
Johann Sebastian Bach
Cromatic Fantasy & Fugue

Presentation of   Hon. G. Oliver Koppell
Elliott-Black Award   Assemblyman,
to Dr. Matthew Ies Spetter   New York State Assembly

Response   Dr. Matthew Ies Spetter

Musical Interlude   Joel Martin

Reception   "Just Ethical Deserts"

The Reception will be held downstairs in Cahill Lounge

THE AMERICAN ETHICAL UNION

is the national federation of Societies and Fellowships for Ethical Culture. It is devoted to the promotion of the knowledge, and love and practice of the right in all relationships of life. It affirms the single belief that the greatest spiritual values are to be found in human relationships through its religious, social action, community service and educational programs.

American Ethical Union
2 West 64th Street
New York, NY 10023

79th National Assembly
held at:
College of Mount St. Vincent
June 18th - 21st, 1986